THE BLACK SHEEP POWER
AS IT PLEASES GOD

DR. Y. BUR

The Black Sheep Power: As It Pleases God®

Unveiling the Divine POWER Hidden in Being an Outcast

Copyright© 2025 by R.O.A.R. Publishing Group. All Rights Reserved.

Visit www.RoarPublishingGroup.com for more information. No part of this publication may be reproduced, stored in a retrieval system, or transmitted in any way by any means, electronic, mechanical, photocopy, recording, or otherwise, without the prior permission of the author except as provided by USA copyright law.

R.O.A.R. Publishing Group
581 N. Park Ave. Ste. #725
Apopka, FL 32704
www.RoarPublishingGroup.com

Published in the United States of America
ISBN: 979-8-9990619-2-8
$22.88

Send *As It Pleases God* ®
Book Series **and** *Workbook* **Testimonies, Donations, Questions, or Orders to:**

Dr. Y. Bur
R.O.A.R. Publishing Group
581 N. Park Ave. Ste. #725
Apopka, FL 32704
ROAR-58-2316
762-758-2316

Dr.YBur@gmail.com

Visit Us At:

 AsItPleasesGodMovement

▶ AsItPleasesGod

🖥 DrYBur.com
🖥 AsItPleasesGod.com

Please Donate

Please DONATE to this *Missionable Movement of God* as a GIVE-BACK to the Kingdom. Thanks for your support. Many Blessings.

AIPG Donation Link

Scan to Pay

As It Pleases God

ASITPLEASESGOD.COM

Available Titles

ASITPLEASESGOD.COM

Table Of Contents

Introduction 11
Chapter One 19
  The First Power 19
    The More Factors 25
    Shift Focus 33
    Reverse Engineering 36
    Transformation of the Heart and Mind 39
Chapter Two 45
  Overcoming Fear and Doubt 45
    Hormonal Health 47
    The Pressure 51
    Bouncing Back 52
    The Learning Process 56
Chapter Three 59
  Dealing With Unsurety 59
    The Point of Origin 69
    Unveiling Our Inner Compass 72
    Building Confidence 85
Chapter Four 93
  The Black Sheep Journey 93
    The Cost 98
    The Label 102

The One Drop Rule 105
Higher Accountability.. 108
Spiritual Tribe 110

Chapter Five 113
Black Sheep Mentality 113
Redefining the Black Sheep 114
The Biblical Mirror.. 122
Union of Oneness 127
Reframing the Narrative 131
Internal Building... 139
Spirit of Overflow 147

Chapter Six.. 151
Leading With Power 151
Divine Light... 153
Breaking The Mold... 156
Think Outside The Box.. 161
Secrets of Unconventional Leadership 166
Beyond The Status Quo 172
Spiritual Reformation.. 177

Chapter Seven..185
The Black Sheep Power 185
Blessed To Be A Blessing... 191
Asking Questions 193
Hearing God.. 195
Finding Our Voices 197
Divine Preparation 202

Chapter Eight 205
- Doing Real Business 205
  - The Significance of Mind Mapping 208
  - Embracing Your Passion 220
  - The Black Sheep Brainstorming 222
  - Finding Real Purpose 229
  - Diamonds In The Rough 234
  - Overcoming Business Doubt 236
  - Business Savvy 240
  - Business Info, Tips, and Know-How 243
  - Writing A Business Plan 251

Chapter Nine 255
- The Divine Advantage 255
  - The Risk 257
  - Overcoming Deceptive Measures 258

Chapter Ten 269
- Freedom of Authenticity 269
  - The Flow 271

Chapter Eleven 277
- Strength In Community 277
  - The Spiritual Moth 280

Chapter Twelve 283
- The Power of Intent 283
  - Spiritual Loop 285
  - Baited Hook 287
  - Pruning Hook 290

ntroduction

Are you experiencing a sense of disconnection? Has being *Blacksheeped* become your middle name? Are you searching for your Tribe? Are you tired of trying to fit in where you do not belong? Well, with this book, the buck stops here! The goal of *The Black Sheep Power* is to encourage individuals to honor their true selves humbly, authentically, and *As It Pleases God*, rather than bend to the expectations, judgments, frailties, and limitations of others.

This book, *The Black Sheep Power: As It Pleases God*®, is not at all about possessing dominating power; it is about extracting the Divine POWER that is already hidden within. This thought-provoking read invites us to look inwardly, emphasizing that TRUE POWER, *As It Pleases Him*, does not lie in control or supremacy, but in the humble Divine Energy and Purpose that resides within each of us for the Greater Good of mankind.

At the core of our being, most of us are preoccupied with the pursuit of dominance, authority, and outward displays of strength and resilience. Well, with *The Black Sheep Power: As It Pleases God*®, it offers a refreshing Spiritual Perspective on how to take Divine Dominion over what is rightfully yours without becoming negatively dominant or a control freak.

So, here is my question: 'Would you prefer to look powerful? Or, 'Would you prefer to be authentically powerful

Introduction

in and out of the Kingdom of God?' Based on these two questions, this book challenges the conventional philosophies of power and its true meaning from a Spiritual Perspective.

The truth of the matter is that God has placed your Divine Blueprinted Instructions within you, with the *Freedom of Authenticity* flowing through your veins. As you think, act, and live in your Heaven on Earth Experience, it is your responsibility to embrace your individuality instead of conforming to the societal norms or cave in to what people say, think, or believe about you. When you wholeheartedly accept who you are with the Divine Will of God at the forefront, you should not allow anyone or anything to dumb you down to their level, regardless of whether you feel you are on their level, below it, above it, or it is not applicable.

Before we go any further, I have a few more questions for you: 'What are you trying to prove?' Then again, 'Who are you trying to prove it to?' Wait, wait, wait, before you answer these questions, let me say this: We are all different, having different beliefs, values, mindsets, opinions, or behaviors in the Eye of God...So, is it not Him that we should be trying to PLEASE, *Spirit to Spirit*?

With your diverse threads of experiences, perspectives, and talents, in the beauty of your differences according to the Heavenly of Heavens, there is always MORE. More of what you have, more of what you do not have, and more of what you do not need, making it extremely difficult to let go of circumstantial control of outcomes. The *More Factors* hidden within the DNA of mankind are no joke, but must be respected and contained, while remaining on the righteous side of the *More Factors* while aiming to PLEASE and TRUST God.

Introduction

Why must we aim to PLEASE and TRUST Him instead of pleasing and trusting ourselves? Selfish pleasures, whether good, bad, or indifferent, contain a sense of disconnection or veiled understanding when you do not govern them properly, or *As It Pleases God*. Really? Yes, really!

The truth is that most of us are Spiritually Veiled, but do not realize that we are, which denies full access to our Inner Power, allowing the psyche to do its thing. For this very reason, as Dr. Y. Bur, The WHY Doctor, I skillfully blend Spiritual Teachings based on the Word of God and the psychological components based on our DNA. Furthermore, with this Spiritual Combo, having actionable steps, *As It Pleases God*, we can receive relevant and sustainable results that are up to Kingdom Standards without compromise.

With this Divine Approach and empowering manifesto, we as Believers can become and remain BALANCED. According to the Heavenly of Heavens, by surrendering to this Spiritual Processing Classroom, *As It Pleases God* and *Spirit to Spirit*, we can become Proverbially and Wisely Balanced, Mentally, Physically, Emotionally, and Spiritually, without becoming so Heavenly Minded that we are no earthly good.

In paving the way for greater relevance in or out of the Kingdom of God, this book is designed to UNVEIL the unlikely, making them likely. What is the difference? In *The Black Sheep Power: As It Pleases God*®, the difference in making the unlikely likely is always hidden in the agreement, processing, training, praying, and development.

In the quest for authenticity and relevance from within, you are not here to blend into the background or to fit into predefined molds. As a *Black Sheep*, you are here to stand out amid your strengths, weaknesses, and quirks, teaching and

Introduction

mentoring others to do likewise for the Greater Good. In *The Black Sheep Power: As It Pleases God®*, the first step in doing so is recognizing that your uniqueness and weaknesses are hidden strengths.

The second step is to use the Fruit of the Spirit in a pluralized form, for instance, in this book, *The Black Sheep Power*, they will be referred to as FRUITS OF THE SPIRIT. Clearly, this is not a mistake, and we have free will to use the singular or pluralized form. Nevertheless, this is how the Holy Spirit revealed these Divine Revelations to me, and this is how the multiple perspectives will come forth through the use of them to bring us into a state of ONENESS. Rest assured that Philippians 1:11 advocates, *"Being filled with the fruits of righteousness which are by Jesus Christ, to the glory and praise of God."*

So, being that we, as a people, are not there yet, we are all a work-in-progress, and we are not all the same, dealing with different issues, let us pluralize and multiply to become fruitful, *As It Pleases God*. Even if we willingly choose not to pluralize and multiply, it is still okay. On the other hand, if we find ourselves trying to correct the one who has MASTERED the Fruits of the Spirit according to the Heavenly of Heavens, while not knowing how to use them correctly ourselves, or *As It Pleases Him*, then this is why we are here! *"Therefore, bear fruits worthy of repentance."* Matthew 3:8.

Furthermore, if God wanted us all to be the same, He would have made us robots, right? Being that He created each of us with free will, it means we possess creativity, innovation, and a deeper understanding of ourselves, even if we are veiled at the moment. Just keep in mind, veil or no veil, our fruits do not lie; even Matthew 7:20 gives us a heads up, saying, *"Therefore by their fruits you will know them."*

Introduction

In the microwave world of today, where instant gratification reigns supreme and social interactions are often condensed into bite-sized exchanges. It is all too easy to feel lonely, unliked, rejected, outcasted, and disconnected, especially when there is truth involved. Despite being more connected than ever through technology and social media, an unsettling observation has arisen. In the irony of it all, it amazes me that people enjoy being lied to, deceived, bogusly hyped up, or gaslit.

When we are secretly or openly driven by negativity or debauchery, it is time for a check-up from the neck up. Why do we need a check-up? The fascination with drama and conflict that destroys innocent lives stirs and desensitizes our emotions, making them addictive and toxic.

Regardless of how we perceive ourselves, whether as a *Black Sheep* or as someone who follows the pack, there exists a UNIVERSAL TRUTH: The cloak of negativity, disdainment, or disobedience in the Eye of God can pump the brakes on our Divine Purpose, Mission, Creativity, and Usability, especially when being *Blacksheeped* due to debauchery, ill will, or rebellion. As I Spiritually Align this, here is what Isaiah 59:2 says, *"But your iniquities have separated you from your God; and your sins have hidden His face from you, so that He will not hear."*

Painstakingly, the curated representations of happiness lead to increased feelings of anxiety, depression, and unworthiness due to constantly comparing ourselves instead of preparing ourselves, *As It Pleases God*. Be it known or unknown, the constant comparison with others can create a sense of inadequacy, diverting our focus from self-improvement to self-criticism. Above all, the denial of this makes our reprobate condition worsen Mentally, Physically, Emotionally, and Spiritually. How is this humanly possible? I would say it is more like humanly probable.

Introduction

Of course, unpreparedness can be daunting for some, especially when being a people pleaser. In this book, *The Black Sheep Power: As It Pleases God®* provides an excellent Spiritual Roadmap on how to Spiritually Prepare ourselves, *As It Pleases Him*, with guaranteed results. Besides, it can also become the best thing for our Spiritual Growth efforts. Moreover, it can also contribute to a shift in our mindsets, allowing self-awareness and self-exploration to occur, *As It Pleases God*.

The Black Sheep Power: As It Pleases God® harnesses a Divine Mentality that is designed to unlock the Divine Secrets, Treasures, Wisdom, and Lessons, bringing forth a life of Divine Purpose and Fulfillment! In the same breath, it is also designed to withhold them as well. What is the purpose of withholding what we need desperately? Until we are ready in the Eye of God, it is withheld for our protection.

The true essence of connection lies in embracing our reality for what it is instead of what it is not, while developing a strategic plan for Divine Change, Elevation, and Growth. Building strong relationships as *The Black Sheep* can become challenging, mind-boggling, heart-wrenching, or outright gut-wrenching at times. But, for a time such as this, with the right Spiritual Principles, *As It Pleases God*, it can become your Hidden Power and Strength in plain sight. This strategic method is not just about luck; it is about intention, Divine Intention to be exact.

In this book, *The Black Sheep Power: As It Pleases God®*, is designed to deal with a few things, but not limited to such:

- ☐ Navigating Conflict with Grace
- ☐ The Transformative Power of Forgiveness
- ☐ Building a Legacy of Love

Introduction

We often proclaim that we are graceful, but in the Eye of God, we are not. We sometimes say that we have forgiven ourselves or someone, but our words, actions, beliefs, and thoughts say otherwise. We assert that we are loving or full of love, but we have all types of conditions that place us and others in bondage with a deprivation of free will.

In a world that often values perfection over authenticity, it is crucial to shift your focus from flaws to the unique qualities hidden within the Spiritual Gifts that make you who you are. As a Spiritual Vessel of the Most High God, I am genuinely interested in who you are beyond the surface level.

Each of us will carry a Divine Blueprinted Purpose from within, containing Spiritual Instructions to guide, provide, and protect. All of which come with Spiritual Conditions, Contingencies, and Constraints that are listed within the pages of this book. According to our Divine Design, no two Spiritual Blueprints are exactly the same, due to our individualized experiences, beliefs, mindsets, aspirations, cultural backgrounds, traumas, and inner chatter. However, the underlying Spiritual Principles, Protocols, Procedures, and the Word of God bind them and us together as we become ONE in Christ Jesus. Now, for your Heaven on Earth Experience in Earthen Vessel, you need to know them according to Kingdom Standards, not man-made ones.

Here is the deal with *The Black Sheep Power: As It Pleases God*®, first, I am concerned about whether you are a real work-in-progress, *As It Pleases Him.* Secondly, I am also concerned whether you are Kingdomly Usable, Humble, and Obedient. Thirdly, I am also concerned about whether you can consistently use the Fruits of the Spirit and behave Christlike.

Why these attributes and concerns? Most Believers proclaim to be powerful, but when yoked or negatively challenged, they cannot hit a lick at a crooked stick. This southern colloquialism means that someone is unable to do

Introduction

something successfully or is lacking in skill or ability, especially when it comes to work or effort. As a result, they must depend on others to do what they should learn how to do for themselves.

How do we know when we are dealing with someone powerless, pretending to be strong? They will quickly revert to anger, fussing, fighting, cussing, rolling their eyes, making faces, insulting others, or confusing factual statements as being complaints to avoid accountability. Whereas, in a light-hearted manner, they should be approaching people, places, and things rationally, strategically, and wisely with a smile, using the Fruits of the Spirit and behaving Christlike.

In the Eye of God, if you do not lapse under pressure, with a little refinement, *As It Pleases Him*, you will come forth as the RAREST DIAMOND from the Heavenly of Heavens.

Still, *The Black Sheep Journey* is no joke, nor is it a laughing matter. So, when *Dealing With Unsurety* in the dusting and buffing process, I need you to rise above the challenges, ask fact-finding questions, set a Spiritual Guard over your mouth, use the Fruits of the Spirit, behave Christlike, and follow instructions.

In a world where self-help books overflow the shelves, finding the right one can feel overwhelming. Yet, if you are reading this, I invite you to open your mind and heart to one book that could genuinely revolutionize your life, GUARANTEED, preparing you for your NEXT. Moreover, this is not just a PROMISE, *Spirit to Spirit*; it is a commitment to unearthing the Cornerstone of Greatness that rests within you.

Chapter One
The First Power

Are you feeling stuck and unfulfilled? Do you feel absolutely powerless? Do you feel stuck in a rut with no way out? Are you ready for real change? Are you ready to take that leap without feeling marginalized or misunderstood? Before embarking on any transformative Spiritual Journey, it is essential to engage in self-awareness and self-reflection.

This Divinely Sacred Path is often riddled with potential, depth, insight, and a connection to something greater than oneself. Still, you must understand the inner landscapes, *As It Pleases God*, to properly prepare yourself while using the right Spiritual Tools to identify personal patterns, strengths, and weaknesses.

As a *Black Sheep*, when dealing with *The First Power*, here are a few things to ask yourself, but not limited to such:

- ☐ What exactly makes me feel stuck?
- ☐ What are my core values?
- ☐ Are my current circumstances aligned with my Divine Purpose, Passion, or Goals?
- ☐ Am I involving God in all things?
- ☐ Am I covering myself with the Blood of Jesus?
- ☐ Am I allowing the Holy Spirit to guide me?
- ☐ Am I repenting and forgiving frequently?

The First Power

By exploring these questions, you can identify the root causes of your thoughts, feelings, desires, beliefs, traumas, and triggers.

We all have untapped potential lying dormant within us, and if we do not take the time to unveil it, we can forfeit *The First Power* that we are all entitled to. All of which serves as a stepping stone, invoking action, inspiring change, guiding us through self-reflection, and empowering us to harness our internal strengths and weaknesses.

What is *The First Power*? According to the Heavenly of Heavens, our *First Power* is GRATITUDE as it applies to our Cornerstone of Greatness and our Predestined Blueprint. Simply put, when we are in Purpose on purpose, *As It Pleases God*, we invoke our Divine Birthright to lay claim to *The First Power*. Whether we deem gratitude as gratefulness or vice versa, it does not deflate its Divine Power.

If there is a *First Power*, there must be a Second Power, right? Absolutely. Our Second Power is to USE *The First Power* through our actionable, wordable, and deedable efforts, *As It Pleases God*. Without incorporating our Heavenly Father in the USE process, we will find ourselves blowing smoke and stalling our progress! Why? He has the details to unlock our true potential, and if we have more knowledge than the ONE who created us, we only deceive ourselves.

Do we really possess power, or are our power plays a bunch of hoaxes? Yes, we do have power, along with strategic power-playing abilities as well. They only become jokeable hoaxes when we attempt to outsmart, prostitute, insult, or think we are above God while playing ourselves short in the interim.

How do I know so much about the power we possess? First, according to Ephesians 3:20, it states: *"Now to Him who is able to do exceedingly abundantly above all that we ask or think,*

The First Power

according to the power that works in us." The key to our internal or external power, and the lack thereof, is based on what is working within us through what we are thinking, saying, and doing. And, if we are living carelessly and fancy-free, doing whatever, whenever, and however, rest assured, our Divine Power is much less than it could be.

Plus, living below our means of power in the Eye of God and according to our genetic potential, makes the psyche an easy trigger switch anyway. With the psyche's unseen and complex interplay of emotions, thoughts, beliefs, and experiences, we can inadvertently allow distractions and detours into our lives to leech off of our power, draining us to the core. More importantly, as *Black Sheep*, if we do not take our power back, *As It Pleases God*, we will 'get got' by the enemy's wiles.

Secondly, when dealing with *The First Power*, God does not like to be mocked. Galatians 6:7 says, *"Do not be deceived, God is not mocked; for whatever a man sows, that he will also reap."* Nor does the Holy Spirit like being blasphemed. Here is what Matthew 12:31-32 says: *"Therefore I say to you, every sin and blasphemy will be forgiven men, but the blasphemy against the Spirit will not be forgiven men. Anyone who speaks a word against the Son of Man, it will be forgiven him; but whoever speaks against the Holy Spirit, it will not be forgiven him, either in this age or in the age to come."*

If blasphemy is occurring, it is an automatic indication of the lack of Spiritual Power due to the elements of disrespect. However, we do have those who go to the dark side to receive a simulation of power, but there is a price to pay for this Spiritual Violation. The power of darkness sets its own price; we may not know what it is until after the fact. Therefore, we should exercise extreme caution when tapping into things of an unknown origin to bypass God Almighty.

The First Power

Thirdly, when dealing with *The First Power*, if selfishness is a part of our method of operation, where we consume our own fruits, rest assured, our superficial powers will bring shame in due season. Here is what Proverbs 1:31 says, *"Therefore they shall eat the fruit of their own way, and be filled to the full with their own fancies."* Why would this happen? God determines why. However, Luke 8:17, says, *"For nothing is secret that will not be revealed, nor anything hidden that will not be known and come to light."*

Now, regardless of what is working inside or outside of us, we must selflessly put in the work, *As It Pleases God*, to harness our hidden powers or unlimited potential. If we are doing this for ourselves only, we once again become limited. Without approaching all things, *As It Pleases God*, our Divine Birthright of *The First Power* to give THANKS, we can indeed CANCEL out our other Spiritual Gifts, Powers, Insights, Wisdom, or whatever.

In Discovering the Transformative Power of Gratitude (*The First Power*), it is imperative to unveil how it can align your life with God's Divine Will and Purpose. Although leading to a path of joy and abundance, it does not negate the process, testing, and training needed to sustain them.

In the Eye of God, cultivating gratitude, *As It Pleases Him*, and experiencing the life-changing benefits of doing so will make a BELIEVER out of anyone. Whereas, on the other hand, ungratefulness and negativity deprive us of our destiny-enriched experiences designed for our benefit, regardless of whether we are the *Black Sheep*, no-sheep, the sheep, or the goat.

Gratitude is not just a nice feeling when giving or receiving. According to the Heavenly of Heavens, it is a powerful and enforceable Spiritual Tool that can transform your life and that of others. In the *As It Pleases God*® Divine Framework, we prepare you to remove the limits from your Mind, Body, Soul,

The First Power

and Spirit to embrace all that God has for you. Now, if you desire half of a portion or no portion, then you have free will to reject gratefulness altogether. When doing so, you have no reason to complain, fuss, or fight about what you willfully rejected while hoping for something or someone better.

Why can a Believer not complain, fuss, or fight, especially when having free will? You can if you like, because no one is exempt from doing so, and this is where self-control comes into play with your human nature or DNA-tical dynamics. Even when someone pisses you off royally, you still have the ability to reel it in positively, kindly, and gratefully. How do I know? It happens to me all the time. I just make a conscious choice to remain kind and well-tempered, while making my best attempts to use the Fruits of the Spirit. In addition, I incorporate a lot of questions while stating facts to calm my nerves. Does it work? It works 80% of the time, and the other 20% is what I allow to fall to the ground as a seed.

What does allowing it to fall to the ground as a seed mean? It means that I do not have all the answers, and if God does not provide an answer, solution, lesson, or Divine Wisdom on the matter at hand, then I do not need to worry about it. I move on to the next thing, freeing my Mind, Body, Soul, and Spirit of this distraction while being gratefully and gracefully about my Father's Business.

Moreover, I do not pretend to be superhuman, as if I am emotionless, hard as a rock, or as if nothing matters. Listen, in Earthen Vessel, I am very human with Supernatural Tendencies that will supersede my humanness if I operate *As It Pleases God* with outright humility, gratefulness, and obedience. And the truth is, you are no different!

Whether you are *The Black Sheep*, a normal sheep, or a self-proclaimed goat, the transformative Power of Gratitude will help you recognize God's Divine Blessings in people, places, things, circumstances, and events, even in your milking or developmental stages of Spirituality. For example, in my younger days, my Spiritual Gifts, Talents, and Abilities worked, but I would miss the target based on my immaturity, lack of readiness, emotions, traumas, mindset, and so on. All of which were training me to become the woman that I am today.

My life of mistakes and failures became the Divine Platform as the WHY Doctor to edify God's precious sheep. According to the Heavenly of Heavens, this ensures that His sheep do not miss the mark due to the time sensitivities of today. In addition, it is also designed for them to understand why they missed the mark, *As It Pleases Him.*

When authentic gratefulness, *As It Pleases God*, ushers in the BEST of the BEST or gets rid of the worst of the worst, you must incorporate humility and obedience to Spiritually Seal this Divine Guarantee. If not, you will become unraveled at the seams of your psyche.

Simply put, when you lose out on a good thing due to negligence or making bad choices, it has a way of messing with your head, leaving you grappling with regret and all types of self-doubt! So, to avoid missed opportunities, it is wise to always exhibit gratefulness in all things to ensure you can extract the lesson, information, understanding, or training involved.

As experience becomes your greatest teacher, you must also simultaneously deal with *The More Factors* associated with living real life. Remember, it is not always about never losing a good thing. As a *Black Sheep*, it is about how you RESPOND and GROW from experiences, turning them into a Testimony for the Kingdom of God, to feed His precious sheep with no regrets.

When difficult circumstances, challenges, or setbacks arise, we can either succumb to despair or rise in FAITH with resilience, grace, and wisdom.

The First Power

The More Factors

Although the key to Spiritual Growth, *As It Pleases God*, is through gratefulness, we cannot take this for granted. As Spiritual Vessels of the Most High God, *The More Factors* must become equated in our equational efforts.

Humanistically, *The More Factors* refer to a multitude of elements and opportunities buried within our DNA that are actively at play beneath the surface. All of which are responsible for contributing to our varying experiences, character traits, unique perspectives, learning capacities, growth potentials, and the lack thereof.

In contrast, *The More Factors* in the Eye of God and according to Kingdom Standards also mean that there is always MORE associated with dealing with Him, our Heavenly Father, *Spirit to Spirit*.

In *The Black Sheep Power: As It Pleases God*®, as we strategically move forward in the Spirit of Excellence, *The More Factors* are also used in the conveyance of the Fruits of the Spirit in a pluralized form. Of course, once again, this is not a mistake; I am a Spiritual Writer, writing on behalf of the Heavenly of Heavens, so as the Holy Spirit reveals Divine Revelations to me, I document accordingly, *Spirit to Spirit*. And this is how I turn on the floodgates of *The More Factors*, with the multiple perspectives coming forth through the use of each FRUIT to bring us into a State of ONENESS.

So, being that we are not in a State of ONENESS as of yet, let us follow instructions with pluralizing and multiplying to become fruitful, *As It Pleases God*. Is this by force? Absolutely not! Everything in this book and beyond is based on free will. But let me back this up with Scripture before moving on: "*For we know that the whole creation groans and labors with birth pangs*

The First Power

together until now. Not only that, but we also who have the firstfruits of the Spirit, even we ourselves groan within ourselves, eagerly waiting for the adoption, the redemption of our body." Romans 8:22-23.

In *The Black Sheep Power*, is pluralizing and multiplying changing the Word of God? Absolutely not! When dealing with REAL Kingdom Power, *As It Pleases God*, we play on a different level with our Spiritual Fruits. If one is not on this type of playing field as of yet, one would not understand fully. Nonetheless, when dealing with *The Black Sheep Power: As It Pleases God*®, Matthew 21:42-44 explains it best: *"Jesus said to them, Have you never read in the Scriptures: 'The stone which the builders rejected has become the chief cornerstone. This was the LORD's doing, And it is marvelous in our eyes'? Therefore, I say to you, the kingdom of God will be taken from you and given to a nation bearing the fruits of it. And whoever falls on this stone will be broken; but on whomever it falls, it will grind him to powder."*

Is grinding someone to powder not a little harsh? Maybe or maybe not, but it is speaking metaphorically. Besides, this is more of a reason to multiply on the qualified righteous side of the spectrum instead of the unqualified negative side of it. So, let us bring forth the LIGHT in the Word with the multiplying factors.

- ☐ *"Then God blessed them, and God said to them, 'Be fruitful and multiply; fill the earth and subdue it; have dominion over the fish of the sea, over the birds of the air, and over every living thing that moves on the earth.' "* Genesis 1:28.

- ☐ *"So God blessed Noah and his sons, and said to them: 'Be fruitful and multiply, and fill the earth.' "* Genesis 9:7.

The First Power

☐ "*Also God said to him: 'I am God Almighty. Be fruitful and multiply; a nation and a company of nations shall proceed from you, and kings shall come from your body.'*" Genesis 35:11.

☐ "*But the children of Israel were fruitful and increased abundantly, multiplied and grew exceedingly mighty; and the land was filled with them.*" Exodus 1:7.

☐ "*For I will look on you favorably and make you fruitful, multiply you and confirm My covenant with you.*" Leviticus 26:9.

☐ "*Now may He who supplies seed to the sower, and bread for food, supply and multiply the seed you have sown and increase the fruits of your righteousness, while you are enriched in everything for all liberality, which causes thanksgiving through us to God.*" 2 Corinthians 9:10-11.

Why is fruitfulness so important in the Eye of God? First, He loves righteousness, peace, and excellence. "*But the wisdom that is from above is first pure, then peaceable, gentle, willing to yield, full of mercy and good fruits, without partiality and without hypocrisy. Now the fruit of righteousness is sown in peace by those who make peace.*" James 3:17-18.

Secondly, without fruitfulness, we will die off from the inside out because the Earth does not see us as a benefit. Hosea 4:6 clearly says, "*My people are destroyed for lack of knowledge. Because you have rejected knowledge, I also will reject you from being priest for Me; because you have forgotten the law of your God, I also will forget your children.*"

The First Power

Here is what happens thereafter, according to Isaiah 5:13: *"Therefore my people have gone into captivity, because they have no knowledge; their honorable men are famished, and their multitude dried up with thirst."* If we feel as if we are in captivity, famished, lukewarm, stiff-necked, dull, or thirsty, we must double-check our multiplying factors, because the math is not mathing in the Eye of God. Without further ado, let us math this thing out.

In our developmental process, when it comes to our Blueprinted Destiny, *The More Factors* will remain hidden until we put in the work, doing what we were called to do and Spiritually Tilling our own ground, *As It Pleases God.* For instance, in Earthen Vessels, when we are limited, even if we pretend we are not, it exposes our *More Factors* to the elements of GREED and DISCONTENTMENT. Whereas, with God, our Heavenly Father, He is unlimited, which can be tapped into through SELFLESSNESS and SERVANTHOOD.

In our materialistic lifestyles, it is very easy to become overwhelmed by the challenges of fitting the bill. For this reason, stressful situations, failures, and setbacks can cloud our sense of good judgment or perception in the Spirit of Righteousness. All of which makes it extremely difficult to see the silver lining or the Greater Good from a Divine Perspective or *As It Pleases God.*

The most profound question about *The More Factor* is, 'How can we obtain more as a *Black Sheeped* Believer without becoming greedy or ungrateful?' When dealing with *The More Factors* as a *Black Sheep*, we must develop a *Spirit to Spirit* connection with our Heavenly Father using a few things, but not limited to such:

- ☐ We must become ONE with the Holy Trinity.
- ☐ We must COVER ourselves with the Blood of Jesus.

The First Power

- ☐ We must INVITE the Holy Spirit into our lives.
- ☐ We must USE and ALIGN with the Word of God.
- ☐ We must INVOKE our Spiritual Instincts.
- ☐ We must APPLY the Fruits of the Spirit.
- ☐ We must BEHAVE Christlike.
- ☐ We must AGREE to be in Purpose on purpose.
- ☐ We must DEVELOP a work-in-progress mindset.
- ☐ We must REPENT, PRAY, and FORGIVE always.
- ☐ We must BECOME Kingdomly Usable.
- ☐ We must LEAD in the Spirit of Excellence.

Can we really complete everything on the above list? Yes, we can. In my opinion, this is the easy part of living a life of fruitfulness. Unfortunately, it is the CHOOSING parts of righteousness that become difficult for us as Believers, especially when dealing with knowledge and insight, *As It Pleases God*. For this reason, Proverbs 3:5-10 says, "*Trust in the Lord with all your heart, And lean not on your own understanding; In all your ways acknowledge Him, And He shall direct your paths. Do not be wise in your own eyes; Fear the Lord and depart from evil. It will be health to your flesh, And strength to your bones. Honor the Lord with your possessions, And with the firstfruits of all your increase; So your barns will be filled with plenty, And your vats will overflow with new wine.*"

Even the Apostle Paul drops Nuggets of Wisdom for us to glean in Colossians 1:9-12. "*For this reason we also, since the day we heard it, do not cease to pray for you, and to ask that you may be filled with the knowledge of His will in all wisdom and spiritual understanding; that you may walk worthy of the Lord, fully pleasing Him, being fruitful in every good work and increasing in the knowledge of God; strengthened with all might, according to His glorious power, for all patience and longsuffering with joy; giving thanks to the Father who has qualified us to be partakers of the inheritance of the saints in the light.*"

The First Power

Whereas, on the other hand, willful disobedience in the Eye of God will indeed make everything and everyone a hassle or seemingly difficult. From a Spiritual Standpoint, the conscious choice to disregard established rules, laws, or moral guidelines makes us stiff-necked, dull, lukewarm, or unstable in the Spiritual Realm. All of which causes us to become easily yoked, utterly soul tied, negatively entrenched, emotionally unstable, waywardly influenced, or outright toxic.

Why would Believers become hassled by God Almighty? He does not physically hassle us, so to speak. Unfortunately, it happens Mentally, Emotionally, and Spiritually with a hands-off and highly effective approach. But let me say this: His silence or rejection allows our enemies and our psyche to have their way, blocking our resilience and clarity. Please allow me to Spiritually Align this according to 1 Samuel 15:23. *"For rebellion is as the sin of witchcraft, and stubbornness is as iniquity and idolatry. Because you have rejected the word of the Lord, He also has rejected you from being king."* This Spiritual Principle was gleaned from King Saul's Experience, and is all the more relevant now than ever.

How do King Saul's Experiences become relevant to us in this day and age? In *The More Factors*, here are a few reasons for its relevancy, but not limited to such:

- ☐ We as a people have become rebellious without realizing we are. Here is what Divine Wisdom teaches us about disobedience and rebellion in Proverbs 17:11: *"An evil man seeks only rebellion; therefore a cruel messenger will be sent against him."*

- ☐ We have become more idolatrous with self-created and man-made idols without realizing we are becoming as such. Jeremiah 10:14 says, *"Everyone is dull-hearted, and*

The First Power

without knowledge; every metalsmith is put to shame by the carved image; for his molded image is falsehood, and there is no breath in them."

- ☐ We have become more manipulative and controlling without realizing it. As a *Black Sheep*, here is what Romans 1:18-19 says about this matter: *"For the wrath of God is revealed from heaven against all ungodliness and unrighteousness of men, who suppress the truth in unrighteousness, because what may be known of God is manifest in them, for God has shown it to them."*

- ☐ We are quick to call people witches or demonic without knowing or understanding the character traits associated. Here is what Galatians 5:19-21 says about this matter: *"Now the works of the flesh are evident, which are: adultery, fornication, uncleanness, lewdness, idolatry, sorcery (witchcraft), hatred, contentions, jealousies, outbursts of wrath, selfish ambitions, dissentions, heresies, envy, murders, drunkenness, revelries, and the like; of which I tell you beforehand, just as I also told you in time past, that those who practice such things will not inherit the kingdom of God."*

- ☐ We are quick to violate Spiritual Laws such as Seedtime and Harvest, the Law of Cause and Effect, and so on, without knowing or understanding anything about them. Proverbs 28:9 clearly says, *"One who turns away his ear from hearing the law, even his prayer is an abomination."* And then we dare to question why our prayers are falling to the ground with zero Spiritual Power.

The First Power

- [ ] We engage in unwise counsel, while leaving God out of the equation as if He does not have a say in the matter. Isaiah 30:1 says, *"Woe to the rebellious children, says the Lord, who take counsel, but not of Me, and who devise plans, but not of My Spirit, that they may add sin to sin."*

- [ ] We are outright resistant without realizing it. Romans 13:2 says, *"Therefore whoever resists the authority resists the ordinance of God, and those who resist will bring judgment on themselves."*

- [ ] We focus more on material gain than Spiritual Gain or Wisdom. Here is what Matthew 6:19-21 advises: *"Do not store up for yourselves treasures on earth, where moths and vermin destroy, and where thieves break in and steal. But store up for yourselves treasures in heaven, where moths and vermin do not destroy, and where thieves do not break in and steal. For where your treasure is, there your heart will be also."* Nevertheless, here is the order of any sort of gain we should follow according to Matthew 6:33, *"But seek first his kingdom and his righteousness, and all these things will be given to you as well."*

Now the question is, 'How do we make *The More Factors* work on our behalf and *As It Pleases God?*' According to the Heavenly of Heavens, we are required to WAKE UP and *Shift Focus*. *"Now Christ is risen from the dead, and has become the firstfruits of those who have fallen asleep."* 1 Corinthians 15:20. Yes, we must shift our focus from worldly to Spiritual while aligning with the Word of God and our Predestined Blueprinted Purpose. So, let us go deeper.

The First Power

Shift Focus

When *Shifting Focus*, we ought not overcomplicate things because it is in simplicity that God makes hard and complex things appear easy and achievable to mankind. Here is the deal: *In The Black Sheep Power: As It Pleases God*®, when building Divine Substance, we *Shift Focus* to our SHARRE Concept, but not limited to such:

- ☐ **S**implicity.
- ☐ **H**umility.
- ☐ **A**uthenticity.
- ☐ **R**elatability.
- ☐ **R**elevance.
- ☐ **E**xcellence.

The Black Sheep Power's SHARRE Concept helps us to build real substance in the Eye of God when it comes to the real acts of sharing. For the record, the inability to share makes us Kingdomly Limited, even though God may use us to a certain extent. However, when dealing with our Divine Purpose, we will have limited access while suffering a longing from within the psyche. Why would the psyche do this to Believers? Because the psyche knows there is something more, but is denied access. If it keeps us blocked, it remains in control, doing whatever it wants and whenever it likes.

Believe it or not, those who lack substance most often do not realize they lack it while appearing right in their own eyes. But of course, no one is exempt from this process; we will all go through this to determine what we are working with, why we are working with it, and for whom. Plus, this is where most of us miss the mark in or out of the Kingdom.

The First Power

Why would we lack substance as Believers? The undeniable and daunting emptiness within the psyche will accompany any form of superficiality or mask. Unfortunately, this is when we must constantly hide who we really are. The more we lean into deceiving ourselves and others, when the mask comes off, we are in for a rude awakening, regardless of whether we are a *Black Sheep* or not.

What is more baffling than all, those who speak the truth in love are rejected and *Black Sheeped* by those who are not authentically themselves. How do I know? Suppose someone is intentionally *Blacksheeping* others, deliberately blocking someone, or outright excluding them. In this case, it means that they are dealing with some form of hidden jealousy, envy, brainwashing, coveting, competitiveness, resentment, or animosity. Really? Yes, really!

As a matter of fact, it is happening in churches among so-called Believers more now than ever in the history of Christianity. How do we make this make sense? First, we have social media connecting and dividing us all at the same time, with transactional and conditional relations. Secondly, we debate over who is right and who is wrong, or who God loves more. Thirdly, when God is giving a right-now, relevant WORD to feed His sheep, if it does not fit into our agenda, make us money, or offend sensitive, yet rebellious ears, we silence the person or refuse to share it with others.

What if the Word is not of God? As Believers, if we are whooping and hollering, we should know the difference; if not, we have work to do! If a broadcast word is tickling our ears without provoking change, *As It Pleases God*, then it does not take a rocket scientist to know the difference! Remember, Spirit knows Spirit.

For example, I ran across a conference being broadcast publicly, where most of the presenters were NOT sent from the Heavenly of Heavens by the Most High God. Clearly, I am

The First Power

not discrediting anyone's sharing of the Gospel because they were doing what they were getting paid to do. Nor am I discrediting anyone's message. Yet, the one MESSAGE that God Divinely Sent was not shared publicly and *Blacksheeped*. At the same time, some dared to say that the sermon or the Word of God was not good, only to crush and shame the Divine Mission of God within this individual.

As a Divine Vessel of the Most High God, I am here to say publicly on this day: The Devil is a liar...the show must go on! God is still moving, and no one can stop the Divine Movement of God, period! Yes, I said it, and I will not back down...I am here to feed God's sheep for real, for real. Nor will I tolerate any form of character assassination against those who are TRULY CALLED and CHOSEN or in Spiritual Training, *As It Pleases God*.

How do I know the difference between who is Called or Chosen? I have the Spiritual Ears to HEAR what most cannot! I have the Spiritual Eyes to SEE what most cannot. I have the Spiritual Voice to SPEAK what most cannot. More importantly, I have the Spiritual Discipline to allow everyone and everything to play their roles to extract and convert the Divine Information hidden within them to feed God's sheep.

My Spiritual Gifts are from the Heavenly Realms that are Divinely Aligned with my Predestined Blueprinted Purpose. In this book, *The Black Sheep Power: As It Pleases God*®, I will share the Spiritual Principles, Protocols, and Procedures on how to do likewise, while KNOWING and RESPECTING the differences in others on their Spiritual Journey as such.

When Spiritually Embarking in such a manner, it is imperative to learn how to master the *Reverse Engineering* Process to analyze our journey backward. Why must we master this process as Believers? First, it prevents us from living backwardly. Secondly, we can identify pivotal moments in our lives, the lessons learned or the ones we did not learn, and the underlying positive or negative patterns that shape us. Then again, we can also pinpoint the people, places, and things that can result in our potential downfall. Thirdly, it helps us to reflect and assess our past experiences and choices without getting stuck in the past or living in regret. Lastly, it helps us gain clarity and direction for our next whatever, with whomever.

Reverse Engineering

When we think about reversing anything, based on our cultural backgrounds or societal norms, we tend to interject all types of demonic or unrealistic taboos, zapping *The First Power*. Once we engage in such taboos, we will begin to get God all wrong, saying He said what He did not say, doing things He did not tell us to do, and becoming nothing like He intended, according to our Predestined Blueprinted Purpose. Plus, we could miss out on our Divine Opportunities due to cultural judgments that have zero relevance and are not Biblical.

To safeguard *The Black Sheep Power: As It Pleases God*®, let us get an understanding of *Reverse Engineering* in the Eye of God. *Reverse Engineering*, from a Divine Perspective, is the process of deconstructing or analyzing ourselves Mentally, Physically, Emotionally, and Spiritually to understand the underlying Spiritual Principles, Laws, and Protocols of God, our Heavenly Father and Creator. This process is designed to help us align or realign our lives accordingly with the end-to-beginning concept, similar to setting a goal and working in reverse to achieve it.

From the Ancient of Days, *Reverse Engineering* as a *Black Sheep* is more than just a technical process. Actually, it is a Spiritual Journey of self-discovery and self-awareness that seeks to align our human understanding, rationale, and know-how

The First Power

with Divine Wisdom, *As It Pleases God*. While simultaneously prompting us to confront fears, doubts, insecurities, and ingrained habits. This process also challenges us to dismantle, analyze, and reconstruct our understanding of our Heaven on Earth Experiences, Predestined Blueprints, and Spiritual Gifts.

In honoring our unique paths and free will options, no one will get the *Reverse Engineering* process right the first time around because Spiritual training must occur, *As It Pleases God*. Those who pretend to get it right all the time are full of fluff and extra stuff. Why is this the case, especially when having it going on and in need of nothing? Regardless of our wants, needs, desires, or status, Divine Wisdom on any level tests, trains, and establishes with Kingdom Protocol, Standards, and Laws for our protection. If we seemingly get everything right with zero corrective measures, BEWARE!

Spiritually Speaking, introspection on your behalf helps you pinpoint or filter your authentic values, desires, and motivations. When *reverse-engineering* your life, *As It Pleases God*, by asking fact-finding questions, you can get the ball rolling in mastering this transformative process. Listed below are a few questions to ask yourself, but not limited to such:

- ☐ What do I truly value?

- ☐ Why do I value it so much?

- ☐ What core beliefs do I hold that shape my views?

- ☐ What beliefs have I inherited, and which are truly mine?

- ☐ Which experiences in my life have had the most significant impact?

The First Power

- ☐ What negative experiences have pushed me to redefine myself?

- ☐ When do I feel most fulfilled and why?

- ☐ What activities make me lose track of time?

- ☐ What role does fear play in my decision-making?

- ☐ In what areas of my life do I feel the most inauthentic or disconnected?

- ☐ How can I better align my actions with my Spiritual Principles?

- ☐ How do I define success, and does that definition align with my true Spiritual Values or Predestined Blueprint?

- ☐ How do I envision my ideal life?

- ☐ What practical steps can I take to align my daily actions to PLEASE God?

Based on your answers, consider journaling them, as well as your thoughts, testimonies, and experiences. Proper documentation in the Eye of God lets Him know that you are serious about your life, decisions, and feelings. In addition, it also allows you to keep a track record or tangible history of your progress, identify patterns, pinpoint struggles, and evaluate their impact on your well-being.

The First Power

What is the purpose of documenting as Believers? First, it helps us to OVERCOME. Here is the Spiritual Seal from Revelation 12:11, "*And they overcame him by the blood of the Lamb and by the word of their testimony, and they did not love their lives to the death.*" Secondly, it helps us confess our hopes through documented reminders. Here is what Hebrews 10:23 advises: "*Let us hold fast the confession of our hope without wavering, for He who promised is faithful.*"

With a *Transformation of the Heart and Mind*, the assurance that God will equip you to overcome will come forth when you embrace a work-in-progress demeanor, *As It Pleases Him*. Now, if for some reason you prefer to equip yourself, then have at it, and give yourself a pat on the back. Trust me, by the time the enemy, the Cycles, and the Vicissitudes of Life are done with you, you will surrender to the Clarion Call.

How can I say such a thing, right? You are here for a reason, and if you do not know what it is or avoid it altogether, then the Cycle of Life will attempt to purge you Mentally, Physically, Emotionally, and Spiritually in hopes that you awaken from your slumber. Even Ecclesiastes 3:1-2 says, "*To everything there is a season, a time for every purpose under heaven: a time to be born, and a time to die; a time to plant, and a time to pluck what is planted.*" The moment you think you are exempt, rest assured, you are sadly mistaken. In the Divine Call for growth and purification, God is requiring you to do your part with your Heaven on Earth Experiences.

Transformation of the Heart and Mind

As we all know, God weighs the Heart and Mind Postures of mankind because they lead to more breached contracts than we could ever imagine. Clearly, these are not physical contracts; they are Spiritual Contracts based on the reason for our being. Here is a prime example from Jeremiah 1:5, saying,

The First Power

"Before I formed you in the womb, I knew you; before you were born I sanctified you; I ordained you a prophet to the nations."

God has put the foreknowledge of His Divine Love and Purpose inside each individual, written on the Tablet of the Heart. Really? Yes, really! Here is what Romans 8:29 says, *"For whom He foreknew, He also predestined to be conformed to the image of His Son, that He might be the firstborn among many brethren."*

Even amid our Divine Foreknowledge, Predestined Blueprint, Spiritual Gifts, and the Conformity of Christ, in Earthen Vessels, we have still forgotten the reasons why we are here in the first place. As a result, we get into the mindset that we can control everything with the mind while losing touch with our hearts. What does this mean? We focus on mind power without knowing what is in our hearts or anything about using the Fruits of the Spirit. In the Realm of the Spirit, this creates an ultimate disconnect in our heart and mind postures, making us confused, disassociated, and irrational. While at the same time, not realizing that we are.

Spiritually Speaking, in the *Transformation of the Heart and Mind*, it has zero tolerance for certain things. When I say zero tolerance, it means that the heart and mind cannot transform as they should when possessing certain character traits that spoil our fruits and those of others.

Picturesquely, certain character traits bump heads like bumping water molecules in boiling water, forming bubbles. Once the bubble pops or erupts, whatever is around it will get splashed. What is really doing the bumping for Believers, especially in the Eye of God? The inner chatter of the heart and mind is bumping against each other. For instance, this is where the mind is saying one thing and the heart is saying another, and a Spiritual Bump is then created. Here is how James 1:8 defines this person: *"He is a double-minded man, unstable in all his ways."*

The First Power

Although we cannot physically see them bumping, the results are imminent if left uncorrected with lukewarmness, or the heat is not reduced by taking some form of corrective action. With this analogy, we can better understand when Revelation 3:16 says, *"So then, because you are lukewarm, and neither cold nor hot, I will vomit you out of My mouth."* Even though we often do not admit being in this condition, our actions, words, body language, and demeanor will rat us out, exposing our heart or mind postures.

Here is a list of a few zero-tolerance items, but not limited to such:

- ☐ The *Transformation of the Heart and Mind* has zero tolerance for those who do not have love for God, themselves, or others. For this reason, 1 John 4:7 says, *"Dear friends, let us love one another, for love comes from God. Everyone who loves has been born of God and knows God."*

- ☐ The *Transformation of the Heart and Mind* has zero tolerance for the shenanigans of those who are not at peace with others. Here is what Colossians 3:15 advises: *"And let the peace of God rule in your hearts, to which also you were called in one body; and be thankful."*

- ☐ The *Transformation of the Heart and Mind* has zero tolerance for those who are extremely impatient, unproductive, unreliable, and unfruitful. Here is what James 1:3-4 says, *"Knowing that the testing of your faith produces patience. But let patience have its perfect work, that you may be perfect and complete, lacking nothing."*

- ☐ The *Transformation of the Heart and Mind* has zero tolerance for those who are unkind, unruly, and blatantly reckless. Here is what Ephesians 4:32 shares with us: *"And be kind to one another, tenderhearted, forgiving one another, even as God in Christ forgave you."*

- ☐ The *Transformation of the Heart and Mind* has zero tolerance for those who are unfaithful, untimely, and unmanageable. Here is what Isaiah 40:31 says, *"But those who wait on the Lord shall renew their strength; they shall mount up with wings like eagles, they shall run and not be weary, they shall walk and not faint."*

- ☐ The *Transformation of the Heart and Mind* has zero tolerance for those who refuse to show any form of goodness whatsoever. Romans 12:21 advises, *"Do not be overcome by evil, but overcome evil with good."*

- ☐ The *Transformation of the Heart and Mind* has zero tolerance for those who are abrasive, rude, or toxic. Titus 2:7 says, *"In all things showing yourself to be a pattern of good works; in doctrine showing integrity, reverence, incorruptibility."*

- ☐ The *Transformation of the Heart and Mind* has zero tolerance for the lack of self-control. Here is how 2 Peter 1:5-7 sums up this key aspect of Fruitful Development, *As It Pleases God*: *"But also for this very reason, giving all diligence, add to your faith virtue, to virtue knowledge, to knowledge self-control, to self-control perseverance, to perseverance godliness, to godliness brotherly kindness, and to brotherly kindness love."*

The First Power

Nevertheless, within our character, behaviors, and purpose lies Divine Revelation and a wake-up call, especially if we pursue living life, *As It Pleases God*. *"Therefore, whatever you want men to do to you, do also to them, for this is the Law and the Prophets."* Matthew 7:12.

Amid awakening from our slumber, we do not lose our identity in Christ Jesus; it only exemplifies the refinement process needed to reflect His Divine Virtues for the Greater Good. Can God really do this for us? Absolutely! Ezekiel 36:26 says, *"I will give you a new heart and put a new spirit in you; I will remove from you your heart of stone and give you a heart of flesh."*

What is the catch with a heart of flesh? There is no catch; there is just a Divine Expectation, yet still available to all mankind. This Divine Expectation is located in Philippians 1:27, saying, *"Only let your conduct be worthy of the gospel of Christ, so that whether I come and see you or am absent, I may hear of your affairs, that you stand fast in one spirit, with one mind striving together for the faith of the gospel."*

How can we truly work on our conduct when life is lifing and the Cycle of Life has us in a tizzy? God has given us the Fruits of the Spirit to work with as He weighs the *Heart and Mind Postures* of all mankind. I am living proof that they work; use them, and they will revolutionize our lives in ways that we can only give Him the glory as we become the Crème de la Crème of Divine Greatness.

In *Transformation of the Heart and Mind*, grace, forgiveness, mercy, humility, and love on our terms do not equate to God's Divine Purpose for them all. If not governed properly, it can make *The Black Sheep* negatively darker, especially when bullied, sucker-punched, ridiculed, or shamefully outed.

Galatians 5:15 says, *"But if you bite and devour one another, beware lest you be consumed by one another."* For this reason, we are going to *Reverse Engineer* this tendency, enabling *The Black Sheep* to

The First Power

become positively POWERFUL, Mentally, Physically, Emotionally, and Spiritually. When done properly and *As It Pleases God*, it helps in keeping all things in the Light of God, with good, anointed oil in our Spiritual Lamps.

As a *Black Sheep* in or out of the Kingdom of God, when it comes to *The First Power* of your Divine Birthright, you are the LIGHT designed to illuminate dark areas with clarity, hope, and guidance. On the other hand, if you do not embrace this significant responsibility, *As It Pleases God*, the darkness of your training or toiling process will embody more confusion, despair, and loss until you awaken from your slumber.

Clearly, no one is exempt from this process. Your role as a seemingly underdog or *Black Sheep* is vital in the training process of how to make wise choices when life is lifing. Listen, the Cycles, Seasons, or Vicissitudes of Life do not stop because we want them to. They will do their job, carrying out the Will of God, with or without our participation, submission, or permission.

Plus, if you think for a minute that you are here in this world just to exist, take up space, or emulate others, you are sadly mistaken! According to your Divine Blueprint, you are here to Divinely Illuminate this world in the area that darkness has trained or attempted to silence you. For this reason, in *The Black Sheep Power: As It Pleases God*®, it is my reasonable service to provide the necessary time-sensitive information on *Overcoming Fear and Doubt*, which has a target on your back.

Chapter Two
Overcoming Fear and Doubt

Are you tired of fear and doubt holding you back? Have you ever felt paralyzed from pursuing your dreams? Are you afraid to speak up for yourself? Are you tired of letting fear and doubt dictate your life? In this chapter, we will discover practical strategies to conquer your inner critic, unveil your Divine Blueprinted Purpose, and unlock your true Divine Potential, *As It Pleases God*. In addition, it will help us break free from the mental barriers and traumas designed to set us back, or prevent us from embracing a life of limitless possibilities.

When we are fearful, we often do not admit it because it makes us appear weak and vulnerable. However, as a *Black Sheep*, in order to *Overcome Fear and Doubt* once and for all, we must understand a few things. First, since the dawn of time, fear has been intricately woven into the fabric of our DNA. Actually, it is a primal emotion, designed to preserve our lives from danger, alerting us to danger, and prompting us to take action. Yet, outside of self-preservation, mismanaged or ungoverned fears have a way of taking lives, or becoming extremely burdensome.

Secondly, fear and doubt have profound physiological implications, particularly on our hormonal balance. Most of us will chop fear and doubt up as emotional imbalances. In the Eye of God and according to our DNA, they have behind-the-

Overcoming Fear and Doubt

scenes implications that we often do not associate with our Spiritual Journey of Enlightenment. Here is the deal: For a time such as this, God is calling for us to learn about the connection between our Physical, Emotional, Mental, Spiritual, and Hormonal State of Being. What does this mean in layman's terms? It is time for Spirituality to meet up with SCIENCE, for real, for real! Our *Hormonal Health* depends upon us to bridge the gap between our Belief System and the Temple of God.

On this Spiritual Journey of connection, understanding, and personal growth, we must recognize some of the underlying factors of the unseen taking place from within. Most often, we find ourselves blaming things on the devil, but really, some things are happening within our bodies due to our lack of understanding. So in this chapter, we are going to take a deep dive into a few things, but not limited to such:

- ☐ Our Hormonal Health.
- ☐ The Pressure.
- ☐ The Bounce Back.
- ☐ The Learning Process.

As a *Black Sheep*, you are indeed the Temple of God, created with Divine Intentions and Purpose, *As It Pleases Him.* In your reclamation process of your Divine Worthiness, there are a few things you must understand about yourself, even if you think you know everything. In essence, to open the doors to *Overcoming Fear and Doubt* associated with or stemming from your past, present, and future, you must get to know the Divine Expectations.

For instance, as the whispers of past mistakes may echo loudly in your mind, you need to know what to do and how to respond. As your present challenges seem to become more

Overcoming Fear and Doubt

daunting by the moment, you must know what to do and how to respond. As the uncertainty of the future looms with swirling threats of destruction, you must know what to do and how to respond. If not, you can place cracks in your own foundation while zapping your own confidence by not knowing the simplicities of the complexities.

For our Heaven on Earth Experiences, according to the Ancient of Days, let us discuss what most Believers avoid talking about.

Hormonal Health

When we experience fear or doubt, real or imagined, our body activates a stress response, often referred to as the 'fight or flight' reaction. This process begins in the brain, where the amygdala detects the threat and signals the hypothalamus to activate the sympathetic nervous system. According to how we were prewired from the Beginning, this triggers the adrenal glands to release a surge of hormones, including adrenaline (epinephrine) and cortisol. Now, regardless of whether we are a Believer or not, this process will occur; however, God has given us the Fruits of the Spirit to counteract the long-term effects of it.

In order to harness *The Black Sheep Power: As It Pleases God*®, there are a few things we must know about our hormonal selves to master our Spirit Man.

- ☐ Adrenaline is the hormone that prepares the body for immediate action. It increases heart rate, elevates blood pressure, and boosts energy supplies. While these effects can be beneficial in acute situations, chronic elevation of adrenaline due to ongoing fear or doubt can lead to fatigue, anxiety, and other stress-related health issues.

Overcoming Fear and Doubt

- [ ] Cortisol is often referred to as the 'stress hormone.' Cortisol helps regulate a variety of processes in the body, including metabolism and immune response. In the short term, cortisol can be beneficial in managing stress; however, prolonged high levels due to continuous fear, doubt, and anxiety can lead to numerous health problems, such as weight gain, cardiovascular diseases, autoimmune conditions, weakened immune function, and digestive issues.

As Believers, the interplay between fear and doubt does not stop with adrenaline and cortisol. They can also affect other hormones if we do not counteract them with the Fruits of the Spirit and behave Christlike. How do we make this make sense? There is no Spiritual Law against the use of the Fruit of the Spirit according to Galatians 5:22-23. Which means, they are designed to coax our human nature that supersedes our understanding.

According to the Heavenly of Heavens, in addition to exercise, meditation, proper nutrition, and sleep, there is more to our hormonal health. The healing powers hidden in Love, Joy, Peace, Patience, Kindness, Goodness, Faithfulness, Gentleness, and Self-Control can indeed help control the adrenaline and cortisol released into our bloodstreams. However, if we know nothing about their use, then who knows what is really going on from within. Who knows what fear and doubt are causing within the human psyche?

What are the other hormones that are being released into the Body of Believers? I am so glad you asked!

- [ ] Fear and doubt affect our INSULIN. Chronic stress can lead to insulin resistance, as high levels of cortisol

Overcoming Fear and Doubt

can interfere with insulin's function in regulating blood sugar. This can increase the risk of developing type 2 diabetes and contribute to weight gain.

- ☐ Fear and doubt affect ESTROGEN and TESTOSTERONE. Chronic fear and doubt may disrupt the balance of reproductive hormones. In women, elevated cortisol levels can lead to irregular menstrual cycles or exacerbate symptoms of premenstrual syndrome (PMS). In men, chronic stress can lower testosterone levels, impacting libido and overall mood.

- ☐ Fear and doubt affect SEROTONIN and DOPAMINE. These neurotransmitters are crucial for mood regulation. Chronic fear and doubt can decrease their levels, leading to increased anxiety and depression. Unfortunately, this, in turn, can create a vicious cycle where the brain's hormonal balance affects emotional health, perpetuating feelings of fear, doubt, trauma, and paranoia.

Being that we as Believers are not taught about *Hormonal Health*, the hormonal consequences are evident, especially among Believers. As a result, we find ourselves between a rock and a hard place with mental disorders, health conditions, and ungodly situations that could be reversed or avoided.

In Earthen Vessels, if we do not prepare ourselves, *As It Pleases God*, the elevated cortisol levels associated with known and unknown stress can lead to anxiety, fear, doubt, and a distorted sense of self-worth. As our bodies are designed to trigger-release cortisol, if we do not take the time to prepare

Overcoming Fear and Doubt

ourselves, *As It Pleases Him*, only to selfishly please ourselves, we may find ourselves overwhelmed, confused, and lost without understanding why.

Similarly, according to our DNA, imbalances in estrogen and progesterone can affect our mood and emotional stability, further complicating our ability to find genuine happiness. All of which can make us feel as if we are the *Black Sheep* when we are not. All in all, it becomes a problem when the mind creates or feeds us images of being *Blacksheeped* when it is an illusion with zero facts or formal truth.

How do *Hormonal Imbalances* occur? Most often, it is because we engage with people, places, and things that are UNPLEASING to God. While at the same time, covering it up as if we have done no wrong. And, sometimes, it is not the action that got us in hot water; it was the acts of disobedience and the cover-up that landed us in trouble, and our psyche traumatized.

Hypothetically, here is an example of how fear and doubt can work against us: Amid the fear of being alone and the doubt of not finding the right person, we decided to play God, fabricating our own miracles to downplay the inner turmoil and shame of being single and alone. Only to find out that we have created our worst nightmare by choosing someone outside of the Will of God.

Can we really create our own nightmare realities when we are on fire for God and covered by the Blood of Jesus? Absolutely. It happened to me...I have made really bad decisions in my life because I was impatient and fearful, wanting what I wanted. It was not that I was a bad person or did not love God; it was that fear and doubt had a chokehold on me that I could not seem to break. In addition, no one had the answers or instructions to help with my dilemma. I really mean no one!

Overcoming Fear and Doubt

Why would no one have the answers, especially when there is nothing new under the sun? First, it was my Spiritual Training Ground and Classroom. Secondly, I had to develop a certain type of *Spirit to Spirit* Relationship with my Heavenly Father to download Divine Information, Instructions, and Revelations. Thirdly, it was a part of my Divine Destiny to provide the Spiritual Answers and Solutions, *As It Pleased God.* And lastly, it is through the Power of my Testimony that I write effectively, relevantly, authentically, and from hands-on experiences. With *The Black Sheep Power: As It Pleases God*®, I have enough Spiritual Power to reach everyone, from the poorhouse to the penthouse, while landing smack dab into the White House, leaving no one behind or untouched through the Law of Reciprocity. Of course, *The Pressure* is no joke, but to save millions of lives, it is worth the effort. So let us talk about this a little more.

The Pressure

From childhood, we are often taught to be brave and strong, while not understanding the components associated with the pressure to maintain a facade of courage without God Almighty. If we do not learn how to CONFRONT and PROCESS our fears, they can work against us by introducing stress, anxiety, and other bodily ailments or sicknesses. Then again, when doubt is added to the equation, it solidifies our fears.

With any form of fear or doubt, there is always a root cause. In the Eye of God, it is our responsibility to pinpoint what it is or is not. For example, 2 Timothy 1:7 says, *"For God has not given us a spirit of fear, but of power and of love and of a sound mind."* So, if this is the case, where is the fear coming from? Do you know? Or, do you even care?

Overcoming Fear and Doubt

Listen, fear, and doubt are illusions that are cleverly disguised as strengths, often holding us back from reaching our full potential. For example, when I am approach by someone slinging power, running their mouth as if they are tough or they are absolutely talking too much, I already know what time it is. For the record, in the Kingdom of God, our strength is wrapped in humility and self-control. If a person prides themself on being the tough guy or girl, it is an automatic indication of a weakness in the Eye of God.

The world often idolizes toughness, and the Kingdom of God conveys meekness as the Lamb of God. Does this not make a Believer a pushover? Maybe or maybe not, but it makes them Divinely Usable, Teachable, and Effective. Above all, it gives them a *Bounce Back* that will make their enemies shake in their boots. Here is what Proverbs 24:16 has to say: *"For a righteous man may fall seven times and rise again, but the wicked shall fall by calamity."*

Bouncing Back

Regardless of how things appear to the naked eye, if we do not exhibit self-control, it says a lot about our character, even if we proclaim earthly power. The goal of *The Black Sheep* is to bring forth the Spiritual Power that we already possess from within, so if we get pushed over, we will have a BOUNCE BACK that confounds human reasoning.

What is the big deal about *Bouncing Back*? In the Eye of God, it is not a matter of getting knocked down, because this is a part of life. Our Spiritual Power and Dominance as being *The Black Sheep* are predicated on getting back up, dusting ourselves off, and helping others to do likewise for the Greater Good.

Suppose our *Bounce Back* is predicated on getting people back, throwing people under the bus, chucking rocks, or

Overcoming Fear and Doubt

dragging people through the mud. In this case, the weight of *The Pressure* will crush us Mentally, Physically, Emotionally, or Spiritually. For the record, we should never impulsively undertake endeavors that can lead to our own downfall or that of another. Nor should we set deliberate traps to trip someone up or to expose them.

Here is what Ecclesiastes 10:8 says about the potential repercussions of our choice to dig and plot: *"He who digs a pit will fall into it, and whoever breaks through a wall will be bitten by a serpent."* Due to these dangerous tendencies of digging and plotting, we are forced back into the Spiritual Classroom for more training on Spiritual Etiquette.

Why are we forced back into the Spiritual Classroom, especially when having free will? It is due to an underlying coveting quirk in our character. Here is where I found this information: Proverbs 12:12 says, *"The wicked covet the catch of evil men, but the root of the righteous yields fruit."* When we set intentional traps or make an attempt to trip someone up, there are elements of coveting involved. We can deny this all we like, but within the human psyche, coveting is a key factor and will affect our *Bounce Back* efforts.

Coveting, from a Spiritual Perspective, often refers to an intense desire for what others have. Which can include possessions, relationships, lifestyles, or qualities that can lead to feelings of jealousy of what belongs to us, envy of what does not belong to us, dissatisfaction in all things, and a disconnection from our Predestined Path, Promise, Passion, or Purpose. Are they not all the same? It depends on what we are working with, or our Spiritual Status or Level.

Simply put, if we are on Spiritual Milk, our Predestined Path, Promise, Passion, or Purpose could be the same on that specific predestined level. Whereas, when we are on Spiritual Meat, *As It Pleases God*, they may vary depending on our level of

Overcoming Fear and Doubt

Bounce Back and Spiritual Growth Process. Therefore, we must have Spiritual Balance and Discipline, knowing the difference between them all. If not, we can indeed stub our toes and trip over ourselves.

As a *Black Sheep* on any level, here are a few tips, but not limited to such:

- ☐ Our **Predestined Path** is associated with our Spiritual Journey or Walk with God, our Heavenly Father. Moreover, our path's identity will not look like someone else's. We have different experiences, fingerprints, eyeprints, and footprints for a reason, and this happens to be one of them. It amazes me how this unique path is marked by faith or the lack thereof. With God's Divine Plan of predestination, there is no in-between in this matter. Still, through His Divine Grace and Mercy, it is filled with Divine Intention, Guidance, and Wisdom, helping us to regulate our faith properly. If we stay on the Predestined Path, *As It Pleases God*, rest assured that we are never alone.

- ☐ Our **Predestined Promise** is the Spiritual Covenant between the Promiser (God, our Heavenly Father) and the promisee (An Individual, Tribe, or Community) that may or may not be known by others outside of the Holy Spirit. Most often, this will come with Spiritual Contingency Clauses. These are conditions or understandings that govern the expectations and responsibilities of both parties involved. Regardless of any clauses, obedience is better than sacrifice, according to 1 Samuel 15:22. The Spiritual Framework of any Predestined Promise, *As It Pleases God*, is always a commitment filled with Trust, Love, and Purpose. If a

Overcoming Fear and Doubt

promise is filled with distrust, hate, and distractions, we should exercise extreme caution.

- [ ] Our **Predestined Passion** is what we enjoy doing with little or no effort, training, or coaching. Then again, it could be our Genius Ability or Creativity that is hidden under a weakness or some form of trauma. Spiritually Speaking, this is often where our Spiritual Gifts are hidden, but not always, depending on our Spiritual Level or the Spiritual Training needed to facilitate it. For example, with my Predestined Passion for writing on a Divine Level on behalf of the Heavenly of Heavens, most people could not withstand the intense pressure associated. Nor could they deal with the Spiritual Accountability of leading God's sheep with Divine Precision and Accuracy. Therefore, their Spiritual Developmental Process of their Predestined Passion would take less time and effort in comparison to mine.

- [ ] Our **Predestined Blueprint** is an internal, yet Divine Plan of God with Spiritual Instructions, Layouts, and Specifications. In addition, it also contains the Provisions, Protection, and Facilitation needed to bring forth our reason for being. Just like an architect's plans for a building, we have this capacity as well. In Earthen Vessel for our Heaven on Earth Experiences, everyone has a Predestined Blueprint, even if they are clueless about it. However, we must seek a deeper understanding of our Divine Purpose along with the essence of our existence.

  Our Predestined Blueprint comes with Spiritual Guidance through our conscience, intuitions, feelings, senses, or insight, creating a unique Spiritual Compass for us. Plus, it has a unique way of directing our choices

Overcoming Fear and Doubt

and experiences to enrich and promote our growth for the Greater Good of mankind.

In order not to crack under *The Pressure* and to *Bounce Back* quickly while becoming better equipped, we must learn how to exhibit the Fruits of the Spirit and behave Christlike, allowing God to be God. If out of our own free will, we decide to become the gods of our own lives, then have at it...I am not here to stop anyone; I am here to advise, educate, share *The Learning Process*, and Divinely Illuminate the WAY, *As It Pleases God*.

The Learning Process

Most often, what we fear or doubt can teach us invaluable lessons if we choose to confront them, *As It Pleases God*. Why do we need to add Him into our fears and doubts? They may have our Divine Wisdom, Purpose, Instructions, or Blessings attached.

For me, fear makes me look for the underlying root or dangling fruit. Whereas, having doubts about anything or anyone, including myself, makes me ask more of the right questions, ushering in Divine Illumination, *As It Pleases God*.

For the record, if someone proclaims to be fearless or doubtless, they are lying. How do I know? Unbeknown to most, it is the elements of fear and doubt that spark our Creative Genius to solve problems, create solutions, and overcome anything. Nevertheless, it is our God-Given Duty to redirect them for the Greater Good using the Fruits of the Spirit. If not, fear and doubt will make us insecure; I mean very insecure, especially when dabbling in the lesser good, unrighteousness, and unfruitfulness. As *The Black Sheep*, in

Overcoming Fear and Doubt

order to become the Cornerstone of Greatness, it behooves us to leave no stone unturned.

How is it possible to leave no stone unturned when we are clueless about the stone concept altogether? Each stone represents a situation, circumstance, person, place, thing, or event that needs dissecting from human reasoning to a Spiritual Understanding. For instance, in the dissecting process, the fear of failure can become a source of motivation to push beyond our self-imposed limitations, especially when adding God into the equation, *As It Pleases Him*. Pushing in such a manner prepares us more thoroughly by learning new skills, asking the right questions, training effectively, and strengthening our outcomes if we understand how to identify fear and doubt.

As a *Black Sheep*, in the *Learning Process*, the goal is to keep things simple to ensure that we do not overcomplicate people, places, things, and life itself. In the Eye of God, simplicity is not about dumbing things down; rather, it is about conveying, painting mental pictures, or understanding with a few items, but not limited to such:

- ☐ **Clarity**: Is it clear?
- ☐ **Relateability**: Is it relatable?
- ☐ **Relevance**: Is it timely or relevant?
- ☐ **Retainability**: Is it worth retaining?
- ☐ **Graspability**: Is it easy to catch on?
- ☐ **Engageability**: Is it engaging?
- ☐ **Accessibility**: Is it accessible?

The essence of *The Black Sheep Power: As It Pleases God*® is wrapped in simplicity, ease, and inclusivity, leaving no willing man behind, regardless of their background, mistakes, or beliefs. When we make people feel welcomed, wanted,

Overcoming Fear and Doubt

respected, supported, and valued, it opens the Divine Floodgates of untapped potential, from the least to the greatest, igniting a COLLECTIVE POWER. Here is what Matthew 18:19-20 says about this: *"Again I say to you that if two of you agree on earth concerning anything that they ask, it will be done for them by My Father in heaven. For where two or three are gathered together in My name, I am there in the midst of them."*

In the *Learning Process*, especially when *Dealing with Unsurety*, it is wise to always lean on Ecclesiastes 4:9-12. *"Two are better than one, because they have a good reward for their labor. For if they fall, one will lift up his companion. But woe to him who is alone when he falls, for he has no one to help him up. Again, if two lie down together, they will keep warm; but how can one be warm alone? Though one may be overpowered by another, two can withstand him. And a threefold cord is not quickly broken."*

Chapter Three
Dealing With Unsurety

Do you ever feel lost and uncertain about your life's direction? Are you still hiding yourself under a rock? Do you feel as though you have a unique purpose, but you are unsure what it is? In today's time, it is easy to feel like we are hiding under a rock, sheltering ourselves from worldliness and our true potential because we are outright unsure, different, misunderstood, or feel out of place. Well, as *The Black Sheep* or when *Dealing With Unsurety* that is lurking in the background or the forefront, we must take the time to look from within to analyze why we do what we do and why we are not doing what we should.

Most would feel ashamed when *Dealing With Unsurety*, but it is all part of the process. Believe it or not, I used to feel lost, unfulfilled, and confused as well. Plus, I still get confused, as it is a part of living real life. But I have mastered several ways to seek Divine Clarity by asking fact-finding questions and getting a proper understanding of whatever, whomever, or however, *As It Pleases God*.

For the record, we should never leave confusion as-is...it is WISE to seek Divine Clarity due to the seed associated with fusing a cunning narrative into the equation. Is confusion really designed to interject a cunning narrative into our lives as Believers? Absolutely! Con is to persuade, and fusion is to join two or more things together...And there we have it—Confusion.

In the Realm of the Spirit, confusion or chaos is a RED FLAG for the conscience and senses to pay attention or to become extremely alert. If it is not counteracted, *As It Pleases God*, it can penetrate or sift us, similar to what happened in the Garden of Eden.

What is the big deal about chaos and confusion? They deprive us of peace, causing the Holy Spirit to lie dormant at times because we have forgotten who we are in Christ Jesus. Nonetheless, know this: *"When a man's ways please the Lord, He makes even his enemies to be at peace with him."* Proverbs 16:7.

After making a mess of my life through various acts of disobedience and recklessness, I embarked on a Spiritual Journey of self-discovery that transformed my life and the lives of others. Here is what Proverbs 2:3-5 taught me: *"Yes, if you cry out for discernment, and lift up your voice for understanding, if you seek her as silver, and search for her as for hidden treasures; then you will understand the fear of the Lord, and find the knowledge of God."*

In this chapter, I will share Divine Secrets, Treasures, and Nuggets of Wisdom I learned along the way. Additionally, I will share a DIY process, based on the Word of God and Kingdom Standards, on how you can discover meaning and purpose.

How do we *Deal With Unsurety*, especially as Believers? First, we must make our best attempts to shed all forms of negativity, debauchery, or ill will with a Romans 12:2 mindset to become a *Messenger of Change*: *"And do not be conformed to this world, but be transformed by the renewing of your mind, that you may prove what is that good and acceptable and perfect will of God."*

Secondly, we must wholeheartedly embrace our quirks and uniqueness, acknowledging that our Spiritual Journey and

Dealing With Unsurety

Divine Blueprint will differ from those around us. Doing so gives us the ability to look within ourselves and run our own race without having to compare ourselves with others. Here is what 2 Corinthians 10:12 advises: *"For we do not dare to class ourselves or compare ourselves with those who commend themselves. But they, measuring themselves by themselves, and comparing themselves among themselves, are not wise."*

Thirdly, we must engage in better relations with God, ourselves, and others, in this order, without passing judgment. Then again, if we are going to pass judgment or make accusations about someone or something, it is best to ask fact-finding questions first. Proverbs 18:15 clearly says, *"The heart of the prudent acquires knowledge, and the ear of the wise seeks knowledge."*

The reason why this is so important for Believers to ask questions is that without questions, it is extremely hard to get accurate feedback, right? What is the big deal here? In the Eye of God, false information has a measuring stick. Really? Yes, really! Matthew 7:1-2 says, *"Judge not, that you be not judged. For with what judgment you judge, you will be judged; and with the measure you use, it will be measured back to you."*

As my ear has been to the ground, there are a lot of so-called prophets proclaiming to be Prophets of God, using recycled information for clicks, likes, and followers. In the Eye of God, a prophet of uncertainty or unsurety is considered a prophet of doom. Who am I to judge, right? No judgment intended. I am only documenting my findings, *As It Pleases God*, and to feed His precious sheep.

If we are unsure about what God said or is saying, then DO NOT say it in HIS NAME. We have free will to use our name or the name of the person we gleaned from, but leave Him out of it if He did not say something. Furthermore, Jeremiah 14:14

even says, "*And the LORD said to me, 'The prophets prophesy lies in My name. I have not sent them, commanded them, or spoken to them. They prophesy to you a false vision, divination, a worthless thing, and the deceit of their heart.'* "

What is a prophet of uncertainty or unsurety? They proclaim that God is giving them the 411 on the lives of others, but for some odd reason, they do not get the revelation for their own lives. For the record, for the True Prophets of the Most High God, He will do a clean sweep of their lives first to develop Divine Clarity, Authenticity, and Alignment. With a self-mirroring effect, they absolutely believe in Matthew 7:3-5. "*And why do you look at the speck in your brother's eye, but do not consider the plank in your own eye? Or how can you say to your brother, 'Let me remove the speck from your eye'; and look, a plank is in your own eye? Hypocrite! First remove the plank from your own eye, and then you will see clearly to remove the speck from your brother's eye.*"

Of course, God will use anyone or anything to accomplish His Divine Will or Purpose. Still, when *Dealing With Unsurety*, we can place ourselves on a slippery slope. To add insult to injury, I have encountered many of them passing judgment about me without asking me one question or even knowing my name. Yet, in their uncertainty, they stood firm on saying the Holy Spirit revealed this or that about me, or He revealed some type of bogus intentions.

As I listened without responding or defending myself, I often wondered why someone would broadcast negative information without getting the facts first. Nevertheless, when people are unsure about people, places, and things, they will begin to make up stuff, hoping something will stick or provoke a response. Why? Like clockwork, a hit dog will holler!

Dealing With Unsurety

What is the purpose of not responding? I do not have to respond to or defend lies; I just silently reject them. We do not need to tell people they are lying; they already know it! They do not need my confirmation, agreement, or participation in their lies, debauchery, or erring. Instead, I activate Psalm 141:3: *"Set a guard, O Lord, over my mouth; keep watch over the door of my lips."*

In *Dealing With Unsurety*, what I have found is that profiling people does not make us a prophet in the Eye of God. Nor does it make us accurate. What if we are well-versed in psychology? Unfortunately, when dealing with Divine Prophets, a psychological analysis may not be accurate. Why not? It is like man-made wisdom versus Divine Wisdom...it is not a match. The questions must be asked; if not, our assumptions with make us look like boo boo the fool.

Now, if they were well-versed in using the Fruits of the Spirit, they can pick up on our method of operation. How so? The Fruits of the Spirit do not lie.

In addition, if they were really operating with the Holy Spirit, He would have advised them about my Spiritual Ranking because Spirit knows Spirit. Plus, if they were not able to RECOGNIZE or RESPECT the Divine Anointing on my life, it means their Spiritual Compass is keeled. To be clear, I am the most humble person who truly uses the Fruits of the Spirit. Nor do I toot my own horn, and if the Holy Spirit does not reveal my Spiritual Status to someone, nor will I.

However, when a person steps up to me as a self-proclaimed prophet or real Prophet, they must come correct because the Teacher within me is ready, willing, and able to take notes to feed God's sheep. Why? I am held to a higher accountability than most, and I must report my findings to the

Heavenly of Heavens as an even exchange for Divine Wisdom, Treasures, and Secrets. Therefore, I look for Spiritual Principles, Protocols, and Standards...and if we are representing the Kingdom of God, certain expectations must be met. If not, it is time to go back into the Spiritual Classroom for Divine Updates. In addition, Matthew 7:15 also warns: *"Beware of false prophets, who come to you in sheep's clothing, but inwardly they are ravenous wolves."*

Is it not a double standard to Spiritually Analyze without asking them one question? It would be if they DID NOT open their mouth. But, once we open our mouths to speak or take action...that is all I need to Spiritually Analyze, *As It Pleases God*. Here is what Proverbs 18:21 says, *"Death and life are in the power of the tongue, and those who love it will eat its fruit."*

In all simplicity, regardless of whether they are sure about what they are saying or not, I have the right to read their fruits to determine whether they are good or bad, righteous or unrighteous, just or unjust, and so on. For this reason, James 1:26 clearly says, *"If anyone among you thinks he is religious, and does not bridle his tongue but deceives his own heart, this one's religion is useless."*

What does better relations have to do with anything? Some of us are content with superficial connections over authentic ones, while getting upset and blaming God for having multiple and fleeting relationships that lack substance. For this reason, Proverbs 3:5-6 advises: *"Trust in the Lord with all your heart, and lean not on your own understanding; in all your ways acknowledge Him, and He shall direct your paths."*

What if Proverbs 3:5-6 says nothing about a relationship? According to Kingdom Standards and Protocols, Proverbs 3:5-6 serves a dual purpose, both personal and communal,

Dealing With Unsurety

transcending mere religious doctrine to pinpoint our trust or the lack thereof. Then again, it also indicates whether we trust in God, ourselves, or others. How so? First, it emphasizes the importance of considering the literal day-to-day choices we make, whether good, bad, or indifferent. And secondly, at its core, it makes us aware of the relational pathways we choose to walk in, through, or toward.

Realistically, on our Spiritual Journey through life in Earthen Vessels, the choices and decisions we make and the relationships we cultivate significantly shape our experiences, cultures, mindsets, and outcomes. As a *Black Sheep*, rather than being consumed by anxiety, fear, frustration, or overthinking our circumstances, we can opt to trust God for real. However, we must know what He is expecting from us to facilitate this type of trust. What does this mean? Most of us say that we trust God, but we do not. How do I know? Listed below are a few indications along with the Divine Expectations, *As It Pleases God*, but not limited to such:

- ☐ When we have our hands on the wheel of our lives, it indicates who is running the show. *"A man's steps are of the Lord; how then can a man understand his own way?"* Proverbs 20:24.

- ☐ When we do not use the Fruits of the Spirit, it indicates who is running the show. *"He who follows righteousness and mercy finds life, righteousness, and honor."* Proverbs 21:21.

- ☐ When we are unrepentant or unforgiving, it indicates who is running the show. *"For if you forgive men their trespasses, your heavenly Father will also forgive you. But if you*

Dealing With Unsurety

do not forgive men their trespasses, neither will your Father forgive your trespasses." Matthew 6:14-15.

- ☐ When we are unloving, uncaring, rude, or unmerciful, it indicates who is running the show. "*Let not mercy and truth forsake you; Bind them around your neck, Write them on the tablet of your heart.*" Proverbs 3:3.

- ☐ When we are chaotic or abusive, it indicates who is running the show. "*Let all bitterness, wrath, anger, clamor, and evil speaking be put away from you, with all malice. And be kind to one another, tenderhearted, forgiving one another, even as God in Christ forgave you.*" Ephesians 4:31-32.

- ☐ When we are nasty, unkind, or envious, it indicates who is running the show. "*The merciful man does good for his own soul, but he who is cruel troubles his own flesh.*" Proverbs 11:17.

- ☐ When we are impatient, manipulative, or cunning, it indicates who is running the show. "*Rest in the Lord, and wait patiently for Him; Do not fret because of him who prospers in his way, because of the man who brings wicked schemes to pass.*" Psalm 37:7.

- ☐ When we are prideful, disobedient, or lack self-control, it indicates who is running the show. "*Do not be wise in your own eyes; fear the Lord and depart from evil. It will be health to your flesh, and strength to your bones.*" Proverbs 3:7-8.

Dealing With Unsurety

- [ ] When we are consumed with power, money, sex, status, fame, likes, and clicks, it indicates who is running the show. *"Do not lay up for yourselves treasures on earth, where moth and rust destroy and where thieves break in and steal; but lay up for yourselves treasures in heaven, where neither moth nor rust destroys and where thieves do not break in and steal. For where your treasure is, there your heart will be also."* Matthew 6:19-21.

- [ ] When we are unwilling to agree to the Will of God in our lives, it indicates who is running the show. *"See then that you walk circumspectly, not as fools but as wise, redeeming the time, because the days are evil. Therefore do not be unwise, but understand what the will of the Lord is."* Ephesians 5:15-17.

- [ ] When we lack trust and faith in God, our Heavenly Father, it indicates who is running the show. *"Trust in the Lord with all your heart, And lean not on your own understanding; In all your ways acknowledge Him, And He shall direct your paths."* Proverbs 3:5-6.

- [ ] When we are dull, stiff-necked, lukewarm, or double-minded, it indicates who is running the show. *"He who keeps instruction is in the way of life, but he who refuses correction goes astray."* Proverbs 10:17.

- [ ] When we are destructive, negative, or combative, it indicates who is running the show. *"These six things the Lord hates, yes, seven are an abomination to Him: a proud look, a lying tongue, hands that shed innocent blood, a heart that*

Dealing With Unsurety

devises wicked plans, feet that are swift in running to evil, a false witness who speaks lies, and one who sows discord among brethren." Proverbs 6:16-19.

In *The Black Sheep Power: As It Pleases God*®, this list does not mean that we are bad, evil, or unusable. It only means that we have work to do in order to withstand and maintain the Spiritual Power from the Heavenly of Heavens. Proverbs 12:15 says, *"The way of a fool is right in his own eyes, but he who heeds counsel is wise."*

By becoming a work-in-progress on this Spiritual Path as a *Black Sheep*, we can usher in the help needed to develop our relational skills. God is looking for usable, willing, and trainable vessels who are ready to put in the work, prioritizing servitude and humility, *As It Pleases Him.* As the call for authenticity and purpose echoes louder than ever, He is requiring us to up the ante on our people skills. Whether through small acts of kindness, lending a listening ear, offering a helping hand, or simply being present in the moment for others, we as a people must rise to the occasion.

When navigating interpersonal relationships, whether they are familial-related, social-related, friend-related, church-related, or work-related, communication is a must. With the *Strength in Community*, each path we take is not just about our individual journeys, but it also encompasses the relationships we form along the way.

In all reality, every choice we make affects not just our lives but the lives of those around us. In doing so, we must trust God always to develop viable substance and understand *The Point of Origin*, even when it does not feel good. Although it may require a lot of courage, with God, *As It Pleases Him*, all things are possible through Christ Jesus.

The Point of Origin

The inferiority complex associated with being *The Black Sheep* has hidden treasures and genius abilities associated, camouflaged with seeming negativity by Divine Design. Why does God camouflage things in Believers? According to Kingdom Standards, to Divinely Forcast, *As It Pleases Him*, we must understand, endure, and survive the outcasting phase to develop our character traits of compassion, empathy, and mercy. Proverbs 17:3 gives us a profound clue about this: *"The refining pot is for silver and the furnace for gold, but the Lord tests the hearts."*

What is the purpose of being tested when seeking out *The Point of Origin* as Believers? First, if we do not develop our character, we will find ourselves throwing God's sheep away or to the wolves without lending a helping hand. Then again, we may also find ourselves spitefully leading or pointing them in the wrong direction, causing them to experience failure. Not realizing that our contribution to their failure planted a seed for our own demise or to plague our Bloodline.

Secondly, it is extremely difficult to PREPARE, *As It Pleases God*, especially if we are not tested or put through the fiery furnace like Shadrach, Meshach, and Abednego in Daniel 3:16-28. Nor will we be able to distinguish whether or not the Fourth Man is in the fire with us. More importantly, if we lack preparation from a Spiritual Perspective, we will begin to place our perceptions on others, depriving them of their free will to choose. As a result, their issues can become ours.

Dealing With Unsurety

Really? Yes, really! This costly transfer happens all too often, especially when there is jealousy, envy, or coveting involved, while pretending there is not.

In the cautionary tale of sibling rivalry, this one ruthless, smart sibling was super envious of the other one, who was labeled as not so smart and unsure at times. As the envy lurked beneath the surface, they hid it from their parents because they were brought up to love each other unconditionally.

In this narrative, we have a sibling who feels overshadowed by the achievements and accolades. Still, while presenting a façade of support and love, the internal gator-like torment was eating away at their soul, constantly gnawing away at their peace of mind. Therefore, they concocted a plan to isolate and scatter anyone getting close to their sibling, whom they secretly envied. In their quest to undermine their sibling, they unwittingly initiate a seedful chain reaction that wreaks havoc on their own life.

What was *The Point of Origin*? The desire for CONTROL was the underlying seed. They were accustomed to being considered as being the best of the best. When threatened with becoming the second choice or the second best, it provoked an uncontrollable beast from within. This deep-seated need for validation and superiority made them feel inferior and insecure, ready to snap anyone's head off who poses a threat. Their secret bouts with anxiety amplified their desire for control, prompting them to act defensively and irrational at times, similar to having a temper tantrum.

In addition, the negative comparisons led to a sense of inadequacy, igniting a FEAR that they may lose their esteemed position as being the best, smartest, and most elite. All of which ignited a hormonal imbalance that caused them

Dealing With Unsurety

to do things they would not normally do without being triggered.

As a twist of fate with this devious plan, their actions led to unforeseen consequences. Unfortunately, they inadvertently scattered their own home, losing their spouse, job, home, and reputation. These unfortunate events, ultimately reshaped their life in ways they never anticipated, causing them to trust God more than ever. They were not restored until they REPENTED of this underhanded behavior that secretly stifled their sibling.

Through this process of Spiritual Atonement, *As It Pleased God*, they begin to grasp the destructive nature of envy. It was not merely a harmless feeling in the Eye of God; it was poison that contaminated their Spiritual Fruits, Gifts, and Relational Bonds. You see, in seeking to stifle their siblings' success, they had inadvertently stifled their own joy and growth. By acknowledging their wrongdoings, they opened the door to change, healing, and a renewed relationship with mutual support and authentic communication.

How is it possible for someone's failure to become our own when we are two different individuals? Spiritually Speaking, doing the wrong things or misleading others intentionally will cause us to fail in the Spiritual Classroom, zapping *The Black Sheep Power* from us or transferring the Divine Mantle to another Bloodline. Matthew 15:14 says, *"Let them alone. They are blind leaders of the blind. And if the blind leads the blind, both will fall into a ditch."*

Can we really fall into a ditch by giving bad, wrong, or deceptive advice? Absolutely! Here is what Jeremiah 23:1-2 says about this: *"Woe to the shepherds who destroy and scatter the sheep of My pasture!" says the Lord. Therefore thus says the Lord God of*

Dealing With Unsurety

Israel against the shepherds who feed My people: 'You have scattered My flock, driven them away, and not attended to them. Behold, I will attend to you for the evil of your doings,' says the Lord."

When truly *Dealing With Unsurety*, often we fail to pinpoint *The Point of Origin* to *Unveil Our Inner Compass*. In *The Black Sheep Power; As It Pleases God*®, it is only fair to discuss this matter in detail to ensure you have the information you need for a time such as this.

Unveiling Our Inner Compass

When *Unveiling Our Inner Compass*, and while living real life, many of us find ourselves at crossroads, grappling with decisions that shape our present situations and our futures. But what do we do when we look around and see our family members, friends, and peers achieving more than we are? What do we do when they are becoming successful, living out their dreams, while we feel lost, confused, helpless, or stagnant? Wait, wait, wait, do not answer these questions yet, let us talk for a moment.

Our Inner Compass (The Heart) is the guiding force of our values, beliefs, and the essence of who we are, with a myriad of choices, consequences, and experiences. Often enough, we may inadvertently fall into a common pitfall, which is the urge to help God out, as if He made a mistake with us or in our lives. Of course, we may not admit to the underlying urge to help God out, but it can become detrimental if not governed accordingly.

How do we recognize if we are attempting to force God's hand? The first indication is when we attempt to control every aspect of our lives and the lives of others, violating their free will. The second indication is present in our actions, thoughts, beliefs, desires, responses, and traumas, stemming from underlying fear, self-doubt, and unsurety. The third

Dealing With Unsurety

indication is when we fail to trust the process, while becoming impatient, manipulative, or diabolic, while willfully introducing generational curses into our Bloodline.

According to the Heavenly of Heavens, as *The Black Sheep*, when *Unveiling Our Inner Compass*, we must pay attention to the quiet nudges and feelings that guide, block, or provoke us. Then again, it may require us to take a step back to Spiritually Analyze when the urge to override the Will of God presents itself. When this urge appears, it is always best to seek Divine Clarity to better understand what is going on from within and what is taking place between our two ears, while at the same time, pinpointing our WHY. In addition, it also gives us an opportunity to ask ourselves fact-finding questions to ensure that we are on one accord, Mentally, Physically, Emotionally, and Spiritually with the Will of God while using the Fruits of the Spirit.

In discussing this topic, I have a perfect story to drive my point home. In the Book of Genesis, I am beginning my version of this story in Chapter 25:19. Jacob and Esau, the sons of Isaac and Rebekah, are woven with themes of sibling rivalry, love, and Divine Destiny.

From the start, there was tension and rivalry brewing with their family dynamics as Jacob was said to have grasped Esau's heel as he was born, foreshadowing competition between the two. In ancient times, their firstborn Birthrights held immense value, conferring status, material wealth, and a greater BLESSING from the father. Throughout their lives, their contrasting personalities became evident, with Esau being a skilled hunter and Jacob being more of a homebody, hanging around the tent all day, helping with domestic chores.

Respectfully speaking, Jacob was more like a mama's boy. Although his mother, Rebekah, pampered him immensely, as she had no clue that she was making him weak in the Eye of God. From the womb, Jacob came out wanting everything his

Dealing With Unsurety

brother had without desiring and working for his own. To be clear, all children will have this tendency, but Jacob had it really bad...and he was not taught to do otherwise.

Actually, Jacob was encouraged by his mother because God told her, *'The older shall serve the younger'* in Genesis 25:23. So, my question is, 'Was Rebekah's favoritism of him over his brother based on this statement from God?' Better yet, I have another question: 'Why was she not preparing him to lead instead of being on the take?'

The flaws of pampering our children too much can warp our *Inner Compass* or properly lead as parents. Jacob's relationship with his mother, Rebekah, unearthed patterns of behavior that would follow him throughout his life, which invite a deeper examination of the ramifications of permissive parenting and favoritism.

Rebekah's seemingly innocent affection and unrestrained favoritism morphed into an enabling force, nurturing an entitled mindset in Jacob. So much so, it was to the point where he failed to appreciate the value of hard work and effort. While at the same time, always taking the easy way out without sharing and brotherly cooperation. Plus, he was not taught independence and resilience, which inadvertently hindered him from being Spiritually Used by God to become truly Great at that time. Why? He lacked the fortitude that comes from facing challenges head-on.

According to the Heavenly of Heavens, a certain degree of struggle, discipline, decision-making, testing, and even disappointment is necessary for cultivating strength and character. However, his brother Esau was getting this in, doing his thing, being a little rebellious, but very selfishly responsible, to say the least. How do I know? Simply put, he was a hunter...a good one at that!

Although we do not talk about Esau much, the bottom line is that it takes physical and mental skills with a little

Dealing With Unsurety

toughness to be a hunter, especially when dealing with wild game. Here are a few skilled qualities of Esau, but not limited to such:

- ☐ He had Patience: Hunting often involves waiting for extended periods, requiring the ability to remain calm and still.

- ☐ He had Observation Skills: A keen eye for detail helps hunters notice subtle signs of animal movement, tracks, and behavior.

- ☐ He had Physical Fitness: Good physical condition is essential for hiking, climbing, and carrying equipment in diverse terrains.

- ☐ He had Endurance: The ability to withstand long hours in challenging conditions is crucial for hunting expeditions.

- ☐ He had Knowledge of Wildlife: Understanding animal behavior, habitats, and seasonal patterns aids in successful hunting.

- ☐ He had Stealth: The ability to move quietly and avoid detection by wildlife is vital for getting close to animals.

- ☐ He had Adaptability: Conditions can change rapidly in the wild, so being able to adjust strategies is important.

- ☐ He had Problem-Solving Skills: Quick thinking and the ability to find solutions in unexpected scenarios can make a significant difference.

Dealing With Unsurety

- ☐ He had Marksmanship: Proficiency in shooting and using weapons safely and accurately is crucial for ethical hunting.

- ☐ He had Attention to Detail: Small changes in the environment can indicate animal presence, so attention to detail is paramount.

- ☐ He had Mental Toughness: The ability to stay focused and resilient, especially during challenging hunts, is essential.

- ☐ He had Safety Awareness: Understanding the importance of safety measures and being aware of surroundings can prevent accidents.

- ☐ He had Planning Skills: Strategic thinking about routes, times, and conditions is vital for successful hunts.

- ☐ He had Persistence: Continued efforts despite setbacks and failures are often required to achieve hunting goals.

- ☐ He had Wilderness Skills: Knowledge of survival skills, first aid, and navigation can be lifesaving in remote areas.

- ☐ He had Emotional Control: Managing emotions, especially in stressful situations, helps in making sound decisions.

Dealing With Unsurety

In addition to Esau's developed skills, in *Unveiling Our Inner Compass*, he also had a few disdaining negative flaws that were UNPLEASING to God. Listed below are a few of them, but not limited to such:

- ☐ In *Unveiling Our Inner Compass*, Esau liked a lot of foreign women. In a cultural context, sexual immorality and violating God's design for relationships are often highlighted as sinful. Placing anything above the true God is viewed as an abomination.

- ☐ In *Unveiling Our Inner Compass*, He was very impulsive, willing to disobey his parents, defying cultural roots, family values, and formidable traditions. *"He who is slow to wrath has great understanding, but he who is impulsive exalts folly."* Proverbs 14:29.

- ☐ In *Unveiling Our Inner Compass*, Esau lacked foresight, not being able to see beyond what he wanted, which benefited him. *"A prudent man foresees evil and hides himself; The simple pass on and are punished."* Proverbs 27:12.

- ☐ In *Unveiling Our Inner Compass*, He was reckless, doing whatever he wanted without wise counsel. *"Ponder the path of your feet, and let all your ways be established. Do not turn to the right or the left; remove your foot from evil."* Proverbs 4:26-27.

- ☐ In *Unveiling Our Inner Compass*, He was prideful. Humility is valued, and arrogance or pride is often condemned. *"Everyone proud in heart is an abomination to the Lord; though they join forces, none will go unpunished."* Proverbs 16:5.

Dealing With Unsurety

- [ ] In *Unveiling Our Inner Compass*, Esau lacked a trusting relationship with God; therefore, he depended on himself more than God. "*Trust in the Lord with all your heart, and lean not on your own understanding; in all your ways acknowledge Him, and He shall direct your paths.*" Proverbs 3:5-6.

- [ ] In *Unveiling Our Inner Compass*, He possessed a neglectful attitude. Failing to show compassion and support for those in need is contrary to the values of faith. "*So then, because you are lukewarm, and neither cold nor hot, I will vomit you out of My mouth.*" Revelation 3:16.

- [ ] In *Unveiling Our Inner Compass*, Esau was stubborn, lacking motherly guidance to develop a balance of respect for all mankind. "*He who is often rebuked, and hardens his neck, will suddenly be destroyed, and that without remedy.*" Proverbs 29:1.

- [ ] In *Unveiling Our Inner Compass*, He lacked the Spiritual Fruits needed to move the Heart of God. "*But the fruit of the Spirit is love, joy, peace, longsuffering, kindness, goodness, faithfulness, gentleness, self-control. Against such there is no law.*" Galatians 5:22-23.

- [ ] In *Unveiling Our Inner Compass*, Esau was rebelliously overconfident. "*Yet they did not obey or incline their ear, but followed the counsels and the dictates of their evil hearts, and went backward and not forward.*" Jeremiah 7:24.

Dealing With Unsurety

- ☐ In *Unveiling Our Inner Compass*, He lacked self-control. *"The heart of the righteous studies how to answer, but the mouth of the wicked pours forth evil."* Proverbs 15:28.

- ☐ In *Unveiling Our Inner Compass*, Esau indulged in a lot of self-gratification. *"But My people would not heed My voice, and Israel would have none of Me. So I gave them over to their own stubborn heart, to walk in their own counsels."* Psalm 81:11-12.

All of these character traits led to regret and brokenness. Why were regret and brokenness associated? Esau did not vocalize or work on his internal struggles as he tried to mask them pridefully. However, they were noticed in his actions, thoughts, beliefs, and demeanor. How do I know? He was easily triggered with anger and frustration.

Esau's underlying anger could have resulted from his mother favoring his little brother over him. It could have been from being exhausted from seeking his father's approval and competing for his love. It could have been from Jacob constantly irritating him, getting under his skin, while internalizing his pain and feelings of betrayal. Then again, his propensity for anger could have been derived from a sense of dissatisfaction with his life choices. Who knows, besides Esau himself?

In my opinion, to be highly skilled as a hunter and easily triggered is a recipe for disaster. How so? Although Esau was not labeled a trickster like his brother, he had the potential to take someone out at the drop of a dime without giving it a second thought. Beneath all of that toughness lie unaddressed wounds, unchecked anger, obvious recklessness, and silent familial battles, which can definitely lead to destructive outcomes. *"So then, my beloved brethren, let every man be swift to hear, slow to speak, slow to wrath; for the wrath of man does not produce the righteousness of God."* James 1:19-20.

On the other hand, when it came to Jacob, he was a little too soft and passive to lead, but he had a deep-rooted flaw of being very manipulative. So, the question is, 'Was Jacob envious of Esau, his elder brother, because he was a skilled hunter and outdoorsman?'

From my perspective, it seems to me that Jacob had a little bit of something going on from within, especially with coveting and competitiveness taking place. How do I know? Jacob attempts to take things from his brother continually, which indicates that he was battling with a little jealousy, envy, pride, greed, coveting, and competitiveness.

Most of all, he was having an underlying identity crisis that his mother and father did not recognize he was having. In my opinion, his desire to be first was secretly driving him insane, without realizing he already possessed everything he needed to succeed.

Although Jacob was quieter and more contemplative, in my opinion, he had too much time on his hands to think about how to outdo his brother. Above all, the intricate web of family dynamics and deception has indeed provided a great story in *Unveiling Our Inner Compass*.

From an early age, Jacob learned the art of deception and the lack of integrity from his mother, who learned it from her Bloodline, *The Point of Origin*. To say the least, Isaac could have stopped this generational curse, but he did not. Rebekah could have stopped this generational curse, but she did not. Jacob could have stopped this generational curse, but he did not. So, here we are...the cycle continued!

One day, after a long hunt, Esau returned home famished. He was so desperate for food that he could barely think straight. Jacob, who was resourcefully cunning, was cooking

Dealing With Unsurety

stew and saw a moment of weakness within his brother that he could capitalize on. As the opportunity presented itself, Jacob offered Esau a bowl of the delicious stew in exchange for his birthright as the firstborn son. Without thinking about the long-term consequences, Esau agreed to do so. Why would he do such a thing? He did not have VALUE in his Divine Birthrights. Frankly, this is nothing new. We are still doing this in today's day and age without realizing it. But let us continue with this story.

Their mother, Rebekah, was a woman of sharp wit. She was extremely manipulative and steeped in a tradition of trickery. Her upbringing had sculpted her into a figure who did not shy away from manipulation when the stakes were high. In her Bloodline, deception was not just a tool, but a necessity to attempt to control the narrative.

From Genesis 27, Isaac, believing he was nearing death, sought to bless Esau with his final blessing. Rebekah, wanting to secure the blessing for her favorite child, Jacob, devised a cunning plan to steal Esau's blessings. So, she dressed Jacob in Esau's clothes and covered his arms with goat skins to mimic Esau's hairy skin, so that he would feel and smell like his brother.

How can a mother do such a thing to her child? Did she even have a conscience when placing one child over another to steal? The answer is NO! She knew exactly what she was doing because she said, "*Let your curse be on me, my son; only obey my voice, and go, get them for me.*" Genesis 27:13. She knew she was invoking a curse, but encouraged her favorite child to engage in this deceitful act anyway. This is indeed a story of ambition over righteous love...She shows incredible conviction in her belief that Jacob deserves the blessing over his brother Esau, and she was willing to do anything to force the Hand of God, throwing honesty and integrity out the window. So my question is, 'How does her son deserve something he has to steal?'

Nevertheless, when Jacob approached his elderly father, due to his blindness, Jacob outright fooled him. As a result, Isaac bestowed upon Jacob the blessing meant for Esau.

When Esau discovered the vicious acts of deception and the ultimate betrayal, he was heartbroken, disappointed, and furious. As a result of the betrayal of his little brother, he vowed to take revenge on Jacob, thus forcing him to flee for his safety.

As we reflect on this ancient story, Rebekah lost her family...she lost her favorite son, she lost the son she betrayed, and she lost the trust of her husband, who had trusted her and relied on her counsel. In my opinion, this is one of the worst kinds of hurt, for a mother to intentionally wreck her home over selfish ambitions to reap division and loss. While simultaneously thrusting her favorite child into a den of wolves as a *Black Sheep*, that he was not properly prepared or trained for.

Now, due to the lack of proper parental guidance, Jacob is instantly thrust into a life of loneliness without the comfort of his mother. Can you imagine going from having a full-fledged family to having no one, not knowing whether you are coming or going? Then again, not knowing if you were going to live or die?

During his travels, while thinking his life was over, Jacob had a dream of a ladder reaching to Heaven, with angels ascending and descending. This Divine Encounter filled him with hope and reassurance, revealing that he was not alone and that God was with him.

Although the way Jacob went about doing what he did was not right in *Unveiling His Inner Compass*, here is what he said to God: *"If God will be with me and will keep me in this way that I go, and will give me bread to eat and clothing to wear so that I come again to my*

Dealing With Unsurety

father's house in peace, the Lord shall be my God." Genesis 28:20-21. His surrender to the Will of God was indeed his turning point, training him for his next.

Of course, this does not give Jacob a free pass; it just puts him on a Spiritual Learning Curve to deal with the inability to overcome his fears and doubts of not being enough. Jacob also had some good characteristics about him, but the not-so-good ones superseded the good ones. Therefore, He had to deal with a few other items, such as, but not limited to such:

- ☐ He had to deal with the Spirit of Cunning.
- ☐ He had to deal with the Spirit of Trickery.
- ☐ He had to deal with the Spirit of Sensitivity.
- ☐ He had to deal with the Spirit of Envy.
- ☐ He had to deal with the Spirit of Jealousy.
- ☐ He had to deal with the Spirit of Competitiveness.
- ☐ He had to deal with the Spirit of Deceptiveness.
- ☐ He had to deal with the Spirit of Neediness.
- ☐ He had to deal with the Spirit of Codependency.
- ☐ He had to deal with the Spirit of Pride.

Before going any further in this story, Jacob's account with his secret insecurities serves as a reminder that while our roots shape us, it is our choices that determine our path. Simply put, he had a choice to continue in his deceitful antics or bring them to a complete halt. Yet, he made a conscious choice to continue in his deceptive antics, planting all types of debaucherous seeds as if they would never take root. Even though his mother was behind the debauchery, he still had a choice.

After Jacob found himself in a new land where he would continue his Spiritual Journey without his mother's covering, with a Spiritual Mirror facing him, he had to do something different. Simply put, he was force to grow up quickly.

In the region of Haran, Jacob was sent to his uncle Laban's house as a place of refuge. In my opinion, it was his Spiritual Training Ground, but let us continue. He soon fell in love with Rachel as if they were a match made in Heaven. So, he agreed to work for seven years to win her hand in marriage.

Jacob's work involved tending to Laban's sheep, meticulously caring for them and ensuring their well-being. As Laban's flocks grew rapidly, so did Jacob's affection for Rachel, as he was treated like *The Black Sheep* of the family.

Initially, Jacob worked for Laban for seven years to marry Rachel, but Laban deceitfully gave him Leah instead. He was devastated as he felt his past catching up with him. He now felt the sting of betrayal like never before...the woman that he really loved was not the woman he married. As a result of his dire love for Rachel, Jacob then had to work another seven years for the love of his life.

After Jacob worked for Laban for many years, they agreed that Jacob would receive the speckled and spotted sheep and goats from Laban's flocks as payment. Laban, however, removed all the speckled and spotted animals from his flock to ensure Jacob would have fewer to work with, demonstrating his deceptive nature.

During his time in Haran, Jacob had a unique interaction with the sheep and learned to select the strongest among them to breed. He utilized knowledge from a dream that revealed a special breeding technique. Jacob placed branches of poplar, almond, and plane trees in the watering troughs, creating an environment where the sheep would conceive. This dream symbolized God's promise and guidance as Jacob prospered in his work and amassed his own flock.

As years passed, Jacob also faced many challenges and conflicts with Laban because of several acts of deceitfulness.

Dealing With Unsurety

After Jacob decided to leave with his family and possessions, Laban still pursued him, accusing Jacob of stealing his household gods. In my opinion, this was his last opportunity to exert control and instill fear in Jacob.

Yet through it all, Jacob remained steadfast in his faith and continued to care for the flocks. Eventually, he decided it was time to return home, feeling God's call to reconcile with Esau, whom he utterly betrayed.

On the journey back home, Jacob was consumed with all types of anxiety because he was unsure of how Esau would react to his return. However, with the strength he had developed during his years as a shepherd, Jacob approached the reunion with humility and hope. In the end, he and Esau embraced, showcasing the power of forgiveness and familial love.

Jacob's experience with the sheep taught him vital lessons about patience, responsibility, and faith. Each flock he tended became a TESTAMENT to God's Divine Provision in his life, highlighting the deep connection between the SHEPHERD and His sheep—a relationship built on care, trust, and the acknowledgment of Divine Purpose.

Although Jacob made a lot of mistakes along the way, rest assured, his legacy lives on, granting us valuable information to revolutionize our lives for the Greater Good. For me, his story is a great Spiritual Tool designed for *Building Confidence* and Integrity on a level that solidifies our Heaven on Earth Experience.

Building Confidence

When we think about *Building Confidence*, we often associate it with being pridefully arrogant, with a belief in one's abilities. Then again, it can also be the assurance that comes from an understanding of one's worth and capabilities. Conversely,

Dealing With Unsurety

when dealing with confidence, *As It Pleases God*, even though we have free will, it is Spiritually Filtered through Him, by Him, and for Him. Let me explain...

Unbeknown to most, first and foremost, *The Black Sheep Power* is all about in WHOM we are confiding. For instance, if we are confiding in God, our Heavenly Father, *As It Pleases Him*, Proverbs 3:26 gives us a hint about why we should approach confidence in this manner: *"For the Lord will be your confidence, and will keep your foot from being caught."*

Secondly, as our Divine Cornerstone for Spiritual Power, Success, and Fulfillment, *As It Pleases God*, confidence is indeed a REWARD that we can lay claim to, according to Hebrews 10:35. Really? Yes, really! *"Therefore do not cast away your confidence, which has great reward."*

Lastly, once we learn how to embrace confidence, *As It Pleases Him*, we can enhance our Transformative Power to overcome, endure, and move forward in the Spirit of Excellence.

Why do we really need confidence as faithful Believers? Most Believers have a form of faithfulness in their loyalty, commitment, and consistency. But faithfulness without confidence makes us contradict ourselves, come across as uncertain, or appear wishy-washy. For this reason, most worldly individuals think we are extremely hypocritical, unrooted in our beliefs, or outright ungrounded altogether.

For instance, we have a Believer who knows the Word of God like the back of their hand, yet cannot control their emotions, tongue, or thoughts. Nor can they keep their legs closed or britches up. Do we think for a minute that this would not draw skepticism? It would...and, if it does not, then something is definitely wrong!

Confidence is also a willful choice of mankind and an underlying belief in our convictions that must be exercised in

Dealing With Unsurety

order to capitalize, *As It Pleases God*. Here are a few examples of the benefits associated with confidence, but not limited to such:

- ☐ We need confidence to take calculated risks.
- ☐ We need confidence for our Predestined Blueprint.
- ☐ We need confidence to remain focused and astute.
- ☐ We need confidence to pursue our dreams.
- ☐ We need confidence to understand our passions.
- ☐ We need confidence to become authentically creative.
- ☐ We need confidence to remain resilient.
- ☐ We need confidence to become Divinely Wise.
- ☐ We need confidence to overcome obstacles.
- ☐ We need confidence to create win-wins.
- ☐ We need confidence to override doubt and fear.
- ☐ We need confidence to develop self-assurance.
- ☐ We need confidence to inspire and uplift others.
- ☐ We need confidence to redefine our perspectives.
- ☐ We need confidence to maximize our faith, hope, and love.

In the Eye of God, our Heavenly Father, there is a powerful approach to building ourselves, our relationships, and our lives that goes beyond surface-level connections and interactions. With a little guidance, respect, and understanding from a Divine Perspective, we can begin navigating our lives with the Divine Grace needed to bring forth the GREATNESS from within.

In *Building Confidence*, we must do a few things, but not limited to such:

- ☐ We must pursue our PURPOSE or PASSION.
- ☐ We must expand our CREATIVITY.

Dealing With Unsurety

- ☐ We must COMMUNICATE with others.
- ☐ We must set realistic BOUNDARIES.
- ☐ We must LIVE our own lives.
- ☐ We must ENGAGE in selfless acts of kindness.
- ☐ We must BECOME positively proactive.
- ☐ We must REMAIN positively optimistic.
- ☐ We must RESPECT the perspectives of others.
- ☐ We must MASTER solving problems.
- ☐ We must INSPIRE and BUILD others.
- ☐ We must LEAD by example.

In *Building Confidence*, we must begin setting achievable goals. Once done, we must focus on mastering the ability to break down large goals into smaller, manageable ones to create a sense of progress and momentum. By doing so, it helps us to understand our obstacles, hiccups, and setbacks. In addition, we are better able to create positive mental pictures and embrace our challenges without doubting ourselves.

In *Dealing With Unsurety*, stepping outside our comfort zone is a part of the plan. By embracing challenges, taking calculated risks, and learning from failures, we can develop a mindset to create win-wins out of everything and with everyone.

When we celebrate small victories, *As It Pleases God*, He is more willing to unveil the larger ones, especially when cultivating a growth and adaptable mindset.

The Apostle Paul delivers a powerful message during his stay in Athens about the Divine Nature of God, helping us to *Build Confidence*, regardless of where we are in life or what we have going on. "*God, who made the world and everything in it, since He is Lord of heaven and earth, does not dwell in temples made with hands. Nor is He worshiped with men's hands, as though He needed anything,*

Dealing With Unsurety

since He gives to all life, breath, and all things. And He has made from one blood every nation of men to dwell on all the face of the earth, and has determined their pre-appointed times and the boundaries of their dwellings, so that they should seek the Lord, in the hope that they might grope for Him and find Him, though He is not far from each one of us; for in Him we live and move and have our being, as also some of your own poets have said, 'For we are also His offspring.'" Acts 17:24-28.

In stepping up to the plate with God in *Building Confidence*, we must get rid of a few things, but not limited to such:

- ☐ We must get rid of hatefulness, unforgiveness, and mercilessness.
- ☐ We must get rid of unhappiness, joylessness, or unappreciativeness.
- ☐ We must get rid of unrest, weariness, and worry.
- ☐ We must get rid of impatience or rushing all the time.
- ☐ We must get rid of unkindness or lack of compassion.
- ☐ We must get rid of evilness, cruelness, or any form of debauchery.
- ☐ We must get rid of unfaithfulness or doubtfulness.
- ☐ We must get rid of abrasiveness or rudeness.
- ☐ We must get rid of recklessness or disobedience.
- ☐ We must get rid of envy, jealousy, or covetousness.
- ☐ We must get rid of prideful arrogance.
- ☐ We must get rid of the lies, masks, and deception.

What is the purpose of getting rid of the above items? If we do not rid ourselves of specific negative characteristics, it will make us destitute and weak in the Realm of the Spirit.

In *The Black Sheep Power: As It Pleases God*®, all of these negative attributes can block our *Divine Confidence* from the Heavenly of Heavens. Now, if one has store-bought or self-made confidence, then this would not apply, because self-reliance can never equate to Godly Alliance or Reliance. What does this mean? Simply put, store-bought or self-reliant confidence is predicated on these negative attributes.

Even if we appear to have it all together, we subject ourselves to becoming a victim of worldliness if we willfully violate the human psyche. Frankly, due to our lack of understanding of *Building Confidence* in such a manner and *As It Pleases God*, we will find ourselves filling our inner voids with conditional items, superficial things catering to our senses, or pouncing on those appearing above or beneath us.

As the Heavenly of Heavens take note of our behaviors, mindsets, and heart postures, we may overlook the vital elements needed to *Build Confidence* from a Kingdom Perspective. When we are getting what appears to be right in our own eyes, but is deeply frowned upon in the Eye of God, it creates an imbalance within the psyche.

When it is all said and done, we must consider the matters of the heart, our mindsets, and our core values, regardless of our present state of being or how we feel about ourselves and others.

In *The Black Sheep Power: As It Pleases God*®, especially when dealing with *Building Confidence*, we cannot bypass the character-building steps for our Heaven on Earth developmental process. Nor can we neglect our people skills or the *Spirit to Spirit* Connection needed to tap into the Great Unknown. What is the purpose of doing so, particularly when we are all grown up, and we are not children? Fortunately, we are all on a continuous good or bad learning curve, whether we admit it or not.

Hopefully, we remain on the righteous side of a learning curve. Nevertheless, here is what Isaiah 41:10 says about this side: *"Fear not, for I am with you; be not dismayed, for I am your God. I*

Dealing With Unsurety

will strengthen you, Yes, I will help you, I will uphold you with My righteous right hand."

If we veer off to the unrighteous side, remember that there are consequences and repercussions associated. Why are there consequences and repercussions when having free will as Believers? Every charactorial trait we possess has a SEED, bearing much fruit, positively or negatively, in due season. We must deal with whatever or whomever according to the Standards of the Kingdom. If not, we can become swept away by our own devices or the tricks of the enemy. Once again, Galatians 6:7 says, *"Do not be deceived, God is not mocked; for whatever a man sows, that he will also reap."*

Is reaping really applicable to Believers, especially when we are on fire for God? Regardless of whether we are on fire for God or not, this Spiritual Law is in full effect, doing what it is designed to do. Although we do have the Blood of Jesus, and Divine Grace and Mercy working on our behalf, it does not exempt us from the Law of Cause and Effect, positively or negatively. They only exempt us from the penalty of death, not from the relationship between actions and consequences.

For instance, if you plant seeds in fertile soil and care for them, you can expect a harvest, right? The same applies in the Realm of the Spirit, positively or negatively, based on the Spiritual Law of Duality, Seedtime and Harvest, and Cause and Effect.

For some, in or out of the Kingdom of God, sowing and reaping can appear as a straightforward process, but it is not always straight, nor is it always forward. Sometimes, it is a winding road of Spiritual Training and Development full of dead ends, rerouting, and do-overs to deepen or root our faith.

At the core of our seeding, reaping, and harvesting, we often find ourselves overlooking the Spiritual Law of Duality. All this means is that we have good or bad, right or wrong, just or unjust, positive or negative, and selfless or selfish choices in

Dealing With Unsurety

all that we do, say, and become. Whereas, in *Building Confidence*, and being that not all seeds sprout up instantly, it is wise to place God at the forefront of all things, *As It Pleases Him*. Once done as faithful Believers on fire for Him, we can light up the room by using the Fruits of the Spirit and behaving Christlike at all times. The Spiritual Seeding and Fruiting Process ensures our acts of service convey love, hope, and inspiration with a sense of purpose for the Greater Good of all mankind.

What is Spiritual Seeding and Fruiting? As a *Black Sheep*, this is an active service engaging in prayer, repenting, forgiving, fasting on occasion, serving others, and sharing the Gospel. In addition, it also incorporates covering ourselves with the Blood of Jesus and allowing the Holy Spirit to guide us on *The Black Sheep Journey*.

The heart and mind posture behind our actions, thoughts, desires, and beliefs is of the utmost importance in the Eye of God. As we sow seeds and deeds of faith with sincerity, goodwill, and love when *Building Confidence*, irrespective of the immediate outcomes, here is what Galatians 6:9 tells us: *"And let us not grow weary while doing good, for in due season we shall reap if we do not lose heart."*

Chapter Four
The Black Sheep Journey

Have you ever felt like you do not quite fit in? Do you often feel unequally yoked with others? Are you desiring a sense of belonging? Are you tired of feeling lost, burdensome, and alone? Then again, have you ever felt like the odd one in your family? Well, in navigating the struggles of belonging, you are not alone. When on *The Black Sheep Journey*, walking alongside others yet traveling a completely different path is not uncommon, especially when manifesting our Heaven on Earth Experiences.

In Earthen Vessels, familial bonds can be both beautiful, challenging, and sometimes outright complicated. Amid our yearnings for a deep sense of belonging, God did not make a mistake in His choice of family ties. Nor does He operate as if He does not know what He is doing. It is we, as humans, that function in such a manner. And then have the nerve to deflect this on Him when becoming unequally yoked or when trying to avoid the learning process.

Listen, God has made *The Black Sheep Journey* strategic with problem-solving tools hidden within the dynamics of each step. What makes us so special and deserving in the Eye of God? According to 1 Peter 2:9, it says, *"But you are a chosen generation, a royal priesthood, a holy nation, His own special people, that you may proclaim the praises of Him who called you out of darkness into His marvelous light."* Simply choosing the LIGHT (Divine

Illumination) over darkness makes each of us special in the Eye of God. Whereas, based on our free will, if we choose darkness instead, it is viewed as a form of rebellion or disobedience in the Spiritual Realm.

Why are we considered rebellious or disobedient when exercising our free will to choose darkness? We are Spiritual Beings having a human experience. So, before making it into the Earthly Realm, there was a Spiritual Agreement made, which is our reason for being. Once we are born, we will consciously forget about this Spiritual Agreement, suffering Spiritual Amnesia until we are BORN AGAIN in the Spirit. With this Spiritual Veil, the Divine Blueprint remains written on the heart in detail with a longing attached (the feeling of something's missing). Keep in mind, this happens to everyone, and no one is exempt from this process.

Once we are fully aware, beyond the milking stages of life, if we turn away from the LIGHT of this Divine Agreement, it is considered a Breech of Contract in the Realm of the Spirit. Therefore, the Cycles, Vicissitudes, and Seasons of Life will make their best attempts to reset or awaken us from our slumber. If not, we begin dying a slow death from the inside out with regrets, burdens, complications, setbacks, and so on, with all types of negative attributes, thoughts, beliefs, and desires.

If one does not believe what I am saying to be true, then they must check their mind posture. Rest assured, their defensive mental chatter or internal dialogue will say everything they are not bold enough to say out loud. In addition, it will also include elements of skepticism, dismissal, or hostility, especially if they do not fully understand how the Realm of the Spirit works or have experience in this area.

Now, due to our unconventional thinking patterns associated with our survival modes, filled with all types of doubts, fears, and preconceived notions, we tend to avoid the

The Black Sheep Journey

people, places, and things we must confront. Clearly, I am not referring to combative confrontation...I am referring to dealing with the root of matters, Mentally, Physically, Emotionally, or Spiritually.

What matters must we confront as Believers? The biggest issue on the table is confronting our unequally yoked soul ties. We think it is cool to pick up relationships as if they are a conducive pastime, while labeling them as situationships. Whereas, in the Eye of God, the incompatible or mismatched soul ties provide an immediate distraction, extending beyond romantic relationships to friendships, family dynamics, and even workplace interactions. Simply put, whatever we are going through with anyone or anything, be it a relationship, situationship, contemplativeship, or anything in between, it originates from within us.

How do our issues come from us, especially when we are not the culprit? First, regardless of whether we are the culprit or not, the longing for genuine connection remains within all mankind. So, there is a reason for the attraction, regardless of whether it is good, bad, indifferent, or toxic...the seed is there somewhere. The magnetic pull does not lie...we do! The magnetic pull is not a one-size-fits-all phenomenon. The mysterious allure of our seeds draws us toward another person, place, thing, or idea that is rooted in our past experiences, psychological needs, ungoverned biases, chosen ideologies, preferred lifestyles, or cultural trends and societal influences. When on *The Black Sheep Journey*, we must understand this absolute fact; if not, denial and deflection will become our portion.

Secondly, we are wearing our issues on our shoulders. If not, there would be no issues, right? When we become sensitive about everything, it becomes difficult to learn, *As It Pleases God*. In addition, it also becomes a double-edged sword, hindering our Spiritual Growth Process. If we cannot confront opposing viewpoints and entertain new ideas, we become weak and sometimes unusable in the Eye of God. In the Spiritual Pursuit of Knowledge and Wisdom, we cannot wear our feelings on our shoulders because God may call us to HEAL the one who just spat in our face. If we cannot get over our feelings to do what is RIGHT, then it is back to the Spiritual Classroom for more Spiritual Training and Updates.

Thirdly, we cannot deny that our issues are coming from us when we make our lives and the lives of others miserable. When we instigate emotional distance due to a lack of people skills, while pretending to be a great communicator, we deceive ourselves. Communication goes beyond simply exchanging words; it requires the ability to listen, respond, empathize, understand others' perspectives, overcome barriers, and hold our tongues when necessary.

What if we are indeed great communicators? Then my question would be, 'Are we using the Fruits of the Spirit properly?' Better yet, 'Does one know anything about the Fruit of the Spirit?' Well, as *The Black Sheep Power: As It Pleases God*®, we must know what they are and how to use them accordingly. Why? They encompass Supernatural Power in the fundamental aspect of our human experience, and they level the playing field.

For instance, if we play without using the Fruits of the Spirit, we can decrease our effectiveness, *As It Pleases God*. Conversely, if we play with them, *As It Pleases Him*, we increase our effectiveness, even amid seeming defeat to the natural eyes. How does this make sense? For me, I chop everything up into lessons, training, or preparation while documenting my findings. Therefore, on my *Black Sheep Journey*, through humility and obedience, I can overcome anything by the Blood of the Lamb and by the word of my Testimony, according to Revelation 12:11.

The Black Sheep Journey

On *The Black Sheep Journey*, disobedience in the Eye of God is not something we want to play around with or proclaim equal rights, especially when this is a SORE SPOT for Him from the Garden of Eden Experience.

If we want to throw around equal rights in the Kingdom, then let us royally break this down. Disobedience is disobedience, right? Of course, it is! But if we have seen or experienced the Divine Miracles of God, time after time, and still choose to spit in His face, do we think this is equal? Do we? Can we make this make sense to ourselves? Do we think God is a joke?

When playing with God like this without repentance, we will see His Divine Wrath so fast that it will make our heads spin. Why? First, we belong to Him, and He is a Jealous God. More importantly, we can read all about WHY He is jealous in Genesis 34.

Secondly, when we take from a Spiritual Well with deceitfulness to unjustifiably manipulate, hurt, abuse, or cast down another without correcting the divisive attempts or repentance, we become the enemy of God. Here is what James 4:4 says, *"Adulterers and adulteresses! Do you not know that friendship with the world is enmity with God? Whoever therefore wants to be a friend of the world makes himself an enemy of God."*

As Believers, what are considered divisive attempts? The divisive attempts of mankind are to replace God Almighty with worldliness or vain imaginations for our selfish pleasures or gain. Still, do not take my word for it. Here is what 1 John 2:15-17 says: *"Do not love the world or the things in the world. If anyone loves the world, the love of the Father is not in him. For all that is in the world—the lust of the flesh, the lust of the eyes, and the pride of life—is not of the Father but is of the world."*

The Black Sheep Journey

The Cost

Everything that we do that contradicts or opposes the Will of God in our lives or that of another will fall under one or more of these triads of temptation:

- ☐ The lust of the flesh.
- ☐ The lust of the eyes.
- ☐ The pride of life.

Could it be more than these three? No, everything associated with power, money, sex, fame, status, and anything else in between will fall under at least one or more of the three. All of which can affect the Mind, Body, Soul, and Spirit through our conscience, senses, and thoughts before making its way into reality. What does this mean for *The Black Sheeped* Believers? On *The Black Sheep Journey* of Spiritual Growth, and based on our Divine Rights to Spiritual Duality, we have the POWER to counteract, detach, pray, forgive, or repent midair before taking action, opening our mouths, or forming a complete thought. Really? Yes, really!

Listen, there is a GAP between our mental chatter, spoken words, and taking action that is often ignored by most. In this place, we can either make that particular gap transformative or destructive by interjecting positive or negative thoughts, desires, or affirmations. The way in which we reframe this gap is totally up to us. Hopefully, we can keep this gap on the positive side of the spectrum, but when it deviates to the negative unrighteous side, we still must know what to do and why we are doing so. Plus, we must also know and understand how to reverse-engineer the negative side of anything. Why? Once again, there is a COST for not counteracting or reversing a negative into a positive.

The Black Sheep Journey

In a world that often unashamedly glorifies materialism and superficial desires for followers, clicks, baits, and likes, we cannot think for a minute that God is happy about our behaviors and fleeting desires. Nor can we think that life will not test the essence of our being to see what we are made of. Once this occurs, as *The Black Sheep* or not, one of two things will happen:

- ☐ It will become a SEED of elevation, *As It Pleases God*, availing us to our sense of good judgment for the Greater Good.

- ☐ It will become a SEED of degradation to please ourselves or someone else, clouding our sense of good judgment for the lesser good.

Although God can work with both, why should we disrupt our peace for chaos or waste precious time? In my opinion, it is wise to save ourselves the unnecessary stress, headache, heartbreak, or regret proactively.

What makes this so wise in the Eye of God? Impulsive attitudes, desires, and pursuits for instant gratification indicate a lack of self-control, even if we pretend to have it all together. Without formal restraints, from a Divine Perspective, we sometimes unawaringly thrust ourselves into a state of denial about our relationship with God. While at the same time denying our authentic success journey, our desire for worldly recognition, or the price of our superficial indulgence. More importantly, if we find ourselves ashamed of sharing the price we paid for what we have...then this is why wisdom must be sought after.

The Black Sheep Journey

When someone approaches me in a braggadocious fashion with what they have obtained, accomplished, their lifestyle, their possessions, or whatever...I inquire about the cost.

What is the big deal here, especially when there is a price to pay for everything? From my perspective, if it costs someone their soul, then why are they bragging? For me, when viewed through a lens of morality, bragging is not necessary; repentance is, rather than self-promotion. Nevertheless, without judgment and from experience, at the heart of this issue, here is what I want to know:

- ☐ Did it cost them their integrity?
- ☐ Did it cost them their ability to love?
- ☐ Did it cost them their peace?
- ☐ Did it cost them their joy?
- ☐ Did it cost them their ability to be patient?
- ☐ Did it cost them their ability to be kind?
- ☐ Did it cost them their ability to be a good person?
- ☐ Did it cost them their ability to be faithful?
- ☐ Did it cost them their ability to be gentle?
- ☐ Did it cost them their ability to be caring?
- ☐ Did it cost them their sanity?
- ☐ Did it cost them their self-control?
- ☐ Did it cost them their humbleness of heart?
- ☐ Did it cost them their good name?

The bottom line is that inquiring minds, like mine, want to know! What is the purpose of knowing someone else's business? First, we do not want to come into an agreement with someone who has sold their soul. Why not? They are more than willing to take ours without giving it a second thought or in a moment of weakness. Is this really happening?

Absolutely! So, it is only wise to ask good and sound fact-finding questions.

Secondly, if something costs us absolutely NOTHING whatsoever, then we must question the validity of whatever with whomever. Why should we question this matter, especially when God is full of BLESSINGS? Yes, we are Blessed to be a Blessing. Nevertheless, if there is zero VALUE in whatever or with whomever or if it does not involve the sweat of our brows, we must question the SOURCE.

Remember, Genesis 3:19 says, *"In the sweat of your face you shall eat bread till you return to the ground, for out of it you were taken; for dust you are, and to dust you shall return."* All this means is that when it comes to our Predestined Blueprinted Purpose, we are required to Spiritually Till our own ground. Simply put, no one can do this for us; we must put in the work, doing what we were called to do, *As It Pleases God.*

In an era dominated by social media, when dealing with *The Cost*, broadcasting a distorted version of our reality is deception at its finest. Once we engage in deceptive measures to mask our insecurities, satiate a void, or downplay our lack of fulfillment, we contribute to our longings and feelings of emptiness within the psyche. When left undealt with, it has a way of feeding our sense of pride.

Should we not be prideful, instead of broadcasting insecurity? As we navigate this landscape, we have the free will to choose either of the two or none of them at all. Just know that according to Proverbs 16:18, it clearly says, *"Pride goes before destruction, And a haughty spirit before a fall."*

Without exhibiting pridefulness, should we not be proud of what we have or what we have accomplished? Of course, we should. If someone really has it going on...then they should just BE that person with outright humility. Here is what Luke

14:11 says, *"For whoever exalts himself will be humbled, and he who humbles himself will be exalted."*

When we properly equip ourselves to deal with disobedience, without whitewashing our reality, we are less likely to create golden calves to replace our invisible God of the Heavenly of Heavens. If we do, in due time, He will strip us Mentally, Physically, Emotionally, or Spiritually. Really? Yes, really. Then, we will find ourselves covering our nakedness with tangible stuff without using the intangible Blood of Jesus as a Spiritual Covering.

Suppose we do not want our nakedness exposed. In this case, we must willfully and humbly repent, forgiving ourselves and others, turn from all forms of debauchery, and develop a *Spirit to Spirit* Relationship, using the Fruits of the Spirit while behaving Christlike. Although this may seem like a lot to do, it does get easier when used, *As It Pleases God*. Plus, the sacrificial price of using this method is far less and more beneficial than using our own method of operation. Why? *The Label* we create ourselves without God or outside of His Divine Will has a way of sticking to us or showing up in our children when we least expect it.

The Label

As *The Black Sheep* or anything in between, God does not like the ornaments of people, places, and things taking His place, especially when He is the Creator of it all and Who is within us all. Let us interject scripture before moving on. *"Go up to a land flowing with milk and honey; for I will not go up in your midst, lest I consume you on the way, for you are a stiff-necked people. And when the people heard this bad news, they mourned, and no one put on his ornaments. For the LORD had said to Moses, 'Say to the children of Israel, you are a stiff-necked people. I could come up into your midst in*

The Black Sheep Journey

one moment and consume you. Now therefore, take off your ornaments, that I may know what to do to you.' So, the children of Israel stripped themselves of their ornaments by Mount Horeb." Genesis 33:3-6.

What is the purpose of being labeled as *The Black Sheep*? On the surface, being labeled as *The Black Sheep* can carry a negative connotation, implying that one does not fit in or follow societal norms, making them feel isolated, judged, or misunderstood. Then again, it can cause some to rebel or feel inadequate.

However, upon closer examination, *The Label* in the Eye of God is a shrouded stigma with Divine Treasures associated, similar to an undiscovered diamond hiding our Divine Expressions and Creativity. If we dare to change our perception, redefine our narratives, and challenge the status quo, *As It Pleases God*, we will better understand they are designed to do a few things, but not limited to such:

- ☐ Heal us.
- ☐ Break us.
- ☐ Restore us.
- ☐ Teach us.
- ☐ Prune us.
- ☐ Prepare us.
- ☐ Chastise us.
- ☐ Develop us.
- ☐ Protect us.
- ☐ Deliver us.

If we learn how to celebrate our *Blacked Sheeped* differences, they will in return grant us to secret treasures hidden within them. Really? Yes, really! Our differences hold Divine Insight and Extraordinary Potential. So instead of being ashamed of them, we should work on perfecting them, *As It Pleases God*. For me, every weakness, and I mean every weakness I possessed, was a hidden strength in disguise, bringing forth *The Black Sheep Power* to challenge the norm from the least to the greatest.

In unlocking the hidden treasures from within, what do we need to do? Here is the deal: Due to the varying rooted origins of our complexities, we must determine which one is necessary or applicable. We must also approach challenges from angles that others might not consider, identifying opportunities for growth where others see only obstacles. All of which requires original thought, positive mental chatter, the ability to ask relevant fact-finding questions, and to properly articulate creative input.

What if we are not well-spoken? Then, write it! What if we cannot write, then get someone to document for us! What if we do not have anyone? Listen, God will always give us something to work with. As it pertains to *The Black Sheep Power* and self-discovery phase, He will never leave us unequipped, even if it feels that way at times. Please find a way, like the woman who lost one coin in Luke 15:8-10. Trust that it is there somewhere, somehow, or with someone! Then again, if an excuse is what is found, then have at it!

Why must we selflessly search for a way? According to the Nature of God, whatever it is or is not, it is not for you only. It is for the Kingdom of God, *As It Pleases Him*, or to feed His precious sheep.

What is the big deal here? What I had to go through, challenging the status quo, the battle scars I endured, and the rejection I faced to get this information for a time such as this, is not something I joke around with. Thus, I do not settle for excuses! Had I made an excuse not to learn, document, and share this information in my condition, I would be justified in doing so. Nevertheless, for the sake of the Kingdom and our

The Black Sheep Journey

NEXT in line, I pushed through to prepare you in *The Black Sheep Journey*. Yes, you!

As Believers or not, being an outsider or treated as such can be tough on the human psyche. However, with the right mindset, *As It Pleases God*, it can also lead to amazing results, unlocking your true potential and igniting a sense of belonging you never knew existed.

The One Drop Rule

One drop of anything can indeed label or contaminate us. Before we go any further, let me explain: The *One Drop Rule* is a social and legal principle that emerged in the United States during the 19th century, particularly within the context of race relations and the laws of segregation. At its core, the rule suggests that any person with even a single ancestor of African descent is considered Black. Although we all originated from Africa, I digress in explaining how the Garden of Eden Experience is within us all, even if we pretend to be something else.

Okay, I had a moment, so let me get back on track. This social construct played a significant role in shaping racial identity, social status, and legal definitions of race. During the antebellum period, laws were enacted that defined and distract Blackness in such a way that even a minimal degree of African ancestry meant one was classified as Black.

The *One Drop Rule* to this very day influences various court rulings and state laws, including matters related to marriage, property rights, and civil rights, weakening the Divine Pool of the Chosen *Black Sheep*. Why would this happen, especially when the Chosen Ones are Spiritually Marked? It was due to the inability to *Overcome our Fears and Doubts* of racial mixing based on skin colors and not bloodlines, similar to being unequally yoked according to the Bible to invoke privilege amongst certain people, cultures, denominations, and so on. What does this mean? We take the Word of God and make it seem as if He is referring to skin colors, when He is referring to BLOODLINES.

So, here is my question: What is flowing through your veins right now? Is it love or hate? Is it righteousness or unrighteousness? Is it good or evil? Is it blessed or cursed? Is it wise or unwise? What is the purpose of all of these questions? Spiritual Duality is real, and it has a direct target on our Bloodlines. With all due respect, if we have zero knowledge about Spiritual Duality, we are already defeated in the Eye of God.

How can I say such a thing about someone's lack of knowledge, right? First, here is what I have Spiritually Gleaned from Galatians 3:28, *"There is neither Jew nor Greek, neither slave nor free, neither male nor female; for you are all one in Christ Jesus."*

Secondly, if we decide to remain divided, then have at it. When deciding to do so, according to Ephesians 4:4-6, know this: *"There is one body and one Spirit, just as you were called in one hope of your calling; one Lord, one faith, one baptism; one God and Father of all, who is above all, and through all, and in you all."*

Thirdly, regardless of our racial identity, heritage, and social constructs, we cannot *Overcome Fear or Doubt* if we do not know the opposite of them. Colossians 3:1 clearly says, *"But above all these things put on love, which is the bond of perfection. And let the peace of God rule in your hearts, to which also you were called in one body; and be thankful."* In all simplicity, if we are putting on hate, then it becomes the bond of imperfection. If division and unrest are ruling our hearts, then we CANNOT become one body, *As It Pleases God*, nor will we become authentically thankful, tapping into *The First Power*.

The Black Sheep Journey

According to the Heavenly of Heavens, we are quick to point the finger when it comes to politics. However, the *One Drop Rule* has targeted the church in a bad way, and God is not happy about how we are handling His Business with this man-made rule. For this reason, we are going to reel this in from a Spiritual Perspective. For instance, we focus on skin color, and God focuses on the heart and mind postures. We focus on material gain, and God focuses on Wisdom, Inner Wealth, Heavenly Treasures, Divine Secrets, and Predestined Blueprints.

Am I not being a hypocrite, talking about the *One Drop Rule* and saying we are all ONE in Christ Jesus, especially when titling this book, *The Black Sheep Power*? Sheep have multiple colors, such as white, black, gray, brown, red, cream, and silver. Also, they have multiple patterns such as spots, stripes, speckles, and mottled. However, in the Eye of God, we are dealing with the Level of Spiritual Melanin that is influenced by worldly genetics or Kingdom Genetics.

From a Spiritual Perspective and as Spiritual Beings in Earthen Vessels, the more melanin we have, the more Light, Pressure, or Illumination we can handle. Once used properly, *As It Pleases God*, it then becomes Spiritual Melanin with Divine Layers of PROTECTION for us. Plus, we rarely allow God to use us in such a manner due to the lack of knowledge, understanding, and know-how.

So, if I am called a hypocrite using the title *The Black Sheep Power*, it does not faze me at all. Why not? We all have this potential, and we are all *Blacksheeped* at some point in our lives. The only difference is whether or not we OVERCOME or SUCCUMB. More importantly, God will use this Spiritual Method to train the Best of the Best or the Cream of the Crop with this before He grants them Divine Power.

The Black Sheep Journey

When someone approaches me with having a perfect life, I already know they have little or no Spiritual Power, and they will crumble under pressure quickly. Is this not judging someone? Maybe or maybe not, but I will NOT trust my life with someone who will abandon me at the drop of a dime without teaming up to pray with me. Nor will I trust them when exhibiting reckless behaviors contradicting the Will of God for my life. What is the big deal? They are easy prey to become used and manipulated by the enemy, especially when having zero knowledge about the Fruits of the Spirit, how to use them, when to use them, and why they are doing so.

Listen, the enemy will target the weakest link in our lives, and if we are not choosing our link-ups carefully, we will 'get got' by the wiles of the enemy.

According to the Heavenly of Heavens, if we do not use our experiences to expose the True Greatness that is already within, *As It Pleases God*, then we have free will to remain in the sheepfold. In addition, we can never complain about not having the opportunity to become a real Shepherd, leading the Flock of God.

Our common origin is hidden with *The One Drop Rule* based on the Blood of Jesus, and not of man. 2 Corinthians 5:17 Spiritual Seal is applicable and enforceable in this case, saying, *"Therefore, if anyone is in Christ, he is a new creation; old things have passed away; behold, all things have become new."* Based on this, if we desire *Higher Accountability* on a Spiritual Level and *As It Pleases God*, let us dig deeper into this matter.

Higher Accountability

In an age where accountability is often discussed in terms of personal, professional, ethical, or social responsibility, the concept of higher accountability, specifically in relation to our Spiritual Lives and our Spirit to Spirit Relationship with God

The Black Sheep Journey

Almighty, deserves a closer examination. Why? According to the Heavenly of Heavens, when dealing with Divine Accountability, *As It Pleases God*, it has our Spiritual Protection involved in its use or the lack thereof.

Why do we need Spiritual Protection, especially when it is Divine? When dealing with anything or anyone, there is a *Higher Accountability* associated. For this reason, Romans 14:12 says, "*So then each of us shall give account of himself to God.*"

What if this Scripture says absolutely nothing about *Higher Accountability*? The *Higher Accountability* comes into play when we use Spiritual Things as a teacher, mentor, or as a method of conveyance. Here is what James 3:1 says about this matter: "*My brethren, let not many of you become teachers, knowing that we shall receive a stricter judgment.*"

Is it fair to receive stricter judgment, especially when grace is readily available? Absolutely! In the intricate balance between justice, grace, and mercy, we must make our best attempts to do the right things, even when we are tempted, teased, provoked, or tripped up. Sometimes it may feel as if we are penalized for being human, but most often, it is the willful choices that get us into a world of trouble with God, our Heavenly Father. Here is what James 4:17 says about our seedful intents: "*Therefore, to him who knows to do good and does not do it, to him it is sin.*"

Whether we are *The Black Sheep* or not, when it comes to our seedful intents, they have a life of their own, even if we make a mistake or pretend to be a victim. What if we are an innocent victim? Most often, in the Eye of God, yes, we may be a victim, but most often, we are not always innocent. 1 John 1:8 says, "*If we say that we have no sin, we deceive ourselves, and the truth* is not in us." Even Galatians 6:7 states: "*Do not be deceived, God is not mocked; for whatever a man sows, that he will also reap.*"

So, with all due respect, if we do not want more accountability, it is best to stay regular. What is the purpose of staying regular in or out of the Kingdom of God? First, to answer this question, let us take it to Scripture. Luke 12:48 says, "*But he who did not know, yet committed things deserving of stripes, shall be beaten with few. For everyone to whom much is given, from him much will be required; and to whom much has been committed, of him they will ask the more.*"

Secondly, Divine Greatness demands a *Higher Accountability* once awakened. Whereas, staying regular offers comfort zones, a sense of safety, complacency, and predictability, but it will keep us in a state of mediocrity, full of limitations. In addition, we will also miss out on opportunities for Spiritual Growth and Improvement, *As It Pleases God.*

Lastly, when we are unwilling to embrace change as a *Black Sheep*, we can place a damper on our usability, innovations, creativity, and advancements, even on a regular level, while making us quite unstable or unreliable. As a matter of fact, James 1:8 says, "*He is a double-minded man, unstable in all his ways.*" For this reason, if we encounter someone who is always late and cannot keep a commitment, we should exercise extreme caution. On the other hand, if this is you... It is time to step up your game or find your *Spiritual Tribe* to help you become better, stronger, and wiser, *As It Pleases God!*

Spiritual Tribe

Many of us, including myself, will find ourselves at some point in life searching for our *Spiritual Tribe*. As we all have an

The Black Sheep Journey

internal sense of belonging that must be quenched at some point, or when the timing is right, to keep us uplifted. Now, before we say that we do not need anyone, here is what Ecclesiastes 4:9-10 says, *"Two are better than one, because they have a good reward for their labor. For if they fall, one will lift up his companion. But woe to him who is alone when he falls, for he has no one to help him up."*

What is a Spiritual Tribe in the Eye of God? It is a group, community, or society of like-minded individuals or Believers who understand and accept us for who we truly are. In addition, they also help us become a better version of ourselves, according to our Predestined Blueprinted Purpose, with a Proverbs 27:17 Mentality: *"As iron sharpens iron, so a man sharpens the countenance of his friend."*

Finding *Your Tribe* is all about discovering your place in the world, surrounded by people who love, understand, support, and accept you for who you truly are, with all your flaws. Is it really possible to find our *Spiritual Tribe*? Of course. We are all here for a reason, and whatever the reason is, God has already made Spiritual Provision to accommodate and facilitate, which includes our Tribal Network(A Familial or Ancestral Community).

Although we may pick and choose our Tribal Terminology, when dealing with *The Black Sheep Power: As It Pleases God*® and for *The Black Sheep's Journey*, we use a Tribal Mindset to tap into the Tribe of Judah Blessings, Promises, and Anointing.

The Beauty of Finding *Your Tribe* is knowing a few things, but not limited to such:

- ☐ All things are possible with God, our Heavenly Father.
- ☐ When placing God first, we gain FAVOR with Him.

The Black Sheep Journey

All in all, *The Black Sheep* has an internal Spiritual Guide or Compass to pinpoint where they belong and where they do not.

The Power of a Tribe is nothing new. Actually, it is ANCIENT, but newly forgotten by us. Why? We have instant access to this and that, with social media links, causing us to disconnect from those in our immediate circle of relations.

For example, I have seen families at dinner on their phones texting and scrolling without communicating with those at the table. They feel more connected by the internet than by BLOOD. Where I am from, we say, 'Blood is thicker than water.' However, I must update this to an up-to-date version: 'Blood is much thicker than any likes, clicks, baits, apps, or any streams.'

In the Eye of God, we must master how to relate to others, even if they do not like us, hate our guts, reject us, or cannot stand the ground we walk on. Why must we master relating to those who do not give a rat's tail about us? According to the Heavenly of Heavens, it is our training ground. If we cannot relate to them, God will not trust us to relate to His sheep. Why not? Most of His sheep will not like us at first sight. Nor do they want to hear what we have to say. In fact, they will watch us first before allowing us the opportunity to speak or join their tribe.

Chapter Five
Black Sheep Mentality

Is your *Black Sheep Mentality* making you a victim or an easy target? Are you allowing your condition to become a negative hindrance for you? As a bona fide *Black Sheep* with real Spiritual Power, *As It Pleases God*, I have been tested and approved to write this book to lead His sheep back into the Spiritual Fold.

Why must we be a *Black Sheep*...Why can we not be another color? We can choose to be whatever color we like because a sheep is a sheep in or out of the sheepfold. However, *The Black Sheep* is a symbolic analogy referring to those who stand out or do not fit into societal norms. In addition, it is also designed to keep us from blending in with the herd. In my opinion, this is similar to a Chosen One having a Spiritual Mark on their bodies.

Is a Spiritual Mark the same as a birthmark? They may look the same, but in the Realm of the Spirit, they are not equated as being the same. Plus, they have different meanings or carry a certain level of Divine Protection. However, it does require Spiritual Insight to decode the Divine Marking, but the bearer of it will possess a higher Spiritual Mentality than most that they may or may not know about or understand as of yet.

Spiritually Speaking, those who possess a Spiritual Marking will encounter a little more rejection than those who are not Divinely Marked. They will also possess heightened sensitivity to the energy around them, allowing them to perceive and understand emotions and intentions on a deeper level. In my opinion, this is similar to how lions communicate with each other when hunting without having to say one word. Is this humanly possible? Of course, it is highly probable for those who develop a *Spirit to Spirit* Relationship with our Heavenly Father. Let me say this again, 'Spirit knows Spirit!'

While dealing with *The Black Sheep Mentality*, if we cannot handle rejection, we will become limited in the Kingdom of God. Yes, He may use us for certain things, but when dealing with real Spiritual Power on a high level, we are limited in this capacity. Is this fair? Absolutely.

Every Spiritual Disciple in the Bible who was used in a major way suffered some form of rejection. If they could not handle it, God would place them in a Spiritual Classroom or a Spiritual Desert for more training until they were able to handle the weight of rejection.

When we embrace our true selves, *As It Pleases God*, we attract others who appreciate our authenticity. If they do not appreciate who we are, then keep it moving in the Spirit of Excellence.

Redefining the Black Sheep

In *Redefining The Black Sheep*, we must understand what money can and cannot buy. As we seek to redefine what it means to be a *Black Sheep* and how to unveil our Spiritual Power, we must recognize that it requires introspection, self-awareness, and authenticity.

Our Spiritual Power emerges when we align our actions, thoughts, language, and beliefs with our true selves, unapologetically embracing who we are and our reason for being. The moment we come into AGREEMENT with these two things, we open ourselves up to the Divine Training Process designed to handle our Predestined Blueprinted Purpose. In Genesis 1:31, *"God saw everything that He had made, and indeed it was very good."* Thus, we have the Divine Right to embrace the goodness that resides within us...Plus, it is our responsibility to bring it forth anyway!

Do we really have a Spiritual Blueprint? Absolutely. Once again, God did not make a mistake when He created us, and as His stamp of approval, He provided a detailed Blueprint as Divine Proof. Here is what Romans 1:20 says, *"For since the creation of the world His invisible attributes are clearly seen, being understood by the things that are made, even His eternal power and Godhead, so that they are without excuse."*

Keep in mind, when we are fake, we lose power and inner strength by default, even if we pretend to be strong. Why would this happen to us as Believers? Simply put, it takes energy to be fake. With this depletion, we must draw the energy from elsewhere. For this reason, we will find that most of those who are fake or wearing masks are typically users, accusers, and abusers.

Why are fakers consumed with using, accusing, and abusing people? First and foremost, it is the nature of the beast. Secondly, they CANNOT be fueled by their own self-love, acceptance, and courage; therefore, they must depend on an outside source. Thirdly, they are exhausted by their psyche doing a number on them through the lust of the eyes, the lust of the flesh, and the pride of life. Lastly, the desire for power, money, sex, status, and fame has them in a chokehold, gasping for dear life for the people, places, and things money cannot buy.

What can money not buy, especially when we have it going on in real time? In *Redefining The Black Sheep*, it cannot buy God, the Holy Spirit, the Blood of Jesus, the Fruits of the Spirit, and

Black Sheep Mentality

Christlike Character. The moment we attempt to do so, the ultimate smackdown will occur from within the psyche, reflecting in our thoughts, beliefs, desires, actions, and reactions.

Why are we smacked down when money answereth all things? In the Eye of God, it is disrespectful to attempt to manipulate Him with what He classifies as mammon. Besides, He is not a prostitute; He is not for sale, nor does He like being pimped out. "*In His hand is the life of every living thing, and the breath of all mankind.*" Job 12:10.

What is God really expecting from us? He is expecting a *Spirit to Spirit* Relationship from us. Here is what Psalm 50:12-15 has to say about this matter: "*If I were hungry, I would not tell you; For the world is Mine, and all its fullness. Will I eat the flesh of bulls, or drink the blood of goats? Offer to God thanksgiving, and pay your vows to the Most High. Call upon Me in the day of trouble; I will deliver you, and you shall glorify Me.*"

When developing or redefining ourselves, *As It Pleases God*, listed below are a few other items money cannot buy, but not limited to such:

- ☐ In *The Black Sheep Power: As It Pleases God*®, our money cannot buy inner serenity of peace, and comfort with God, ourselves, and others for edification, *Self-Control*, and a direct connection to the Realm of the Spirit. Nor can it help us invoke Supernatural Faith, uncommon favor, or the unique, fashionable style of our Divine Blueprint.

- ☐ In *The Black Sheep Power: As It Pleases God*®, our money cannot buy inner charactorial conviction or correction with justifiable truths hidden in the Power of Repenting, Forgiving, Fasting, and Praying.

Black Sheep Mentality

- ☐ In *The Black Sheep Power: As It Pleases God*®, our money cannot buy inner guidance with a grid-worthy distinction, making the Word of God applicable to our daily living in or out of our Divine Anointing.

- ☐ In *The Black Sheep Power: As It Pleases God*®, our money cannot buy the empowerment of our Inner Genius, overriding or nullifying our toxic influences.

- ☐ In *The Black Sheep Power: As It Pleases God*®, our money cannot buy the ANOINTING of our Gifts, Talents, Calling, Creativity, or Fruits. Nor can it UNVEIL our Spiritual Eyes, Ears, and Mouth to obtain our Kingdom Credentials.

- ☐ In *The Black Sheep Power: As It Pleases God*®, our money cannot buy the guidance of the Ready Writer from within. Nor can it buy or strategize our Plan of Action or our next move relating to the FULL PORTION of our Divine Blueprint without Spiritual Guidance.

- ☐ In *The Black Sheep Power: As It Pleases God*®, our money cannot buy the Inner Revelation of the Great Unknown, unveiling our Spiritual Folds.

- ☐ In *The Black Sheep Power: As It Pleases God*®, our money cannot buy the unspeakable inner joy, quenching thirsts, or pangs of hunger within the human psyche.

- ☐ In *The Black Sheep Power: As It Pleases God*®, our money cannot buy the Infallible Teacher in or out of our Q and A Sessions or Spiritual Classroom.

Black Sheep Mentality

- [ ] In *The Black Sheep Power: As It Pleases God*®, our money cannot buy the inner or outer voice of Divine Utterance, Reasoning, Prophecy, or Intercession.

- [ ] In *The Black Sheep Power: As It Pleases God*®, our money cannot buy the gifted spark of genuine creativity, wisdom, understanding, and knowledge from God's Divine Perspective.

- [ ] In *The Black Sheep Power: As It Pleases God*®, our money cannot buy Spiritual Illumination, unveiling the elements of our Eternal Life now.

Clearly, in *The Black Sheep Power: As It Pleases God*®, our money can provide a comfortable lifestyle with tangible stuff; however, if we do not master the intangibles, *As It Pleases God*, the tangibles will not matter after we adapt to them or endure the traumas associated. Here is what we must know when building and redefining ourselves, in addition to why we need to obtain what money cannot buy.

- [ ] In *The Black Sheep Power: As It Pleases God*®, "Hell and Destruction are never full; So the eyes of man are never satisfied." Proverbs 27:20.

- [ ] In *The Black Sheep Power: As It Pleases God*®, "The righteous eats to the satisfying of his soul, But the stomach of the wicked shall be in want." Proverbs 13:25.

- [ ] In *The Black Sheep Power: As It Pleases God*®, "For the eyes of the greedy man are never satisfied; He heaps up wealth for himself, But does not know who will gather it." Ecclesiastes 4:8.

Black Sheep Mentality

- ☐ In *The Black Sheep Power: As It Pleases God*®, "But those who desire to be rich fall into temptation and a snare, and into many foolish and harmful lusts which drown men in destruction and perdition." 1 Timothy 6:9.

- ☐ In *The Black Sheep Power: As It Pleases God*®, "The leech has two daughters—*Give and Give! There are three things that are never satisfied, Four never say, 'Enough!': The grave, The barren womb, The earth that is not satisfied with water—And the fire never says, 'Enough!'* " Proverbs 30:15-16.

While it is undeniable that financial resources are crucial for meeting our basic needs and enjoying certain types of comforts. Nonetheless, it is also equally important to understand that our bank accounts do not dictate our self-worth or God's love for us. Our bouts with materialism should never cause us to want to end our lives, destroy our mental health, sabotage good relationships, or abandon our joyous happiness.

To obtain and sustain *The Black Sheep Power*, this toxic and dangerous mindset must be redefined, *As It Pleases God*. If not, we will find ourselves doing what we never thought we would do to sustain an image or illusion while hiding our hands.

From the bottom looking up and from the top looking down, I have seen certain things that have rocked me to the core. To say the least, it was not their actions and lack of integrity that rocked me. It was the COVER-UP in the Name of God that rocked my being to the core. I must admit, with a crisis of integrity, boldly lying on God took the cake for me. But what was more unsettling, they did not even attempt to lie on the devil, saying, 'The devil made me do it!' Nor did they attempt to deflect the blame or excuse their behaviors. Instead, from my perspective, they seemingly glorified their actions under the guise of Divine Approval, as if God were endorsing it.

Listen, in a world where our faith often intertwines with our morals, if you are going to do something foul, I mean, real foul, leave God out of it! For the record, you have free will to leave Him out of something you have to lie about. The moment you bring Him into your debaucherous efforts without repentance, it changes the rules of the game.

Why do the rules change, especially when a lie is a lie? It is due to operating with secrecy and deception, as if God would not know about it. Unfortunately, this is exactly how King Saul lost the Kingdom. Instead, they would have been better off operating with transparency and repentance, similar to King David's method of operation. If you did not know this previously, well, now you know...

What was the cover-up all about? It was for money and the opportunity to look rich! Not to BE rich, but to LOOK RICH. As an Oracle of the Most High God, to know the TRUTH, and still be kind to them with a smile on my face was one of the biggest tests of my life, but also the Greatest Teacher as well. So, we must establish fulfillment outside of wealth, and once we become wealthy, our fulfillment is already established. If not, we will confuse the two or become consumed by them.

Without fulfillment from the inside out and *As It Pleases God*, with or without money...you will never be satisfied! So, as a Word to the Wise, if you target the fulfillment factors associated with your Divine Purpose or Predestined Blueprint for the Greater Good, the void or emptiness will cease to exist.

How do we know whether or not fulfillment is established in our lives? It will vary from person to person, situation to situation, trauma to trauma, and so on. However, if in a moment of distress, we have feelings and thoughts of giving

Black Sheep Mentality

up, then it indicates that the fulfillment in whatever or whomever is not established completely. For instance, if what we are doing, saying, or becoming is a part of our reason for being, we do not give up easily. We dig our heels in or get all boots on the ground and do what it takes to get the job done, while overcoming our known and unknown obstacles.

The relentless pursuit of money with God at the forefront overshadows other essential aspects of our lives that really need our attention. Listen, we all need something, and we should never give up on ourselves, regardless. In *Redefining The Black Sheep*, here is how to get the ball rolling on the internal fulfillment process, but not limited to such:

- ☐ Find a quiet place to be alone with God.
- ☐ Develop a *Spirit to Spirit* Relationship with God.
- ☐ Pray, repent, forgive, and fast on occasion.
- ☐ Read the Word of God and meditate on it.
- ☐ Engage in some form of worship.
- ☐ Invite the Holy Spirit in to mentor, guide, and provide.
- ☐ Cover yourself with the Blood of Jesus.
- ☐ Ask questions and document the answers.
- ☐ Give thanks in all things.
- ☐ Remain humble and respectful at all times.
- ☐ Use the Fruits of the Spirit continuously.
- ☐ Behave Christlike at all times.
- ☐ Set a guard over your mouth.
- ☐ Speak and think positively.
- ☐ Engage in acts of kindness regularly.
- ☐ Maintain a work-in-progress mindset.
- ☐ Master creating a win-win out of everything.

If you make a mistake or miss one of them, do not give up; simply rinse and repeat. I cannot tell you how many times I had to redo this process, but still, I did not give up, and nor should you.

According to the Heavenly of Heavens, there is more to life, and it is our responsibility to hone in on the more factors. There is more IN HIM...There is more IN YOU...There is more IN LIFE...There is more IN PURPOSE. And, most of all, there is more IN US. Here is what Matthew 4:4 says, *"But He answered and said, 'It is written, Man shall not live by bread alone, but by every word that proceeds from the mouth of God.'"*

If we downplay or omit the Holy Trinity in our daily living, or if we refuse to cover ourselves with the Blood of Jesus as Spiritual Atonement, it may cause us to doubt or secretly reject ourselves when we mess up. In addition, when doing so, it is known for creating a vicious cycle of déjà vu, self-sabotage, or self-righteousness.

As *The Black Sheep*, we are created to learn from anything and everyone, deciphering through the information, choosing the positive, and discarding the negative to create a win-win. And if we are Spiritually Blind, Deaf, or Mute, we will begin to miss out on the simple things in life.

In addition, if we fail to redefine ourselves, *As It Pleases God*, doubt and confusion will unawaringly become our motivating factors, creating all types of known and unknown Spiritual Disasters. Then again, they may cause us to become accident-prone. So, we really need a *Biblical Mirror* of reflection to ensure we are on the up and up with God, ourselves, and others.

The Biblical Mirror

When I refer to *The Biblical Mirror*, most think that I mean hitting ourselves and others over the head with the Bible with a checklist of do's and don'ts. *The Biblical Mirror*, for me, represents living my life through the Word of God while living

Black Sheep Mentality

by example and embodying Spiritual Principles and Protocols in my actions, thoughts, beliefs, desires, and interactions.

In all simplicity, I allow my character, attitude, demeanor, etiquette, words, and people skills to do my bidding to uplift rather than condemn. Of course, this does not mean that I am perfect; however, I have master the ability to self-correct at the drop of a dime by reflecting on *The Biblical Mirror* set forth in the Word of God.

In *The Black Sheep Power: As It Pleases God*®, as our lives become a Living Testimony, rest assured that compassion, humility, kindness, understanding, and outright integrity are at the very CORE of *The Biblical Mirror* and its teachings.

According to the Heavenly of Heavens, the Bible serves as a Spiritual Mirror, revealing Divine Truths about who we are, why we are, and our relationship with God. What if we opt out of using it? If we decline its use, here is what James 1:23-24 has to say: *"For if anyone is a hearer of the word and not a doer, he is like a man observing his natural face in a mirror; for he observes himself, goes away, and immediately forgets what kind of man he was."*

As we all know, actions often speak louder than words, but rest assured, they both speak volumes in the Eye of God. Although words are powerful, the interplay between words and actions can reveal our true intentions, establish or break our trust, foster deeper relational connections, and, most of all, reveal our character. When dealing with a *Biblical Mirror*, there is nothing wrong with:

- ☐ Exhibiting love when we are hated.
- ☐ Being patient when we are frustrated.
- ☐ Exhibiting peace in a chaotic situation.
- ☐ Showing kindness to unkind people.
- ☐ Extending grace to someone who wronged us.
- ☐ Sharing goodness when we are served lemons.
- ☐ Being faithful when those around us are unfaithful.

Black Sheep Mentality

- ☐ Showing gentleness when we are treated abrasively.
- ☐ Exhibiting self-control when others are being reckless.
- ☐ Being truthful when lies surround us.
- ☐ Showing authenticity when fakeness bombards us.
- ☐ Reversing negatives into positives.
- ☐ Speaking life to yourself and others amid threats.
- ☐ Showing up or being supportive in a time of need.

The Spiritual Principles of *The Biblical Mirror* have a Clarion Call for us to do more than just adhere to rules. It requires us to pursue Divine Transformation in our heart and mind postures to an *As It Pleases God* Mindset, to include integrity and accountability.

We are often our biggest enemy from the inside out based on our thoughts, actions, beliefs, reactions, behaviors, words, lack of conscience, fruits, and character traits. The enemy from within subjects us to becoming the enemy of another, keeping the cycle of deception or lies going. Although no one is perfect, we must become accountable for what is happening inside us, spreading outwardly, affecting, infecting, or traumatizing others, especially the innocent.

If we dare to align our lives with the Word of God, we will find our lives becoming better and strategically aligned with our Divine Blueprint. With all due respect, we often find ourselves not understanding the Bible to the fullest because we are Spiritually Asleep. Therefore, we must AWAKEN our Spirit to become One with the Holy Spirit, covering ourselves with the Blood of Jesus while forgiving and repenting consistently. Why is this approach feasible for Believers? It helps us to MIRROR our lives, giving us a reflection through the Eye of God, as well as the eyes of man. Plus, it helps to tame the human psyche, ensuring it stays respectful and in its rightful place.

Black Sheep Mentality

How can *The Biblical Mirror* help us? If we take the Bible, asking the right fact-finding questions related to us personally, we can better understand how it provides the Spiritual Therapy that money cannot buy. Blasphemy, right? Wrong! When dealing with the human psyche, we must know the Spiritual Principles of God to avoid creating Spiritual Taboos in our Bloodline, playing ourselves short, or playing mind games, causing us to become played in the end. How does this work? Although we are all different, listed below are a few pointers helping us to get started, but not limited to such:

- ☐ We must be willing to step into the Spiritual Classroom with the Holy Trinity (The Father, Son, and Holy Spirit) in charge.

- ☐ We must be willing to pray, repent, forgive, fast on occasion, and meditate on the Word of God, while using positive affirmations as well.

- ☐ We must engage in a *Spirit to Spirit* Connection with our Heavenly Father in our alone time, perfecting our Spiritual Vision, Hearing, and Language.

- ☐ We must document what we are Spiritually Seeing, Hearing, and Speaking with our inside voice.

- ☐ We must ask fact-finding questions when reading the Bible, extracting 'What' happened, 'Why' it happened, 'Where' it happened, 'When' it could happen to us, 'How' to deal with it or overcome, and with 'Whom' to attract, avoid, share, build up, or cast down.

Black Sheep Mentality

- ☐ We must replace negativity with positive affirmations or scriptures, counteracting any form of evil, negative distractions, manipulation, or waywardness.

- ☐ We must get rid of any form of disobedience or rebellion that takes us out of the Will of God.

- ☐ We must question our behavior by aligning it with the Fruits of the Spirit consistently.

- ☐ We must pride ourselves on exhibiting Christlike Character, even when things are not going our way or people are treating us like junkyard dogs.

- ☐ We must be willing to stick to the Promises of God, even when we cannot see our way through.

- ☐ We must listen, learn, grow, and sow back into the Kingdom of God when called upon.

- ☐ We must be willing to pursue righteousness, even if worldliness becomes very tempting to our senses, habits, and lusts.

Now, before we go any further, let us align: *"Take this Book of the Law, and put it beside the ark of the covenant of the LORD your God, that it may be there as a witness against you; for I know your rebellion and your stiff neck. If today, while I am yet alive with you, you have been rebellious against the LORD, then how much more after my death? Gather to me all the elders of your tribes, and your officers, that I may speak these words in their hearing and call heaven and earth to witness against them."* Deuteronomy 31:26-28.

Black Sheep Mentality

Of course, we are no longer under the Law to bring forth punishment or death. Through the Blood of the Lamb, the Spiritual Principles and Protocols are now designed to bring forth the LIGHT, illuminating our paths, taking us from legalism to Spirituality. While at the same time, allowing us to open our hearts and minds to promote love, mercy, compassion, forgiveness, gratitude, and understanding, *As It Pleases God.*

The Biblical Mirror serves as a Guiding Light in our *Union of Oneness*, while having its own built-in hidden roadmap. As a beacon of hope and introspection, it also provides clarity and direction, especially for those who are willing to receive and bring forth the true nature of their Higher Calling for the Greater Good, and *As It Pleases God.*

Union of Oneness

In an age where division, chaos, and conflict often dominate headlines, the concept of the *Union of Oneness* with God serves as a vital reminder that interconnectedness still exists. By embracing this Sacred *Spirit to Spirit* Connection can profoundly deepen our Spiritual Journey, going from ordinary to extraordinary.

In our *Union of Oneness*, it behooves us to engage in private sessions with God, developing our *Spirit to Spirit* Connection. As a form of exercise for the conscience, we can indeed develop our *Black Sheep Mentality* in ways that supersede human reasoning. From the Ancient of Days to the present, this forgotten Spiritual Art of private sessions with God has profound meaning in the Realm of the Spirit. Yet, if we do not take advantage of this practice, our conscience will suffer the consequences.

What can exercising the conscience do for us? In the same way that physical exercise strengthens our bodies, private sessions with God will fortify our Spirits in our moments of reflective solitude. A sanctuary away from the noise, hustle, and bustle of life to develop a *Union of Oneness* with our Heavenly Father will help develop our Spiritual Senses, Fruits, and Character with a better understanding of our inner selves. Plus, with an intimate dialogue as such, it also assists in revamping our psyche to become merciful, forgiving, gracious, unselfish, and compassionate.

What if we avoid our *Spirit to Spirit* alone time with God? We have free will to engage or disengage. This private session with Him is not by force. However, if we do not develop our conscience, *As It Pleases Him*, we will find ourselves judging and condemning people, places, things, and events for the same things we are openly or secretly guilty of. Then again, we may become jealous, envious, greedy, selfish, prideful, competitive, covetous, and operate underhandedly without realizing we are behaving in such a manner.

In our *Union of Oneness*, here is what 2 Chronicles 30:8-9 says about this matter: *"Now do not be stiff-necked, as your fathers were, but yield yourselves to the LORD; and enter His sanctuary, which He has sanctified forever, and serve the LORD your God, that the fierceness of His wrath may turn away from you. For if you return to the LORD, your brethren and your children will be treated with compassion by those who lead them captive, so that they may come back to this land; for the LORD your God is gracious and merciful, and will not turn His face from you if you return to Him."* 2 Chronicles 30:8-9.

According to the Heavenly of Heavens, for your private sessions with God, your Heavenly Father, He is not really picky as most would think. If you dare to remove the limits, your private sessions with Him, *Spirit to Spirit*, can take on many forms, such as, but not limited to:

Black Sheep Mentality

- ☐ Worshipping: Listen to Spiritual or uplifting music that inspires reflection and connection. Create a playlist of songs that speak to your Spirit Man. Then again, regardless of your vocal abilities, you can also sing to God to deepen your connection with Him. Besides, He loves it when we sing to Him, especially when we dialogue with intimacy and affection.

- ☐ Meditation: Spend time in quiet meditation, focusing on your breath and inviting a sense of peace. Meditation is one of the best ways to calm the Mind, Body, Soul, and Spirit, allowing you to heal and develop. If you cannot sit still with your thoughts without them bouncing all over the place, then it behooves you to get somewhere and calm down!

- ☐ Prayer: Speak openly with God, sharing your thoughts, feelings, and desires, and seeking guidance. When in prayer, *Spirit to Spirit*, this is the time to release pent-up emotions, frustrations, and qualms while giving thanks. Just make sure this does not become a begging session.

- ☐ Journaling: Write down your thoughts, feelings, desires, passions, reflections, prayers, visions, answers, instructions, or dialogues with God to capture your Spiritual Journey in writing.

- ☐ Scripture Reading: Explore the Word of God, especially what resonates with you, allowing the teachings to inspire, guide, and align you. 2 Timothy 3:16-17 says, *"All Scripture is given by inspiration of God, and is profitable for doctrine, for reproof, for correction, for instruction in righteousness, that the man of God may be complete, thoroughly equipped for every good work."*

- ☐ Sitting in Silence: Use intentional breathing exercises, breathing in and out, to center yourself and invite stillness in to calm the Mind, Body, Soul, and Spirit, allowing space for God's Divine Voice to be heard.

- ☐ Nature Walks: Spending time in nature helps us Divinely Connect back to the Source of our being. Observing the beauty of nature stimulates the Mind, Body, Soul, and Spirit in ways that Science has yet to understand fully.

- ☐ Gratitude Practice: In our *First Power*, list the simple things you are grateful for, acknowledging the BLESSINGS in your life.

- ☐ Visualization: Imagine a peaceful scenario with God or a moment of Divine Connection with a positive outcome, allowing it to fill you with serenity.

- ☐ Creative Expression: Create art, whether through painting, drawing, writing, or music, as a form of worship and connection to God, your Heavenly Father.

- ☐ Speaking Affirmations: Speak positive affirmations that align with your Spiritual Intentions and Aspirations or the Word of God.

In our *Union of Oneness*, we cannot limit God; all we need to do is carve out a special time with Him, faithfully relax in that moment, and He will take it from there. By consciously

Black Sheep Mentality

investing time in our *Spirit to Spirit* Relationship with God, we can transform our lives in ways beyond human reasoning. When we open ourselves to an enriching Spiritual Experience, it leads to a better understanding of who we are, why we are here, and what we need to do, *As It Pleases Him.* During these moments, we need to focus on *Reframing the Narrative* to become stronger, wiser, and usable in and out of the Kingdom, feeding God's precious sheep.

Reframing the Narrative

The Ultimate Reset is here...Yes, it is upon us right now in this very SEASON. We as a society, especially the so-called Shepherds, are doing the most, without being righteous about what we are doing, saying, and becoming, particularly those in positions of Spiritual Authority.

Ezekiel 34:2-3 says to us today with a Divine Warning and Accountability, *"Son of man, prophesy against the shepherds of Israel, prophesy and say to them, 'Thus says the Lord GOD to the shepherds: Woe to the shepherds of Israel who feed themselves! Should not the shepherds feed the sheep?'"* When we are entrusted to care for and protect God's precious sheep, we cannot prance around here slipping. What does this mean? When we prioritize our own needs over God's flock, He sees this as a NEGLECT OF DUTY in the Realm of the Spirit.

Listen, the Divine Echos are LOUD and our self-serving behaviors are on the Spiritual Table as we speak, and we cannot think for a minute that God is not watching. The moment we think a shakedown cannot hit our houses, it will hit us, shaking us to the core, beginning from the weakest links. No, we are not here to save the world, but we are required to do our part in the Spirit of Righteousness and Decency.

Black Sheep Mentality

So, my question today is, 'What is your motivation behind your actions?' 'Are you acting in the best interest of God's precious sheep?' 'Are you doing what you need to do to fulfill your self-interests at the price of neglecting or defying the innocent?' Or, 'Are you here to serve or be served?' As Shepherds, we must answer these questions; if not, our Divine Portions will be served without our input. Really? Yes, really!

Here is a prime example of how Jesus helped Simon Peter *Reframe the Narrative* in John 21:15-17 regarding his Divine Portion: *"So when they had eaten breakfast, Jesus said to Simon Peter, 'Simon, son of Jonah, do you love Me more than these?' He said to Him, 'Yes, Lord; You know that I love You.' He said to him, 'Feed My lambs.' He said to him again a second time, 'Simon, son of Jonah, do you love Me?' He said to Him, 'Yes, Lord; You know that I love You.' He said to him, 'Tend My sheep.' He said to him the third time, 'Simon, son of Jonah, do you love Me?' Peter was grieved because He said to him the third time, 'Do you love Me?' And he said to Him, 'Lord, You know all things; You know that I love You.' Jesus said to him, 'Feed My sheep.' "*

Most would think these are repetitive questions, but they were designed to provoke deep thought regarding the Divine Commission. Not only was this for Simon Peter, but it is also for us in this day and age to help (prepare) the upcoming lambs (the children), tend to the needy, and feed (teach) the unfortunate, Mentally, Physically, Emotionally, and Spiritually.

Why would Jesus keep repeating Himself, especially when Simon Peter answered Him? It was designed to *Reframe the Narrative* with Simon Peter. Sometimes our mindsets get stuck based on our thoughts, beliefs, conditioning, biases, traumas, and quirks. As a result of this mindset, we may think it is better to make people suffer, especially those appearing beneath us. Unfortunately, in the Eye of God, this is one of the quickest ways to get DOWNGRADED and REPLACED in

Black Sheep Mentality

our Heaven on Earth Experiences. Here is what Proverbs 22:16 says, *"He who oppresses the poor to increase his riches, and he who gives to the rich, will surely come to poverty."*

What if we are not responsible for other people's problems? As Shepherds, we cannot assume this title or role without people. As a matter of fact, their problems come with the territory. But know this, if the sheep really cry out, for real, for real, it can indeed move Heaven and Earth on their behalf, so beware. These are not my words; it is the BIBLE. Exodus 22:22 says, *"You shall not afflict any widow or fatherless child. If you afflict them in any way, and they cry at all to Me, I will surely hear their cry."*

What do we need to do? The bottom line is that we as a people are required to make our best attempts to protect the most vulnerable with compassionate measures. Here is what we need to know according to Proverbs 14:31: *"He who oppresses the poor reproaches his Maker, but he who honors Him has mercy on the needy."* It is always wise to extend mercy because we will never know when we are going to need it. Plus, it is not a matter of if, it is a matter of when!

Economic struggles, social injustices, and systemic neglect are everywhere, and it is only a matter of time before this type of risk comes knocking on our doors. We must ensure that when it does, we have good seeds planted in the ground. On the other hand, if bad seeds are planted, then we do not need a rocket scientist to advise on this matter. Simply put, *"Do not oppress the widow or the fatherless, the alien or the poor. Let none of you think evil in your heart against your brother."* Zechariah 7:10.

When it comes to God's sheep, we must come with a clean, unbiased, or neutral mindset because every sheep will need something different. Therefore, we cannot use the last sheep experience on the upcoming sheep experience. Why not? Simply put, we were all created differently; therefore, we can rely on the Holy Spirit for instructions instead of our own tainted instructions.

If we are clueless about Spiritual Instructions, just repeat Luke 4:18 over and over as many times as needed: *"The Spirit of the Lord is upon Me, because He has anointed Me to preach the gospel to the poor; He has sent Me to heal the brokenhearted, to proclaim liberty to the captives and recovery of sight to the blind, to set at liberty those who are oppressed."* Once the Spiritual Instructions are received, then document them, leaving a paper trail of Divine Information for the next in line.

Why is this approach so effective when dealing with God? Our psyche will protect itself, doing whatever it likes until it is put on blast, in the same way that we are prone to put others on blast when they get our time wrong. So, if we request Spiritual Instructions while documenting the dialogue, *As It Pleases God*, it opens us up to a Divine Realm of infinite possibilities based on trustworthiness.

On the other hand, if we selfishly opt not to request and document, *As It Pleases God*, then we become limited to infinite possibilities due to the propensity for misuse. Is this fair? Absolutely. When we do not do anything with the information, or it will get lost in the probabilities, Divine Wisdom is withheld by default.

Then again, if we have a track record of abusing power, the system, or people, especially God's Chosen Ones, the Realm of the Spirit will pump the brakes on our Divinity until we awaken from our slumber. Frankly, this is how we get a lot of Believers with a good word or who can talk the talk, but have zero Spiritual Power and cannot walk the walk, *As It Pleases Him*. Above all, they are yoked to the core with all types of rotten fruits and do not realize it because they are Spiritually Blind, Deaf, and Mute. Nor can they break the yokes holding their loved ones captive.

Black Sheep Mentality

Who am I to judge who can break yokes and who cannot, right? No judgment intended, I am only the MESSENGER, Divinely Ordained from the Heavenly of Heavens to read the Fruits of the Times and assist in *Reframing the Narratives*. Nonetheless, as Shepherds leading God's sheep, we must become real yoke breakers to protect the flock in or out of the fold. For instance, if someone comes for me and mine, it means gloves off in the Realm of the Spirit, and I do not play around with nonsense or injustice.

How is it possible to develop such Spiritual Tenacity as Believers? According to 1 Peter 5:2-3, here is how: *"Shepherd the flock of God which is among you, serving as overseers, not by compulsion but willingly, not for dishonest gain but eagerly; nor as being lords over those entrusted to you, but being examples to the flock."* First, when we live by example, *As It Pleases God*, He will move Heaven and Earth on our behalf, protecting any and everything that belongs to us or is associated with us. Secondly, when we willfully oversee God's sheep as a servant, He will make sure He provides for us. Thirdly, when we humbly operate in the Spirit of Excellence with truth, self-control, and authenticity, we will always have Spiritual Backup, ready, willing, and able to assist us. Lastly, when we use the Fruits of the Spirit and behave Christlike, it develops our Spiritual Integrity to do what it righteously takes to possess the Promises, Blessings, and the Land.

According to the Spiritual Law of Seedtime and Harvest, Seeds will produce the fruits of likeness in different situations until we learn the lesson, regraft the root, or prune whatever or whomever. At the same time, the Root of Disobedience is NOT a fruit that we want to feed continuously. Why not, especially when having free will? The Spiritual Taboos associated with disobedience have the potential to run deep into our lineage, annihilating our Bloodline or invoking a generational curse, especially if we give in to haughtiness.

Black Sheep Mentality

What does haughtiness have to do with our Bloodline? Unbeknown to most, this sort of bullseye is placed upon two types of people, primarily if they are not extremely careful:

- ☐ The Boastful.
- ☐ The Wicked.

For this one, I do not wish upon my worst enemy; therefore, allow me to take it to scripture. *"I said to the boastful, 'Do not deal boastfully,' and to the wicked, 'Do not lift up the horn. Do not lift up your horn on high; Do not speak with a stiff neck.' For exaltation comes neither from the east nor from the west nor from the south. But God is the Judge: He puts down one, and exalts another."* Psalm 75:4-7.

Who is protected from this bullseye? The opposite category can justifiably invoke protection over their Bloodline without praying amiss, which are:

- ☐ The Humble.
- ☐ The Righteous.

To be clear, this does not mean perfection; it is willful and workable humility and fully repenting or authentic righteousness. More importantly, here is what we need to know: *"All the horns of the wicked I will also cut off, but the horns of the righteous shall be exalted."* Psalm 75:10. For this reason, before we toot our horns on any level, it is imperative to know and understand our antonyms.

Why do we need to know antonyms when dealing with Spirituality? When approaching *The Black Sheep Power: As It Pleases God*®, knowing our opposites helps us counteract negatives with positives, evil with good, unjust with just,

Black Sheep Mentality

wrong with right, and so on. When we fail to understand Spiritual Duality or the differences, we can become easily deceived, confused, misunderstood, and frustrated in our communicative efforts.

The minute we are unable to counteract positively, we become susceptible to the wiles of the enemy because *"Those who live according to the flesh set their minds on the things of the flesh, but those who live according to the Spirit, the things of the Spirit."* Romans 8:5. Listed below are a few susceptibilities when the Holy Spirit is NOT present, but not limited to such:

- ☐ We will revert to the path of least resistance or become increasingly lazy. *"The lazy man buries his hand in the bowl; it wearies him to bring it back to his mouth. The lazy man is wiser in his own eyes than seven men who can answer sensibly."* Proverbs 26:15-16.

- ☐ We will let our guards down, downplaying our instinctual nature while becoming hateful from the inside out. *"He who hates, disguises it with his lips, and lays up deceit within himself."* Proverbs 26:24.

- ☐ We become less likely to convert or look for a win-win due to our hidden inner defeats. *"Whoever has no rule over his own spirit is like a city broken down, without walls."* Proverbs 25:28.

- ☐ We will show our true selves with zero accountability while playing the blaming game, digging deep ditches, or setting traps out of spite. *"Whoever digs a pit will fall into it, and he who rolls a stone will have it roll back on him."* Proverbs 26:27.

Black Sheep Mentality

- ☐ We become prone to jealousy, envy, and coveting, contributing to our own slumber. *"Do not be envious of evil men, nor desire to be with them; for their heart devises violence, and their lips talk of troublemaking."* Proverbs 24:1-2.

- ☐ We will constantly have a bout with ungratefulness, contention, and greediness. *"It is better to dwell in a corner of a housetop, than in a house shared with a contentious person."* Proverbs 25:24.

- ☐ We are less likely to forgive, having mercy upon another without instigating some form of ruckus. *"He who sends a message by the hand of a fool cuts off his own feet and drinks violence. Like the legs of the lame that hang limp is a proverb in the mouth of fools. Like one who binds a stone in a sling is he who gives honor to a fool."* Proverbs 26:6-8.

- ☐ We are prone to wallowing as a victim or becoming a talebearer. *"The words of a talebearer are like tasty trifles, and they go down into the inmost body."* Proverbs 26:22.

- ☐ We become a magnet for confusion, chaos, and debauchery. *"The great God who formed everything gives the fool his hire and the transgressor his wages. As a dog returns to his own vomit, so a fool repeats his folly."* Proverbs 26:10-11.

- ☐ It becomes challenging to develop or maintain a Positive Mental Mindset as we become bombarded by the Vicissitudes of Life, feeling right in our own eyes. *"Do you see a man wise in his own eyes? There is more hope for a fool than for him."* Proverbs 26:12.

Black Sheep Mentality

- [ ] It becomes easier to player-hate or meddle while developing loose lips, saying and doing anything, or operating without a conscience. *"He who passes by and meddles in a quarrel not his own is like one who takes a dog by the ears. Like a madman who throws firebrands, arrows, and death, is the man who deceives his neighbor, and says, 'I was only joking!'"* Proverbs 26:17-19.

- [ ] It becomes easier to compete in or out of our field of expertise while finding fault in others or negatively outing them for developing their Gifts, Calling, Talents, Creativity, or being in Purpose on purpose. *"Debate your case with your neighbor, and do not disclose the secret to another; lest he who hears it expose your shame, and your reputation be ruined."* Proverbs 25:9-10.

If we wet our whistles with the Word of God instead of tooting our own horns, we are better able to contend on a level most cannot. What is the big deal about tooting our own horns? Although we use positive affirmations to build ourselves up in Earthen Vessel, pompousness will not get it, especially when the enemy is ready to make an example out of us. Here is what the scripture has to say to us, *"Do not boast about tomorrow, for you do not know what a day may bring forth. Let another man praise you, and not your own mouth; a stranger, and not your own lips."* Proverbs 27:1-2.

Internal Building

In the *Black Sheep Mentality*, it is imperative to focus on *Internal Building* before building ourselves up externally or pursuing external validation or success. Even 2 Corinthians 4:16 tells us exactly what to do and why: *"Therefore we do not lose heart. Even though our outward man is perishing, yet the inward man is being renewed day by day."* Now, if for some reason we are having a hard time believing the daily renewal process, just repeat Psalm 51:10 over and over, *"Create in me a clean heart, O God, and renew a steadfast spirit within me."* Does it work? Absolutely. I am living proof!

Embracing this renewal process helps us understand our values, beliefs, strengths, weaknesses, and quirks. Plus, it allows us to become a work-in-progress without becoming a sell-out to the elements of darkness, lacking clarity.

If we do not build our inner man and remain in the LIGHT, *As It Pleases God*, we will begin to follow any wave of doctrine or find ourselves entertaining wolves in sheep's clothing. Here is what Ephesians 4:14 warns: *"That we should no longer be children, tossed to and fro and carried about with every wind of doctrine, by the trickery of men, in the cunning craftiness of deceitful plotting."*

Plus, with deceitfulness, we never want to get to a place of no return, Mentally, Physically, Emotionally, or Spiritually. Why not? It is a dark place, and the enemy will have a field day with the Mind, Body, and Soul, where we take pleasure in corrupting, destroying, or devastating others. What if this is all we know? In the Eye of God, we have the power to unknow it as well.

For example, a parent can have two children in a negative environment, one choosing to remain like the parent, perpetuating negative cycles for the lesser good of mankind. And the other one refuses to initiate another life cycle of daunting trauma. So, this particular sibling made a conscious choice to break the negative cycle and the generational curse associated.

Although some people do not believe in generational curses, with *Internal Building*, we must discuss this highly

Black Sheep Mentality

debatable topic for many Believers. Suppose a negative pattern or cycle is not reversed and covered by the Blood of Jesus as Spiritual Atonement. In this case, it remains attached to a particular Bloodline, regardless of whether we understand it or not. Yes, Jesus is the Mediator according to Hebrews 12:24, saying: *"To Jesus the Mediator of the new covenant, and to the blood of sprinkling that speaks better things than that of Abel."* However, if we want that Blood to come alive on our behalf or speak on our behalf, we must do our part. What is our part? Our part in reversing the effects based on the LAW of Spiritual Duality derived from the Garden of Eden through Adam and Eve.

What is Spiritual Duality? It is a concept that explores the existence of two opposing forces, like light and darkness, good and evil, positive and negative, love and hate, right and wrong, just and unjust, or blessings and curses. Simply put, one does not exist without the other, and Divine Wisdom requires us to know and understand both. If not, when life throws us a curveball, it will smack us right in the face, as if we did not see it coming, targeting our homes and children the most.

For example, we will never have to teach a child how to do wrong; it is in their nature. Now, in order to break this cycle, we must teach them how to do the right things, even when wrong things are happening. For this reason, Proverbs 22:6 says, *"Train up a child in the way he should go, and when he is old he will not depart from it."* We must break the cycle or generational curse from the Garden of Eden...We can play on words or make a generational curse an improbability, but the yoke is taking our children down by the masses.

Here is my question: how is it that we know so much about curses but know very little about the FRUITS used to break them? How is it that we do not know that the Fruits of the Spirit are designed to break generational curses? Why do we not know that the Fruits of the Spirit can balance the interplay of opposites? On this note, if I were to ask someone who proclaims that curses are not real, how to reverse a negative into a positive, they would trip over their words. Why would this happen? All of the hoopla is rehearsed!

How do I know that the hoopla exists among Believers? When someone proclaims, 'The devil made me do it,' I then ask, 'Did the devil force your hand?' The answer is, 'No, he did not.' I then ask, 'How did he make you do something without laying a finger on you?' Of course, he (the devil) may plant the seed, similar to what happened to Eve, but he does not make us take action...we do it on our own. In the same way we take action, is the same way we can deactivate it or not act upon the seed of thought. Thus, making Spiritual Duality real, relevant, effective, and useful for all mankind.

Let me say this: Some cultures do not play around with this type of Spiritual Negligence. But for some odd reason, we entertain this type of foolery while bound with negative charactorial traits or conditions passed down through our Bloodline, while justifying and rationalizing the means. Regardless of whether it stems from trauma, addiction, mental health struggles, or unhealthy relationships, the redemptive power of Jesus Christ can break chains and restore us when it is confronted and dealt with, *As It Pleases God.*

Can we make this subject a little more palatable? I am not here to sugarcoat anything because it was that type of teaching that caused me to stub my toe when contending in enemy territory. If it were not for the GRACE and MERCY of God Almighty, I would be barking like a dog right about now! Yet, I am still here in my right mind, so let us continue. Nonetheless, what I have found is that we are so spooked out about people cursing us. But the truth is, we are most often the culprit initiating the cycle of curses without knowing it.

Black Sheep Mentality

Proverbs 18:21 clearly says, *"Death and life are in the power of the tongue, and those who love it will eat its fruit."*

For me, I can tell where a person is at or what they are dealing with by what comes out of their mouth. Before going any further, here is what James 3:9-10 says, *"With it we bless our God and Father, and with it we curse men, who have been made in the similitude of God. Out of the same mouth proceed blessing and cursing. My brethren, these things ought not to be so."*

How did the one sibling break the negative cycle? First, they decided to address negative cycles and the manipulative lies. Secondly, they decided to become positive, fruitful, kindhearted, and loving with God at the forefront, using the Fruits of the Spirit and behaving Christlike consistently. Thirdly, they decided to create a new path and teach others to become better, stronger, and wiser for the Greater Good.

Just like these two siblings coming from the same parents, we also have a choice to continue a negative cycle or break it. If a negative cycle is not confronted, reversed, or broken through *Internal Building*, we will begin breaking down the people, places, and things around us instead of building, creating, and establishing. What makes this so important for Believers? Proverbs 25:28 clearly says, *"Whoever has no rule over his own spirit is like a city broken down, without walls."*

It may take time and a lot of work to make the necessary changes according to Kingdom Standards, but it is doable in the Eye of God. Listen, there is goodness within everyone, and the Fruits of the Spirit, according to Galatians 5:22-23, will help fine-tune them, *As It Pleases Him*. How so? There is no Spiritual Law against their use. Whereas, all else contains a SEED with a Spiritual Law attached.

Why is there no Spiritual Law against the use of the Fruits of the Spirit? Simply put, Love, Joy, Peace, Patience, Kindness, Goodness, Faithfulness, Gentleness, and Self-Control are

Black Sheep Mentality

already in our DNA, even if we do not know about them or use them. According to the Heavenly of Heavens, they are prewired within us, and we only need to use them to activate the healing associated with their use. Listed below are a few picturesque examples, but not limited to such:

- ☐ There is no law against using our natural eyes; we need them to see, so all we need to do is use them. However, the misuse and abuse of our eye gates invoke the Spiritual Laws associated. In addition, the Spiritual Eye of mankind does have Spiritual Laws across the board regarding its use. With this, if one does not understand it, they should not play around with it.

- ☐ There is no law against using the brain; we need the brain to function properly in a normal capacity, even if we only use less than 10% of it. Without its use, we are considered brain-dead, even on life support. On the other hand, if we have a desire to outsmart God with the workings of the brain, there lie Spiritual Laws that should not be violated. Why? Most of the brainial functions we do not use are mostly Spiritual; therefore, certain elements of the brain we should not touch unless we have Spiritual Permission from the Heavenly of Heavens.

- ☐ There is no law against using the mind normally; it works with or without our permission. However, there are Spiritual Laws associated with expanding the mind.

- ☐ There is no law against the normal use of our limbs; we need them to function. Still, there are Spiritual Laws governing the expanded use or the lack thereof.

Black Sheep Mentality

- There is no law against using the mouth normally; we need it to speak, eat, and drink to sustain life. Whereas the overuse, underuse, and abuse of the mouth, which has nothing to do with sustaining life, contain Spiritual Laws.

Conversely, if we opt NOT to use the Fruits of the Spirit, then the Spiritual Laws associated with NOT using them will apply. What is the purpose of being penalized in such a manner? In my opinion, it is not being penalized, so to speak; it is called lacking DISCERNMENT.

Without the use or first-hand knowledge of the Fruits of the Spirit, your Spiritual Compass will become somewhat keeled from the least to the greatest. Matthew 7:20 says, *"Therefore by their fruits you will know them."*

More importantly, by your fruits, you will get to know yourself as well, which is a valuable opportunity for introspection. By examining your own fruits, you can gain Divine Insight into your character and Spiritual Condition, first. Here is how I would examine my own fruits, but not limited to such:

- What is the purpose of this fruit?
- Why am I using this particular fruit?
- How does this fruit apply to my situation?
- Is this the best fruit to use?
- What fruits am I producing?
- Are my fruits positive or negative?
- Are my fruits just or unjust?
- What can I do to enhance the quality of my fruits?
- Is God pleased with my fruits?
- Are my fruits making a positive impact?

Black Sheep Mentality

- ☐ Are my people skills aligning with good fruits?
- ☐ Am I growing my fruits with integrity?

What is the purpose of questioning our fruits in such a manner? Simply put, we have not because we ask not! I make my fruits speak to me, helping me to self-correct at the drop of a dime. How is this humanly possible? Our Spiritual Fruits have a VOICE that can speak through our conscience, senses, red flags, and picturesque glimpses. The bottom line is that our Spiritual Fruits will use anything and anyone to get our attention, especially when we have a listening ear to hear.

Now, here is the deal: If you are reading the fruits of others and not reading and perfecting your own with a work-in-progress mindset, it will not be long before hypocrisy knocks on your door. Here is what James 3:17 advises about this matter: *"But the wisdom that is from above is first pure, then peaceable, gentle, willing to yield, full of mercy and good fruits, without partiality and without hypocrisy."*

Even if we cannot quickly rebound, we have the Word of God as our point of refuge until we develop and strengthen our Spiritual Muscles or Wings of Righteousness. Is this Biblical? Of course, it says, *"For to be carnally minded is death, but to be spiritually minded is life and peace. Because the carnal mind is enmity against God; for it is not subject to the law of God, nor indeed can be. So then, those who are in the flesh cannot please God. But you are not in the flesh but in the Spirit, if indeed the Spirit of God dwells in you. Now if anyone does not have the Spirit of Christ, he is not His. And if Christ is in you, the body is dead because of sin, but the Spirit is life because of righteousness."* Romans 8:6-10.

What is the purpose of building ourselves from the inside out? We must build ourselves Mentally, Physically, Emotionally, and Spiritually. The Bible tells us to: *"Prepare your*

Black Sheep Mentality

outside work, make it fit for yourself in the field; and afterward build your house." Proverbs 24:27. When omitting the building process from the inside out, we will break easily amid the Vicissitudes of Life or when placed under pressure, forcing us to get out of character instead of putting on the Whole Armor of God.

In operating with the *Black Sheep Power: As It Pleases God*®, we must deal with the human psyche through Spiritual Means to apply Divine Wisdom. Using this Spiritual Approach, *As It Pleases Him*, assists in dealing with worldliness without running for cover with our tail between our legs as if He is not on the Throne.

Why would we run as if God is not God? Most often, it is out of fear, doubt, lack of understanding, or immaturity. However, it is *"Through wisdom a house is built, and by understanding it is established; by knowledge the rooms are filled with all precious and pleasant riches. A wise man is strong, Yes, a man of knowledge increases strength; for by wise counsel you will wage your own war, and in a multitude of counselors there is safety."* Proverbs 24:3-6.

Spirit of Overflow

We are designed to make a difference for ourselves and those who are following suit. For this reason, we must take our lives seriously, making the most out of everything and with everyone, as we become a Fountain of Wisdom, as our Spiritual Portions run over. When overflowing in such a manner, Blessings will follow us everywhere we go.

For example, a person possessing the *Spirit of Overflow* can walk into a business where it is so slow with little or no customers. Then, all of a sudden, there is an influx of customers coming in to patronize this business. To be clear, this is not a one-time overflow; it is a constant overflow of Blessings following this individual, spilling over onto anyone around them as well. Does this really happen? Absolutely!

Black Sheep Mentality

When operating *As It Pleases God*, and when in Divine Purpose, our BLESSINGS become evident, shifting atmospheres. Once we are in Purpose on purpose, the Spiritual Seal in Joshua 1:3 becomes automatic: *"Every place that the sole of your foot will tread upon I have given you, as I said to Moses."*

When we are Spirit-led, we do not tread or remain where we do not belong. We keep it moving in the Spirit of Excellence, learning what we need to learn while taking our BLESSINGS with us once the Divine Assignment is over. Here is what I use to Spiritually Align where I place my feet, according to Psalm 1:1-3, *"Blessed is the man who walks not in the counsel of the ungodly, nor stands in the path of sinners, nor sits in the seat of the scornful; but his delight is in the law of the Lord, and in His law he meditates day and night. He shall be like a tree planted by the rivers of water, that brings forth its fruit in its season, whose leaf also shall not wither; and whatever he does shall prosper."* Listed below is how I apply this scripture to real life, but not limited to such:

- ☐ I seek good, sound counsel.
- ☐ I stay in my lane, *As It Pleases God*.
- ☐ I surround myself with those who are stable.
- ☐ I follow Spiritual Principles, Standards, and Protocols.
- ☐ I rehearse and align the Word of God with my life.
- ☐ I quench my thirst with the Word of God.
- ☐ I produce good and shareable fruits.
- ☐ I activate the Law of Reciprocity for the Greater Good.
- ☐ I know and understand that my hands are BLESSED.

As a Word to the Wise, according to the Heavenly of Heavens, we should extend peacefulness and harmony everywhere we place the soles of our feet. When operating in the Spirit of Excellence, if we are not careful, the sliding scale of our communicable efforts has a way of painting a superficial façade to create a sense of awe, instead of allowing us to become openly transparent regarding our reality.

We are a mirror, causing others to secretly or openly emulate us. As a *Black Sheep*, if we are sharing fakeness, superficialities, or cliffhangers, others will follow suit based on their perception of our untruths.

A harmonious demeanor is sought after by many, yet misunderstood by most. So, in the *Spirit of Overflow*, it behooves us to up the ante in this area, ensuring our *A-Game* does not become our *B-Game*. Unbeknown to most, this is when we are operating beneath our Divine Gifting of Greatness encapsulated in our win-win. Only to become subservient to a lesser game, resulting in some form of loss in due time, affecting our bottom lines.

How can we encourage overflow if it is not happening already as Believers? The quickest way is to operate in goodwill consistently and use the Fruits of the Spirit faithfully while repeating Psalm 23:5, *"You prepare a table before me in the presence of my enemies; You anoint my head with oil; My cup runs over."*

Now, on the other side of the coin, we must also exercise caution when operating in debauchery, ill will, or hanging around those who are a magnet for curses, evil, scattering, negativity, chaos, and so on. Listen, the gravitational pull does not lie; therefore, we must exercise extreme caution or quickly get to the root of the matter.

Why should we get an understanding of the people in our environment causing dismay? In my opinion, this is similar to Job's Experience. In the Book of Job, his energy was off due to acts of disobedience and running from God. Clearly, I am not knocking Job, because this was once my story as well.

Energy is transferable, especially if we are weak, sick, traumatized, or inexperienced. Then again, if we are condoning disobedience or supporting debauchery, we can

Black Sheep Mentality

become guilty by association. For this reason, our Spiritual Instincts must be up to par, knowing when to hold, fold, or walk away; if not, we can get caught up.

Before ending this chapter on *The Black Sheep Mentality*, here is the Spiritual Decree and Seal: *"I announce to you today that you shall surely perish; you shall not prolong your days in the land which you cross over the Jordan to go in and possess. I call heaven and earth as witnesses today against you, that I have set before you life and death, blessing and cursing; therefore choose life, that both you and your descendants may live; that you may love the LORD your God, that you may obey His voice, and that you may cling to Him, for He is your life and the length of your days; and that you may dwell in the land which the LORD swore to your fathers, to Abraham, Isaac, and Jacob, to give them."* Deuteronomy 30:18-20.

Chapter Six
Leading With Power

Are you tired of the same old leadership advice? Are you ready to unlock the secrets to your unconventional leadership power? Are you ready to learn how to harness your unique strengths to achieve your goals? In a world saturated with the one-size-fits-all leadership approach, the longing from within is seeking more. Although expert advice is only a click away, to say the least, it often feels bogus, repetitive, inauthentic, uninspiring, and rehearsed. Amid being starstruck by the presenter, most must admit that the well-intentioned but ultimately unsatisfying information is missing something.

In seeking genuine inspiration, due to this silent form of idolatry, in the Eye of God, we inadvertently forfeit the information designed to make our babies leap from within. Truthfully, sound information of Divine Wisdom is rejected day in and day out based on who is presenting it.

According to the Ancient of Days, Divine Wisdom is now being rebranded and watered down into a marketing pitch to capitalize on those who have been swept away by titles, status, and fame. So, instead of getting a Divine Roadmap to their Predestined Blueprint with real lasting results, they are sold a bunch of wooden nickels with cookie-cutter methodologies leading to little to no growth, *As It Pleases God.*

When leading *The Black Sheep*, we lead with systems, strategies, and checklists, making it easier to rinse and repeat when making mistakes. What is the purpose of this type of approach? In the Eye of God, our do-overs usually bring most of our power to the forefront. How so? In my book, experience is a keeper and the best teacher. This is one of the reasons why Hebrews 12:11 says, *"Now no chastening seems to be joyful for the present, but painful; nevertheless, afterward it yields the peaceable fruit of righteousness to those who have been trained by it."*

Secondly, in the do-over process, the key to unlocking our true potential is to look within and redo something better than the previous version. Proverbs 15:31-32 says, *"The ear that hears the rebukes of life will abide among the wise. He who disdains instruction despises his own soul, but he who heeds rebuke gets understanding."*

Thirdly, in the do-over process, to give and receive feedback without becoming offended is what God is looking for in this day and age. Proverbs 12:1 says, *"Whoever loves instruction loves knowledge, but he who hates correction is unwise."*

Lastly, in the do-over process, we must actively listen to people, places, things, and most of all, life. Life has a way of echoing things to come. Frankly, this is one of the reasons why Proverbs 19:20 advises: *"Listen to counsel and receive instruction, that you may be wise in your latter days."*

The Black Sheep: As It Pleases God® is designed to bring out the trailblazer from within with a fresh new perspective from a Divine Level of Authenticity. How is this humanly possible? Although we are all different, the Spiritual Principles regarding our Divine Blueprinted Purpose remain the same across the board...and that is, PLEASING GOD. On the other hand, if we are not PLEASING HIM, only to please ourselves or others, we will become limited by default, even if we think we have it going on.

When *Leading with Power* in the Eye of God, we must consistently do a checkup from the neck up because we remain on top of what we are thinking. As leaders, our thoughts shape our actions, and our actions determine our outcomes. For example, if we find ourselves setting traps for others, we will become ensnared ourselves. According to Proverbs 26:27, it concurs: *"Whoever digs a pit will fall into it, and he who rolls a stone will have it roll back on him."*

Conversely, if we build bridges for others, we will have a bridge waiting for us to prevent us from falling. For this reason, Luke 6:38 advises: *"Give, and it will be given to you; good measure, pressed down, shaken together, and running over will be put into your bosom. For with the same measure that you use, it will be measured back to you."* What if there is no bridge awaiting us? When doing good, *As It Pleases God*, there is always a win-win hidden within whatever with whomever. Find it, and I PROMISE that a treasure trove awaits with a *Divine Light* attached, illuminating the way. Just make sure documentation is occurring.

What if we are having difficulty finding the win-win? Repeat Psalm 119:105 over and over, saying: *"Your word is a lamp to my feet and a light to my path."* And then say, 'Speak Lord, your servant is listening.' Or, say, 'Show me the way, O' Lord.'

Divine Light

With *The Black Sheep Power: As It Pleases God*®, the positive and negative consequences that come from your actions, thoughts, beliefs, desires, and words are presently on the Spiritual Table for Divine EVALUATION. When dealing with *Divine Light* from within, harboring ill will or engaging in debauchery, it not only harms those around us but also weighs heavily on the psyche, often filtered through the conscience, senses, and demeanor. For instance, as everyone has a story to tell, some people look like what they have been through, bearing the marks of suffering. And then again, others do not look like what they have been through or are going through, while seemingly untouched by their past traumas. What is the difference? It is the *Divine Light* from within.

When *Leading With Power*, here is what Matthew 5:14-16 says about *Divine Light*: "*You are the light of the world. A city that is set on a hill cannot be hidden. Nor do they light a lamp and put it under a basket, but on a lampstand, and it gives light to all who are in the house.*"

In a world often shrouded in blatant darkness amid divisive politics, social injustices, outright silencing others, character assassination, or personal struggles, your *Divine Light* serves as a beacon of hope for you and the Kingdom of God. As I do my part in authentically documenting this information for you, I need you to do your part in this process while not hiding your *Divine Light*.

The COMMUNITY in question needs you to overcome the fear and doubt that is attempting to cause you to second-guess yourself, your Divine Mission, and your capabilities. From me to you, you have what it takes. I need you to trust God, trust yourself, and trust in the Divine Blueprint that already has your name engraved on it.

What if someone does not have what it takes? God has given us all something to work with, and it is our responsibility to pinpoint and cultivate it, *As It Pleases Him*. Without Him, mediocrity will have its way with us, causing our flames to burn out or flicker in and out with lukewarmness, dullness, and disobedience.

For instance, if my eyes are watching a person thoroughly, it means they possess more than what they can actually see as of yet. It does not mean they are perfect, fully polished, or in Purpose on purpose; it means they have GREAT potential that needs developing, *As It Pleases God*.

Leading With Power

Whereas, if I cannot tolerate watching, engaging, or being around someone or something, and I am heading for the hills, then it means they may possess an internal glitch, layered by multiple masks. It does not mean that they are evil, bad, or unworthy, nor will I treat them less than a Child of God. I will always use the Fruits of the Spirit, behave Christlike, and glean the story to feed God's sheep; however, it does mean a few things:

- ☐ Their Divine Alignment is not palpable as of yet.
- ☐ They are outright out of purpose.
- ☐ They are an undercover dream killer.
- ☐ They are trying to manipulate or bully me.
- ☐ They are a wolf in sheep's clothing.
- ☐ They are trying to play mind games.
- ☐ They want to insult my intelligence.
- ☐ They are attempting to lead me away from my Purpose.
- ☐ They are trying too hard to overcome *The Black Sheep Syndrome*.

The bottom line is that if I am watching and paying attention, it signifies that I see the potential and value within you. Simply put, it means that you are indeed a Diamond in the Rough. I do not care about mistakes, mishaps, shortcomings, or idiosyncrasies, because we all have them as a part of the human experience. Plus, that is what it took for me to Divinely Evolve into who I am today, The WHY Doctor.

Rather than dwelling on your imperfections, setbacks, and failures, you should learn from them and share your findings in the Spirit of Truth. Why should we share? They are stepping stones on your road or path to realizing your hidden, yet Divine Potentiality, Spiritual Gifts, and Blueprinted Purpose. Plus, whether it is sharing your time, resources, knowledge, understanding, or experiences, activating the Law of Reciprocity helps in *Breaking The Mold* of your self-imposed limitations. Once done, *As It Pleases God*, it then assists in unlocking your hidden potential, fostering Divine Connections, and cultivating a work-in-progress mindset, paving the way for our Heaven on Earth Experiences in real time.

Breaking The Mold

When *Breaking The Mold* on our past, present, and future, we often do not speak about our Heaven on Earth Experiences because we think it is a bunch of unrealistic hoopla. Then some believe it is a money-making prosperity tactic full of hype when stepping out of our comfort zones. Still, regardless of how it is perceived, in the Spiritual Developmental process, *As It Pleases God*, we must also understand that we are unique and wonderfully made in His Divine Image. *"For we are His workmanship, created in Christ Jesus for good works, which God prepared beforehand that we should walk in them."* Ephesians 2:10.

All in all, we already possess what we need in Earthen Vessels. It is the UNVEILING of what we possess according to our Predestined Blueprint that becomes the issue. Yet, in the midst of hidden doubtfulness, it (Our Spiritual Blueprint) does not change...It patiently WAITS for us to *Break The Mold* on whatever, with whomever.

God is so good that He proactively laid an unchanging foundation for us, even when we mess up royally. Although there are Spiritual Prerequisites that must be met to unveil what is already, it is still doable, especially when having the right information, instructions, and how-to regarding the Divine Expectations, *As It Pleases God*.

How do we know if our Predestined Blueprint is real? The conscience of mankind already knows; it is asleep and needs awakening, *As It Pleases God*. Here is what Jeremiah 1:5 says, *"Before I formed you in the womb, I knew you; Before you were born, I sanctified you; I ordained you a prophet to the nations."* Simply put, you are the PROPHET to your very own Spiritual Blueprint. No one outside of you, God, and the Holy Spirit will have the exact details. More importantly, it can only be covered by the Blood of Jesus. Blasphemy, right? Wrong.

No other blood covenant will suffice when dealing with your Divine Blueprint unless it is a counterfeit. Rest assured, counterfeits will do two things:

- ☐ Leave you hanging in a cycle of déjà vu.
- ☐ Lead you back to square one to start over again.

As we lean into this truth, *As It Pleases God*, here is what we must know about using the Blood of Jesus as the Mediator: 1 Timothy 2:5 says, *"For there is one God and one Mediator between God and men, the Man Christ Jesus."* In addition, Hebrews 9:15 also says, *"And for this reason He is the Mediator of the new covenant, by means of death, for the redemption of the transgressions under the first covenant, that those who are called may receive the promise of the eternal inheritance."*

God has not changed His mind about you; now the question is, 'Have you changed your mind about Him?' If not, listed below are a few items needed in *Breaking The Mold*, but not limited to such:

- ☐ In *Breaking The Mold* as a *Black Sheep*, we must understand and acknowledge our core Belief System, preferably a Heavenly One; however, we must decide for ourselves. Why must we decide? God has given mankind free will to choose Him, ourselves, or another. He will not force-feed us; we must want it for ourselves. In *Leading With Power*, here is the Divine Petition: *"Behold, I stand at the door and knock. If anyone hears My voice and opens the door, I will come in to him and dine with him, and he with Me."* Revelation 3:20.

☐ In *Breaking The Mold* as a *Black Sheep*, we must make a conscious decision to Spiritually Awaken ourselves from our state of slumber. In *Leading With Power*, here is the Divine Petition: *"And do this, knowing the time, that now it is high time to awake out of sleep; for now our salvation is nearer than when we first believed."* Romans 13:11.

☐ In *Breaking The Mold* as a *Black Sheep*, we must determine 'What' we want in life. We must also define *When, Where, How,* and *Why* we want it as well. From experience, this is best done through Journaling or Mind Mapping daily to extract what is covered by layers of hidden debris, traumas, or biases. It also helps us to avoid pilfering the hard work of another, allowing us to put in the work for ourselves, giving us confidence and staying power in our Divine Calling. In *Leading With Power*, here is the Divine Petition: *"If any of you lacks wisdom, let him ask of God, who gives to all liberally and without reproach, and it will be given to him."* James 1:5.

☐ In *Breaking The Mold* as a *Black Sheep*, we must put away the lies we are telling ourselves and others, sustaining our superficial mask. In *Leading With Power*, here is the Divine Petition: *"Do not lie to one another, since you have put off the old man with his deeds, and have put on the new man who*

Leading With Power

is renewed in knowledge according to the image of Him who created him." Colossians 3:9-10.

- [ ] In *Breaking The Mold* as a *Black Sheep*, we must pinpoint our internal and external motives, adjusting them to the positive side of the spectrum. In *Leading With Power*, here is the Divine Petition: "*Let nothing be done through selfish ambition or conceit, but in lowliness of mind let each esteem others better than himself.*" Philippians 2:3.

- [ ] In *Breaking The Mold* as a *Black Sheep*, we must determine our direction of focus or level of distractions, fine-tuning them accordingly to create a win-win. In *Leading With Power*, here is the Divine Petition: "*Ponder the path of your feet, and let all your ways be established. Do not turn to the right or the left; remove your foot from evil.*" Proverbs 4:26-27.

- [ ] In *Breaking The Mold* as a *Black Sheep*, we must consider 'What' we think of ourselves and others, as well as the reasons 'Why' we allow ourselves to reflect in such a manner. Doing so helps us make the appropriate adjustments or corrections needed to maintain a Positive and Fruitful Mindset. In *Leading With Power*, here is the Divine Petition: "*Finally, brethren, whatever things are true, whatever things are noble, whatever things are just, whatever things are pure, whatever things are lovely, whatever things are of good report, if there is any virtue and if there is anything praiseworthy—meditate on these things.*" Philippians 4:8.

Leading With Power

☐ In *Breaking The Mold* as a *Black Sheep*, we must account for our daily 'Give-Back' into the Kingdom for the conveyance of whatever and whomever we value. In *Leading With Power*, here is the Divine Petition: *"Give, and it will be given to you: good measure, pressed down, shaken together, and running over will be put into your bosom. For with the same measure that you use, it will be measured back to you."* Luke 6:38.

☐ In *Breaking The Mold* as a *Black Sheep*, we must become cognizant of our habits, lusts, weaknesses, vices, and kryptonite, allowing ourselves to become a work-in-progress to avoid a Mental, Physical, Emotional, or Spiritual Derailment when we least expect it. In *Leading With Power*, here is the Divine Petition: *"Therefore we also, since we are surrounded by so great a cloud of witnesses, let us lay aside every weight, and the sin which so easily ensnares us, and let us run with endurance the race that is set before us."* Hebrews 12:1.

☐ In *Breaking The Mold* as a *Black Sheep*, we must become ever so willing to right our wrongs, repent, forgive, let go, and have mercy on ourselves and others. Doing so helps us to allow our mishaps, flaws, or mistakes to make us cohabitantly better without becoming indecisively bitter, particularly as the Vicissitudes of Life continue with or without our permission. In *Leading With Power*, here is the Divine Petition: *"For if you forgive men their trespasses, your heavenly Father will also forgive you. But if you do not forgive men their trespasses, neither will your Father forgive your trespasses."* Matthew 6:14-15.

Leading With Power

- [ ] In *Breaking The Mold* as a *Black Sheep*, we must be willing to learn amid all things without becoming rude, disobedient, abrasive, confrontational, defensive, and combative, disrupting our Personal Power or Spiritual Growth. In *Leading With Power*, here is the Divine Petition: *"Instruct a wise man, and he will be wiser; teach a just man, and he will increase in learning."* Proverbs 9:9.

- [ ] In *Breaking The Mold* as a *Black Sheep*, we must become humble, exhibiting the Fruits of the Spirit and Christlike Character, especially when we are thrown a curveball to distract us or create an imbalance within the human psyche. More importantly, becoming humble helps us to love ourselves and others without trying to control or place them in some form of bondage. Unbeknown to most, *Unconditional Love* bridges the gap in humanity in ways unknown to the human psyche. On the other hand, conditions create yokes, bondage, and enslavement, causing inner rebellion or secret vendettas. So, beware! In *Leading With Power*, here is the Divine Petition: *"And be kind to one another, tenderhearted, forgiving one another, even as God in Christ forgave you."* Ephesians 4:32.

Regardless of how we perceive *Breaking The Mold*, it is not a one-and-done process; it is a continuous Spiritual Journey that requires us to *Think Outside The Box*.

Think Outside The Box

When we *Think Outside The Box*, we also give ourselves the opportunity to think inside, around, through, over, and under the box, leaving no stone unturned. When doing so, *As It Pleases God*, it requires TRUST.

Here is the type of trust that is needed in *The Black Sheep Power: As It Pleases God*®, according to Proverbs 3:5-6: *"Trust in the Lord with all your heart, and lean not on your own understanding; in all your ways acknowledge Him, and He shall direct your paths."*

Philippians 4:6-7 gives us a few hints as well: *"Be anxious for nothing, but in everything by prayer and supplication, with thanksgiving, let your requests be made known to God; and the peace of God, which surpasses all understanding, will guard your hearts and minds through Christ Jesus."* When you *Think Outside The Box*, make sure you do a few things, but not limited to such:

- ☐ Do not be anxious.
- ☐ Pray about everything.
- ☐ Petition the Lord, your God.
- ☐ Give thanks in all things.
- ☐ Make your request known to God.
- ☐ Relax and be at peace with God, yourself, and others.
- ☐ Set a guard over your heart posture, and desires.
- ☐ Set a guard over your thoughts.
- ☐ Cover all things with the Blood of Jesus as Spiritual Atonement.

What if they do not work? Then my question would be, 'What if they do?' Regardless of how we feel, think, or believe, or what is going on in our lives, here is what Proverbs 16:3 tells us to do: *"Commit your works to the Lord, and your thoughts will be established."* We must COMMIT that thing, or whatever it is or is not, to God, and leave it with Him. We do not need to FIX it. He wants us to SURRENDER and THINK without allowing people, places, things, or circumstances to rob us of our peace.

As we journey through life, committing something or someone to God does not mean to forget it or them, while abandoning our responsibilities. Nor does it mean that it qualifies as a twiddling our thumbs session. For the *Black Sheep*, it means GIVE it to Him or ALIGN our actions, thoughts, beliefs, desires, and words with His Divine Will.

In a world filled with uncertainty, as an act of faith on our behalf in the establishing phase, we must begin thinking inside, outside, around, through, over, and under the box to glean Divine Wisdom, Secrets, Understanding, Information, Guidance, or Strategy while proactively preparing, *As It Pleases Him*. There is no need to overthink this process, just humbly ALIGN with a *Spirit to Spirit* Agreement using the Word of God as Divine Leverage.

A sweet soul is the breeding ground for us to *Think Outside The Box*, leaving desirable imprints on the hearts of all we come in contact with. Once again, the human psyche is indeed fickle, yet it can recognize a GENUINE SPIRIT, regardless of our biases, conditioning, or level of denial. How do we know if we are on the right track with *Thinking Outside The Box*? Listed below is a small compilation of a few indicators, but not limited to such:

- ☐ As *Black Sheep*, we become better in our thinking process when we know and understand 'Who' is in charge of our lives and 'Why,' as well as 'What' we believe.

- ☐ As *Black Sheep*, we become better in our thinking process when we own our truth and when we can debunk all forms of deception with the Word of God.

Leading With Power

- ☐ As *Black Sheep*, we become better in our thinking process when our word becomes our bond. Allowing us to set a wise guard over our tongues.

- ☐ As *Black Sheep*, we become better in our thinking process when we become humble and respectful to all.

- ☐ As *Black Sheep*, we become better in our thinking process when we become consciously transparent.

- ☐ As *Black Sheep*, we become better in our thinking process when our soulish nature is honing in on being peacefully patient.

- ☐ As *Black Sheep*, we become better in our thinking process when we learn to love without conditions or biased favoritism.

- ☐ As *Black Sheep*, we become better in our thinking process when we are able to use the Fruits of the Spirit, exhibiting Christlike Character without giving it a second thought.

- ☐ As *Black Sheep*, we become better in our thinking process when we speak life into another without putting them in the grave, Mentally, Physically, Emotionally, or Spiritually.

- ☐ As *Black Sheep*, we become better in our thinking process when we convert negatives into positives to create a win-win.

Leading With Power

- [ ] As *Black Sheep*, we become better in our thinking process when we become astute in the Spirit of Oneness.

- [ ] As *Black Sheep*, we become better in our thinking process when we pride ourselves on becoming obedient, trainable, usable, understanding, and commissionable.

With these indicators regarding *Thinking Outside The Box*, we can pinpoint if we are on the right track to becoming a Representative of the Kingdom.

Are we not all Representatives of the Kingdom as Believers? We all have the potential; however, if we are misrepresenting the Kingdom in any way, shape, or form, we do not need anyone to decide our fate for us. What does our fate have to do with anything? According to the Heavenly of Heavens, we have free will to choose whatever and whomever we like, and for any reason, which determines our Spiritual Portions. When *Thinking Outside The Box*, Proverbs 16:9 clearly says, "*A man's heart plans his way, but the Lord directs his steps.*"

Our Spiritual Portions are comprised of what we serve to ourselves, through ourselves, and with ourselves to God, to the Kingdom, and others. What do our portions have to do with *Thinking Outside The Box*? Unbeknown to most, what we serve to others, we Symbolically Serve back to ourselves or into our Bloodline, be it positively, negatively, or indifferently. Here is what Matthew 7:2 says, "*For with what judgment you judge, you will be judged; and with the measure you use, it will be measured back to you.*"

When *Thinking Outside The Box*, we must first understand and respect the fact that we are all different with different wants, needs, desires, conditions, traumas, and so on. Here is what Romans 12:10 advises: *"Be kindly affectionate to one another with brotherly love, in honor giving preference to one another."*

Secondly, we must also understand that nothing is set in stone and change is available to all. Here is what Ecclesiastes 3:1 shares: *"To everything there is a season, a time for every purpose under heaven."*

Thirdly, as a whole, we must better understand the Spiritual Process the Heavenly of Heavens requires from us according to our Divine Blueprint, *As It Pleases God*. Here is what Ephesians 2:10 points out: *"For we are His workmanship, created in Christ Jesus for good works, which God prepared beforehand that we should walk in them."*

The moment we become God's workmanship, *As It Pleases Him*, we open ourselves up to the *Secrets of Unconventional Leadership* that is unafraid of breaking the norm.

Secrets of Unconventional Leadership

Although life can become a little complex at times, the *Secrets of Unconventional Leadership* remain a hidden and rare commodity. According to the Heavenly of Heavens, it is designed to work in our favor, especially if we begin to understand and respect the Cycle of Life in totality. What does the Cycle of Life have to do with our existence? We were created from the dust of the earth, thus connecting us to the Cycles, Seasons, and Vicissitudes of Life by default.

In dealing with the *Secrets of Unconventional Leadership*, let us talk about the Animal Kingdom for a moment. Plus, when *Leading With Power* as a *Black Sheep*, I am pretty sure that I can drive my point home. Animals have less, living in seemingly atrocious conditions, but they are more connected to God than we are. Blasphemy, right? Wrong.

Leading With Power

We, as humans, lost our Spiritual Covering (Direct Connection) in the Garden of Eden with Adam and Eve, which requires us to be born again in the Spirit. Here is what John 3:3 says, *"Jesus answered and said to him, 'Most assuredly, I say to you, unless one is born again, he cannot see the kingdom of God.'"* Whereas, everything else remains Spiritually Connected to God, our Divine Source.

From my perspective, they have to trust God for everything, including life itself, while standing on guard at all times. Can you imagine having to stay on alert 24/7 for predators, who are doing what they are naturally design to do. What is that? Take out the weak and unsuspecting? For me, it is exhausting and traumatizing to see this process in action, but I am grateful this is not my portion. Nevertheless, as we take a deep dive, listed below are a few things I have noticed about them that could benefit us:

- ☐ Animals do not complain, bicker, fuss, or fight with God about their existence. Nor are they burdened with anxiety regarding their purpose. This type of behavior is totally unlike humans, who often grapple with observational questions, exaggerated doubts, moral drama, and identity crises.

- ☐ They live in the moment, without pondering on questions like: 'Why am I here?' 'What do I need to do?' Or, 'What is my purpose?' Instead, they focus on protecting their Bloodline without giving it a second thought. While simultaneously nurturing their young and fulfilling their roles, and exhibit an innate understanding of their place in the environment.

- ☐ Animals use their instincts to survive, fighting for their right to live without having any qualms with God whatsoever. Their characteristics are so unlike humans, who often voice their frustrations, injustices, and dissatisfactions without giving thanks at all.

- ☐ They pay attention to their surroundings to avoid annihilation. More importantly, whether in packs, herds, colonies, or rolling solo, they have learned how to cooperate with their conditions or environments, to avoid being knocked off their square. Animals grouped by nature understand that teamwork, rather than conflict and competitiveness, fosters survival and growth for them.

- ☐ Animals adapt accordingly, doing what it takes to regenerate against all odds to keep their purity and wisdom as a species. At the same time, trusting in the natural order of things.

- ☐ They make the most of what they have or their habitat, harnessing the resources around them to survive. Their remarkable ability to adapt and thrive is phenomenal to watch in real-time. Animals often find themselves venturing into our domains and setting up shop, making it their own with or without our permission. Their innerborn nature is to take dominion, especially when we as humans have very little Spiritual Knowledge of it.

- ☐ Animals are happy with who they are and where they live, and do not question why they must hunt for food. Unlike us, we complain about missing a meal or experiencing a moment of thirst.

Leading With Power

- Animals eat according to their Divine Design. Each species has been uniquely crafted, with DNA traits that optimize their survival, habits, order, and role in the environment. If, for some reason, we see an elephant become a carnivore (a meat eater) or a lion become an herbivore (a plant eater), something is wrong. There is an imbalance in the system; plus, their digestive systems are not equipped to process them, causing them to die a slow death unless they were created as omnivores (eating meat and plants). Unlike us, if our bodies reject or do not process something, we take a pill and still eat it anyway! Come on now...if our bodies reject a certain type of food, do not eat it!

- They do not go on all types of diets to be a certain size or to fit in a certain clique. Why are they not image-conscious? They still have their Spiritual Covering intact. So they do not see size as being an issue, they do not see what they naturally eat as a problem, nor do they experience shame. Actually, they see their lifeline as a means of survival.

- Animals grow, learn, and do more, building their stability, agility, and strength according to how God created them. What is the purpose of this learning curve? According to the Cycle of Life, it is designed to take out the weak, feeble, or disobedient, making them easy prey. In my opinion, this is really where the strong survive.

- They develop their own mastery, boggling the human mind to outsmart us, especially when we think we have them all figured out. For instance, they instinctively learn our language. Thus, we have yet to learn their communicable dialect, so we can only speculate what they are saying through what they are doing.

Animals are animals, and humans will be humans, right? As humans, we can benefit from observing the behavior of animals. Their natural behaviors will tell us more than we can ever lie about.

The *Secrets of Unconventional Leadership* wants us to know that our POWER is hidden in gratitude, acceptance, and contentment. We do not have to engage in negative or debauched complaints, tactics, frustrations, or conflicts to become POWERFUL. With a COOPERATIVE Spirit, *As It Pleases God*, there is no one or nothing that can stop us from doing what we were called to do. Nor can it deflate our power unless we give it away or allow it to drain us.

The truth is, we have been Spiritually Blessed with more. Up till now, we find ourselves doing less with the Gifts of Life, especially with our Spiritual Instincts and Insight. Am I pointing the finger here? Absolutely not! At times, if we are truly honest with ourselves, as it relates to our human nature, we will also find ourselves giving a rat's tail about anything or anyone outside of ourselves.

A willingness to embrace an animal-like focus on life as it unfolds, *As It Pleases God*, is what He is looking for when *Leading With Power*. It helps us to embrace each moment while accepting our circumstances with a work-in-progress mindset. Then again, it may require us to strive to connect with others without conflict to create win-wins. If not, selfishness will come calling our names or knocking on our doors with trivial matters, growing serious due to the lack of understanding. Once again, God does not make mistakes; we do!

Leading With Power

Why do we behave selfishly and make selfish mistakes? Unfortunately, this mainly happens when the Fruits of the Spirit and Christlike Character are not appropriately used, or we have become openly or secretly abused, used, victimized, or traumatized by something or someone.

What is the big deal about not engaging in character development, especially when we have all experienced the Vicissitudes of Life? According to the Heavenly of Heavens, abuse, victimization, and trauma are the leading causes of unused or underutilized Gifts, Callings, Talents, and Creativity.

Why do negative character traits hold us back as Believers, especially when we should be the head and not the tail, above and not beneath, and the first and not the last? The human psyche is very fickle and controlling. Plus, it tends to rehash whatever will keep us under control. Then again, whatever allows it to remain in charge, the psyche will use it to beat us down from the inside out with negativity, fear, or a simulation of defeat.

The Spiritual Connection of Oneness with the Holy Spirit cannot take place with our soulish nature being in charge of our Mind, Body, and Soul. How can our soulish nature control us, especially when we are devout Believers? It does not matter if we are Believers or not; our soulish nature will oppress us under the victimized guise of pointing the finger as if someone is doing something to us. Or, we may become conditioned to making excuses by saying, '*It is the Devil*,' or '*The Devil made me do it*.' When, in all actuality, we are doing whatever it is to ourselves due to our perception, without backing whatever we are feeling with what is truthful, factual, and positive.

Frankly, in my opinion, this is how we ruin the lives of the innocent to appease a soulish vendetta that appears real. For this reason, we must exercise extreme caution when spreading or engaging in false propaganda, mockery, debauchery, or judgment.

In the *Secrets of Unconventional Leadership*, while making our rounds with *The Black Sheep Power: As It Pleases God*®, we cannot fall for the okey doke. We are required to operate *Beyond The Status Quo* to ensure that we possess what rightly belongs to us.

Beyond The Status Quo

In Earthen Vessels, *Beyond The Status Quo* is sought by all, and misunderstood by most. For *The Black Sheep Power: As It Pleases God*®, our status is NOT dictated by outward appearances; our heart and mind postures determine it. God-Centered living at its core is what is desired from us in Earthen Vessels instead of adhering to worldly standards amid strengths, struggles, and anything in between.

According to the Heavenly of Heavens, the status of the Mind, Body, Soul, and Spirit is directly related to whether we live *Beyond The Status Quo* or below it. True fulfillment in the Eye of God, and according to our Predestined Blueprinted Purpose, comes from within our being, instead of through external validation from people, places, and things. Regardless of where we are in life or societal norms, our attitudes and intentions determine our thoughts, actions, reactions, and mindsets, positively or negatively.

Why is *Beyond The Status Quo* so misunderstood by Believers? According to *The Black Sheep Power: As It Pleases God*®, it requires BALANCE outside of materialism and outward manmade success that leaves us feeling empty and unfulfilled. When operating in such a manner, it creates all types of psychological traps. In essence, the psyche will engage in varying elements of comparison, jealousy, envy, pride, greed, coveting, competitiveness, and despair. As a result, we will

Leading With Power

inadvertently find ourselves competing against coworkers, friends, family members, and even strangers, making foul, unwise, or detrimental decisions with long-term or short-term consequences.

If left unresolved or unaddressed, while chasing a worldly standard of success and happiness, we will begin measuring our worth against unrealistic benchmarks, bogus propaganda, and false ideologies. All of which will underhandedly suffocate us with feelings of inadequacy, detachment, and hopelessness.

To break free from the cycle or chain of comparison, jealousy, envy, pride, greed, coveting, competitiveness, or despair, we must add God into the equation. As *The Black Sheep*, we must add Him into our experiences, struggles, hangups, and triumphs to embrace the treasure trove of POTENTIAL and POWER hidden within them.

When going *Beyond The Status Quo*, we must be 'In The Know' regarding how the Kingdom of Heaven selects and dethrones, *As It Pleases God*. Why must we know this? It is essential for those who OMIT using the Fruits of the Spirit, or those who refuse to use Christlike Character as a Spiritual Platform or Weapon of Warfare. Simply put, in a world dominated by chaos, confusion, negativity, lies, and conflict, to possess True Power, *As It Pleases Him*, we must possess certain charactorial qualities.

Why are Godly charactorial qualities needed on our Spiritual Journey, *Beyond The Status Quo*? First, positive qualities are needed to help us avoid turning on ourselves or becoming cultish. Secondly, it is a preventative method used to prevent the weakening of our own Spiritual Foundations. Thirdly, it is designed to keep us from being unprepared or unequipped to contend with the enemy's wiles. Lastly, it prevents us from dismantling our Spiritual Armor without knowing it.

Leading With Power

With the ongoing battle between good and evil, which is also known as Spiritual Duality, the enemy's goal is to get us out of character negatively. When on this battleground, unprepared with rotten fruits all over the place, we may fall for the ultimate okey doke, stubbing our own toes royally. Then again, we can also cause our own detours or dethroning.

Can we really become dethroned as Believers, especially when we are not on a Throne? Absolutely. The Throne of God is WITHIN, and if we are oblivious to this Spiritual Fact, we can 'get got' or turn on ourselves without knowing it. Why would this happen to us, especially when having good intentions to serve the Kingdom wholeheartedly? We cannot behave like the enemy and expect God to go to battle for us amid our unrepentant debauchery or effortless charactorial corrections.

When we embody the qualities of the Fruits of the Spirit, outlined in Galatians 5:22-23, such as Love, Joy, Peace, Patience, Kindness, Goodness, Faithfulness, Gentleness, and Self-Control, they act as a Spiritual Shield and Weapon when engaging in Spiritual Warfare. For example, when contending on any level, these positive charactorial qualities will give us more leverage over those who do not use them or know nothing about them, regardless of whether we are a Believer or not.

Listen, God wants us to USE the Fruits of the Spirit, *As It Pleases Him*, instead of trying to PROTECT them. Our Spiritual Fruits are ABSOLUTE in the same way that the Spirit of God is ABSOLUTE (Unchanging). Therefore, they do not need our protection; they can take care of themselves because there is no Spiritual Law against them.

The goal is the USE of them, especially when tested, to activate the Absolute Power of PROTECTION. How do we make this make sense? Listed below are a few examples, but not limited to such:

Leading With Power

- ☐ In going *Beyond The Status Quo*, we DO NOT need to protect love; the use of our love protects us. 1 Peter 4:8 says, *"And above all things have fervent love for one another, for 'love will cover a multitude of sins.'"* In addition, Colossians 3:14 says, *"But above all these things put on love, which is the bond of perfection."*

- ☐ In going *Beyond The Status Quo*, we DO NOT need to protect joy; the use of our joy protects us. John 15:11 says, *"These things I have spoken to you, that My joy may remain in you, and that your joy may be full."*

- ☐ In going *Beyond The Status Quo*, we DO NOT need to protect peace; the use of our peace protects us. Isaiah 26:3 says, *"You will keep him in perfect peace, whose mind is stayed on You, because he trusts in You."*

- ☐ In going *Beyond The Status Quo*, we DO NOT need to protect our patience; the use of our patience protects us. James 1:3-4 says, *"Knowing that the testing of your faith produces patience. But let patience have its perfect work, that you may be perfect and complete, lacking nothing."*

- ☐ In going *Beyond The Status Quo*, we DO NOT need to protect kindness; the use of our kindness protects us. Ephesians 4:32 says, *"And be kind to one another, tenderhearted, forgiving one another, even as God in Christ forgave you."*

- ☐ In going *Beyond The Status Quo*, we DO NOT need to protect goodness; the use of our goodness protects us.

Galatians 6:9 says, "*And let us not grow weary while doing good, for in due season we shall reap if we do not lose heart.*"

- ☐ In going *Beyond The Status Quo*, we DO NOT need to protect faithfulness; the use of our faithfulness protects us. Proverbs 3:3-4 says, "*Let not mercy and truth forsake you; Bind them around your neck, Write them on the tablet of your heart, And so find favor and high esteem In the sight of God and man.*"

- ☐ In going *Beyond The Status Quo*, we DO NOT need to protect gentleness; the use of our gentleness protects us. 2 Timothy 2:24-25 says, "*And a servant of the Lord must not quarrel but be gentle to all, able to teach, patient in humility correcting those who are in opposition.*"

- ☐ In going *Beyond The Status Quo*, we DO NOT need to protect self-control; the use of our self-control protects us. 2 Peter 1:5-6 says, "*But also for this very reason, giving all diligence, add to your faith virtue, to virtue knowledge, to knowledge self-control, to self-control perseverance, to perseverance godliness.*"

According to the Heavenly of Heavens, when using the Fruits of the Spirit, *As It Pleases God* to go *Beyond The Status Quo*, we become a Spiritual Magnet to the Nature of God. All of which creates a Spiritual Gravitational Pull inwardly by what we extend outwardly and vice versa.

What if we are not a magnet? Although we have free will, unfortunately, when embracing this inward-outward dynamics, we do not have a choice in this matter. Once we were created from the dust of the earth, we were GRANDFATHERED into the Law of Gravity.

What takes us *Beyond The Status Quo*? When we stop pointing fingers and lifting our hands to help others, we can step up to the next level. When we begin to point the finger judgmentally, we must note that we have three fingers pointing back at us. For this reason, self-examination is critical, preventing us from creating a bed of debauchery, contaminating our Bloodline, or stunting our growth in or out of the Kingdom of Heaven. Why do we need to know this information? According to the Heavenly of Heavens, our daily walk in Spirituality is real, becoming more relevant than what we see with the naked eye. But, at the same time, it also holds the keys to our *Spiritual Reformation*, peaceful sanity, and quality of life.

Spiritual Reformation

In the Eye of God, as *The Black Sheep*, it is imperative to engage in the *Spiritual Reformation* Process when it comes to our Spiritual Awareness or Badge of Honor. When aligning ourselves, *As It Pleases God*, the one-size-fits-all approach is not going to get it! Not now, and not ever! *"But now, O Lord, You are our Father; We are the clay, and You our potter; And all we are the work of Your hand."* Isaiah 64:8.

Being that we all are subjected to the evolutionary process, heightened consciousness is needed to embrace our unique differences to Spiritually Grow and Divinely Develop in Earthen Vessels. However, amid the learning and training process for our Heaven on Earth Experiences, we must also MASTER the ability to remain in our own lanes to reform the reformable and renew the renewable within ourselves and others.

Leading With Power

What is the purpose of *Spiritual Reformation* as Believers who consistently grow and develop, *As It Pleases God*? As we are a diversified people, and for the Kingdom-Ready *Black Sheep*, first and foremost, it helps to bring us into Oneness with our Heaven on Earth Experiences. Secondly, instead of instigating division in a superfluous reality of our own making, we can self-correct quickly. Thirdly, and respectfully speaking, for those who feel misunderstood or out of place, it also reduces the risk of having the Cycle of Life take them out during the RESETTING process. Lastly, it decreases the zapping of our Personal Power due to some form of weakness, vulnerability, disobedience, traumatization, or mockery. To be clear, when veering off the beaten path, I do not wish powerlessness upon anyone...so let us take this a step further, *As It Pleases God*.

Particularly, if we have not mastered the Spiritual Cleansing Process, we must be very cautious. What is the purpose of exercising such caution, especially when faithfully serving the Kingdom of God? Unbeknown to most, compounded negativity becomes our inner kryptonite, spreading outwardly. For instance, in the Kingdom of God, negative cannot cast out negative; it binds together to become more negative, forming intangible kryptonite in the human psyche.

Although we may associate kryptonite with being a fictional substance, when it comes to our cellular DNA, it is real! Even if one is fiction and the other is science, they both can function as a debilitating component for mankind. Now, to avoid the negative effects of kryptonite, we must master the process of releasing the negative back into its original state, counteracting it with some form of positivity to maintain our State of Balance, Neutralness, or Tranquility, *As It Pleases God*.

What is the purpose of counteracting negatives with positives? If negativity remains without a positive counteraction, we become imbalanced by default. For example, if the pH balance in our hair is off, it creates an imbalance leading to unhealthiness within the hair's root, spreading outwardly to the hair shaft. If not rectified accordingly, in due time, this imbalance will eventually display our inner condition outwardly for all to see. In addition, it will outright affect the growth of our hair on a sliding scale, determining what we can or cannot do with our hair.

With the pH sliding scale, the improperly gauged oil flow in the hair follicle will cause our hair to become too oily, weighing it down or causing limpness. In contrast, the lack of it causes it to become too brittle, resulting in some form of breakage. Yet, amid all, in doing our part in counteracting a negative with a positive in our hair's pH balance, regulating it between 4.5 to 5.5, our hair is then adequately equipped to do the rest; or better yet, it will heal itself.

Now, from a Spiritual Perspective, when it comes down to our Spiritual Oil, for it to flow effectively and succinctly, our Spiritual pH System must become adequately balanced as well. Why? It gives us an indication when an imbalance is causing a derailment, we are becoming ineffectively limp, we are on the verge of breaking down, or we are too abrasive in our approach. How insulting is it to compare our hair with all things Spiritual, right? In all due respect, what is coming out of our heads is just as important as the head itself.

Moreover, our hair is a part of our body with many members; therefore, the same pH Principles applying to our bodily functions that cause them to work together for our good also apply to our Spiritual Functions. Our pH is basically a system used to keep us in check; therefore, we cannot omit what is Divinely Designed to work in our favor, especially if we simply pay attention without developing a deaf ear. Also, when dealing with our Spiritual Crowns as *The Black Sheep*, the head is the only member of the body we will place the Mark of Royalty or a Spiritual Seal on, *As It Pleases God*. Thus, if we understand the head, the body will follow!

On the other hand, if we become self-defiant, selfish, or lack self-control while outright negating Spiritual Truths, this cliché will apply: *'If we kill the head, the body dies by default.'* For this reason, to those who willfully neglect their Spiritual Crowns, the Heavenly of Heavens is calling for us to do better.

How can we do better as *The Black Sheep* and *As It Pleases God*? First, in the *Reformation Process*, it is done by making a conscious decision to protect the HEAD. Secondly, we must set a guard over our Mind, Body, and Soul with the help of the Holy Spirit. Thirdly, we must plead the Blood of Jesus in all things while repenting, forgiving, praying, giving thanks, and fasting on occasion. Lastly, we must make our best attempts to become a work-in-progress using the Fruits of the Spirit while behaving Christlike.

Why do we need to go to such an extent in the *Reformation Process*? Without reformation or real change, *As It Pleases God*, in time, all else fails! Besides, human intervention cannot contend with Divine Intervention, *As It Pleases Him*, because selfishness has a way of thwarting our progress. So, it is always best to approach life from a Spiritual Perspective to avoid creating a deficit from within without knowing it.

To Spiritually Absorb all God has for us, we must be willing to open the Gateway of Wisdom, allowing the Heavenly Oil to flow to and through us, reaching the intended targets. Unfortunately, the moment we become close-minded, we cut the flow, becoming temporarily unusable in the Eye of God with a symbolic *'Out of Service'* sign on our foreheads.

Can we really become marked with an *'Out of Service'* sign on our foreheads? Absolutely! It happens all the time, causing us to feel lost, confused, or a little imbalanced. This TESTING phase of perseverance will always happen, especially to the

Leading With Power

'*Best of the Best*' or the '*Cream of the Crop*' who are designed to rise to the top in due season.

Why are we tested when we are considered to be the '*Best of the Best*' or the '*Cream of the Crop*' in the Eye of God? As a part of Spiritual Duality, God tests our free will to see if we will operate in goodness or evilness, justice or injustice, integrity or debauchery, and so on. For this reason, Galatians 6:9 says this: *"And let us not grow weary while doing good, for in due season we shall reap if we do not lose heart."*

What happens if we fail the test? When disconnected from the Source, we then rely on ourselves to do what is intended to be Divine. Once this happens, the ego takes over, causing us to engage when we should be disengaging. How do we recognize when we are becoming self-reliant?

- ☐ When *Leading With Power*, as *The Black Sheep* in the *Spiritual Reformation* Process, we must take note of our motives, whether they are good, bad, indifferent, self-righteous, or self-seeking.

- ☐ When *Leading With Power*, as *The Black Sheep* in the *Spiritual Reformation* Process, we must determine if we have prayed, repented, given thanks, or fasted. These foundational elements not only ground us, *As It Pleases God*, but they also empower us to lead in the Spirit of Excellence with strength, authority, and authenticity.

- ☐ When *Leading With Power*, as *The Black Sheep* in the *Spiritual Reformation* Process, we must decide if we have asked for Divine Intervention and Guidance from the Holy Spirit. Although the Holy Spirit will challenge us to grow, adapt, or step outside of our comfort zones, yet and still, closed mouths do not get fed.

Leading With Power

- When *Leading With Power*, as *The Black Sheep* in the *Spiritual Reformation* Process, we must take into account how we are going about doing what we are doing. Are we deceitful, sneaky, vindictive, conniving, envious, or devious? Negative character traits are real, so beware, primarily when engaging in such a manner.

- When *Leading With Power*, as *The Black Sheep* in the *Spiritual Reformation* Process, we must search the heart for the secret elements of jealousy, envy, coveting, pride, competitiveness, contention, or unforgiveness.

- When *Leading With Power*, as *The Black Sheep* in the *Spiritual Reformation* Process, we must decide if we are using the Fruits of the Spirit and exhibiting Christlike Character in our endeavors.

- When *Leading With Power*, as *The Black Sheep* in the *Spiritual Reformation* Process, we must consider whether we are acting in humility or pompousness.

- When *Leading With Power*, as *The Black Sheep* in the *Spiritual Reformation* Process, we must become aware of how we respond or react, determining if we are respectful or disrespectful in our approach.

- When *Leading With Power*, as *The Black Sheep* in the *Spiritual Reformation* Process, we must determine if we are genuinely helping others or using, abusing, or mistreating them for selfish gain.

Leading With Power

☐ When *Leading With Power*, as *The Black Sheep* in the *Spiritual Reformation* Process, we must become aware of whether or not we create an environment of non-stressing harmony or a chaotic, stressful, and confusing one.

☐ When *Leading With Power*, as *The Black Sheep* in the *Spiritual Reformation* Process, we must know if we are leading by example positively or if we are leading people astray.

☐ When *Leading With Power*, as *The Black Sheep* in the *Spiritual Reformation* Process, we must be honest about whether or not we truly love ourselves from the inside out.

What is the purpose of knowing this information when *Leading With Power* as *The Black Sheep* in the *Spiritual Reformation* Process? Our unification process begins when we can ask fact-finding questions while honestly answering them to keep us in a Spiritual Wave of Learning. If not, we become prone to self-instigated biases and irrelevant conditioning, affecting those we come in contact with, similar to having a contagious virus or cold.

If our Spiritual Immune System is not strong enough to fight off viruses or germs, we inadvertently become affected and infected. Without realizing it, we may repeat the same patterns with others or even infect ourselves and our Bloodline repeatedly.

With this in mind, Spiritual Awareness is definitely needed for our sake, for the sake of the ones we love, and for the sake of others to ensure *The Black Sheep Power* will represent the Kingdom, *As It Pleases God*.

Chapter Seven
The Black Sheep Power

Are you tired of feeling like you do not fit in and are ready to shake the dust off your feet? Then again, are you tired of being labeled and intentionally treated like *The Black Sheep*? If you have found yourself in this position, you are definitely not alone. In finding your place in life, the feelings of powerlessness and lack of acceptance can be overwhelming at times, leading to an extremely deep sense of frustration and loneliness. In addition, it will also leave you questioning your identity and belonging. Nevertheless, based on Spiritual Duality and your Divine Birthrights, you can reverse your powerlessness into Divine Power, *As It Pleases God*. In this chapter, you will learn how to do likewise, whether you are a normal sheep, in a sheepfold, a genuine *Black Sheep*, a self-proclaimed goat, or none of the above.

According to the Heavenly of Heavens, *The Black Sheep* is usually a POWERHOUSE of hidden talents, riddled with profound creativity, innovative ideas, and untapped potential. However, in the Divine Reservoir of Greatness, with *The Black Sheep Power: As It Pleases God*®, we must focus on being about our Father's Business by aligning our lives with His Divine Mission and Blueprinted Purpose.

In understanding Divine Purpose, after Jesus' childhood visit to the Temple, He said to His parents in Luke 2:49, *"Did*

The Black Sheep Power

you not know that I must be about my Father's business?" Although for some cultures, this response appears a little disrespectful, He was fully aware of His Spiritual Identity, Commitment, and Mission. Conversely, for our kids of today, they are full of doubt, confusion, and unsurety due to societal pressures, social media manipulation, academic expectations, and cultural norms. All of which forces them to feel like a *Black Sheep* thrown out of the Spiritual Fold to the wolves with zero sense of direction, with a lot of hypocrisy.

And then, we as Believers have the nerve to judge them and wonder about what happened or why they are in the enemy's chokehold. So, instead of helping them get back on track, *As It Pleases God* with the right Spiritual Tools, Information, and Know-How, we allow them to continue in their folly with zero intervention on our behalf.

What if we cannot change anyone? Of course, we cannot change anyone based on their free will. Still, it does not stop us from putting the information in their hands, giving them the option or opportunity to accept or reject it. Listen, if we give our children nothing whatsoever, is this not why we are in the condition we are in today, as *The Blacksheep*, while pretending we are not in this condition? Is it not time to regain *The Black Sheep Power: As It Pleases God*® back and stop feeling as if we are not enough? I am just asking...

Humbly speaking as a *Black Sheep* by Divine Design, if God Almighty TRUSTS me with Divine Wisdom, Secrets, and Treasures from the Kingdom, doing what most cannot, being enough is an understatement for us. According to the Heavenly of Heavens, I am MORE THAN ENOUGH to write and teach about *The Black Sheep Power: As It Pleases God*®, to shake Heaven and Earth for a time such as this. Plus, I do not have to prove myself to those NOT connected to my Predestined Blueprint, who COULD NOT hit a lick at a crooked stick, or who cannot go toe-to-toe with me in the Realm of the Spirit. So, regardless of how the Vicissitudes and Cycles of my life appear to the naked eye on my Spiritual Journey, I keep it moving in the Spirit of Excellence, doing what I am called to do.

Why such passion with *The Black Sheep Power: As It Pleases God*®? First, I had to turn my passion into purpose to unveil my Divinely Blueprinted Mission. Secondly, I have millions of *Black Sheep* and *Diamonds in the Rough* depending on me, and I am not willing to lose one of God's precious sheep. Thirdly, the show must go on, regardless of what people think of me, how they feel about me, or the obstacles presented before me.

As God had it from back then to now, and being that I was from the country and a *Diamond in the Rough* myself, it was all TRAINING for a time such as this. In my initial phase of becoming wiser, stronger, and more astute, *As It Pleased God*, those who rejected me, picked on me, or snubbed their noses could have helped, educated, or coached me on what to do and what not to do. Above all of the rejection and the intentional crushing, I remained trainable, teachable, and obedient. But instead of them helping me because it was the right thing to do. They chose to attempt to crush me due to my mistakes and naivety, withholding information that could have helped me along the way.

To my amazement, no one ever asked me, 'What happened? Where did you go wrong? How did you get yourself into such a situation? Or, how can I help you?' Instead, they chose to use, abuse, manipulate, bully, or intimidate me to get what they wanted. Then again, some even outright pilfered what they needed because I was a *Black Sheep*, appearing powerless with no one to help me. To add insult to injury, some made money with my ideas without my permission, nor giving back to the CISTERN from which they gleaned. In addition, due to their feelings of entitlement, they did not even repent for the underhanded acts, nor say 'Thank You' or 'I Appreciate You' for putting in the hard work.

Now that God has lifted the Spiritual Veil, that one *Blacksheeped* person they considered as a 'nobody,' is now the 'Cornerstoned Somebody' that they need in real-time. How so? According to the Heavenly of Heavens, the Stolen Ark cannot and will not SAIL without the one who put in the work to build it from the ground up with specific instructions from the Heavenly of Heavens.

What if they attempt to navigate the treacherous waters of the Stolen Ark without the God-Given Originator? It will become like the ship on its way to Tarshish with Jonah, who was hiding and sleeping on it while running from God Almighty to avoid going to Nineveh, doing what he was told to do.

While the potential for chaos exists, the absence of Divine Direction for the Predestined Mission, *As It Pleases God*, taints the Stolen Ark, until its God-Given Originator is on board. What if we do not want anyone to know about them or what happened? God knows! And if He knows and we do not self-correct, *As It Pleases Him*, it could lead not only to physical turmoil but also crises on the Stolen Ark due to them not confronting the Moral and Spiritual Weight of their actions.

What does this mean in layman's terms? Unfortunately, as the spark of introspection is at hand, it is only for those who know the TRUTH. As the tables turned in my favor, their shadiness has been exposed to the world, revealing the hidden, behind-the-scenes *Black Sheep* possessing the REAL POWER from the Heavenly of Heavens.

Sadly, those who proclaimed to be on top of their game, insulting me for not being on top of mine, are now asking me for help or advice. Due to my consistency and kindness, and doing more for the Kingdom of God with less, while they did nothing for the Kingdom with more, they (meaning many of them) openly admit they wished they had helped me more. At the same time, continuing to glean from my reservoir, pretending as if it is from their own.

Amid all this, I did not give up on myself nor hold grudges. Why not, especially when they are capitalizing and reaping where they have not sown? FORGIVENESS is one of my SECRET WEAPONS in grabbing the lessons needed on my Spiritual Journey, keeping my heart from oozing all over the place. Once again, regardless of how my life appeared to the naked eye, here is the deal: I chose DIVINE WISDOM, Secrets, and Treasures over all else. While simultaneously making a vow to God to become a Spiritual Vessel of the Kingdom, unveiling the *Divine Potential* in others, *As It Pleased Him*. With *The Black Sheep Power: As It Pleases God*®, here are some of my vows, but not limited to such:

- ☐ As an ARK BUILDING *Black Sheep*, I vowed to provide ACCESS or OPPORTUNITIES to Divine Information from the Heavenly of Heavens, *As It Pleases Him*.

- ☐ As an ARK BUILDING *Black Sheep*, I vowed to help others learn how to develop and unveil *The Black Sheep Power*.

- ☐ As an ARK BUILDING *Black Sheep*, I vowed to help others to understand and build themselves from the inside out, *As It Pleases Him*.

- ☐ As an ARK BUILDING *Black Sheep*, I vowed to help bring others *In Purpose On Purpose* according to their Divine Blueprint.

The Black Sheep Power

- ☐ As an ARK BUILDING *Black Sheep*, I vowed to help others build an empire with the vital information I gleaned over the years, without having to make or accept excuses, as my GIVEBACK to the Kingdom.

- ☐ As an ARK BUILDING *Black Sheep*, I vowed to be about my Father's Business, *As It Pleases Him*, bringing *The Black Sheep Power* Concept to the forefront.

What is the purpose of making such vows as an ARK BUILDING *Black Sheep*? First, I KNOW Spiritual Laws, Principles, and Protocols without undermining or underestimating my Divine Potential. Secondly, I can use them to my Divine ADVANTAGE if I place the Holy Trinity at the forefront of my life, use the Fruits of the Spirit, operate with Christlike Character, remain humble, repent, forgive, learn, grow, sow, give thanks, and follow the Voice of God. Really? Yes, really!

Do all of this work? Judge for yourself...if you find someone who can authentically emulate my Predestined Blueprint, please let me know. It is not going to happen...I put in the work for myself, so my Spiritual Journey cannot be compared to those who have not walked in my shoes! What makes me so convinced of this fact? We are all UNIQUE in the Eye of God, and my *Spirit to Spirit* walk with Him is what sets my *Divine Potential* apart from that of the next man. As I am indeed *Blessed To Be A Blessing*, I take nothing for granted, especially when harnessing The *Black Sheep Power: As It Pleases God*®. Therefore, in this chapter, we will embark on a Spiritual Journey to explore:

- ☐ The reason that we are *Blessed To Be A Blessing*.

The Black Sheep Power

- ☐ How to master *Asking Questions*.
- ☐ How to magnify *Hearing God*.
- ☐ The importance of *Finding Your Voice*.

Being Divinely Blessed is not merely about receiving, as most would think. In *The Black Sheep Power*, it is more about taking the opportunity to give back, feeding God's sheep, *As It Pleases Him*. Thus, in order to know what PLEASES Him, we must master the art of asking questions, magnifying our ability to hear Him, and finding our voices, so that we create a positive impact on the Kingdom, ourselves, and those around us for the Greater Good.

Blessed To Be A Blessing

My Spiritual Vows and Seals on my Divine Journey of self-discovery changed the trajectory of my life with no shame attached. But it also became a catalyst for change, impacting the lives of others through *The Black Sheeped Power* of my Testimony.

The authentic Fruits of my Testimony, rooted in humility, understanding, and authenticity, are not just mine alone. They are the beacon of hope and a bridge for others like myself to uplift and inspire those facing similar challenges, primarily those who have been *Black Sheeped*, treated like outsiders, and have faced abnormal adversity. Beyond a shadow of a doubt, with the Hand of God on our lives, I am *Blessed To Be A Blessing* to unveil the hidden strength and power that we all possess.

How can I be so sure that I am *Blessed To Be A Blessing*? First, we all are...no one is exempt from this GIFT; we only falter at using it, *As It Pleases God*, opting to please ourselves instead. Here is the Spiritual Seal of Divine Promise to Abraham: *"I will*

The Black Sheep Power

make you a great nation; I will bless you and make your name great; And you shall be a blessing. I will bless those who bless you, And I will curse him who curses you; And in you all the families of the earth shall be blessed." Genesis 12:2-3. Does the Divine Promise really apply to our generation? Absolutely! Once again, we must Spiritually Align ourselves *As It Pleases God*, move in obedient faith, and trust in Him wholeheartedly to Spiritually Capitalize on it while holding Him Divinely Accountable for His Word.

Secondly, based upon the Law of Reciprocity, if we keep open communication with our Heavenly Father, *Spirit to Spirit*, He will provide PROVISIONS for our Spiritual Journey and pinpoint the underground Divine Cisterns or Spiritual Negev. As long as it aligns with our Divine Blueprint while building The *Black Sheep Power: As It Pleases God*®, the Spiritual Manna will not cease. If one does not believe this, here is what Matthew 6:31-33 advises: *"Therefore do not worry, saying, 'What shall we eat?' or 'What shall we drink?' or 'What shall we wear?' For after all these things the Gentiles seek. For your heavenly Father knows that you need all these things. But seek first the kingdom of God and His righteousness, and all these things shall be added to you."*

On this Spiritual Learning Curve, *As It Pleases God*, we need to know a few things about being *Blessed To Be A Blessing* before going any further. Matthew 12:35 gives us a few leveraging facts we should never forget:

- ☐ A good man, out of the good treasure of his heart, brings forth good.

- ☐ An evil man, out of the evil treasure of his heart, brings forth evil.

The Black Sheep Power

☐ For out of the abundance of the heart, his mouth speaks.

The Spiritual Sealing encapsulated in this scripture requires that we know the difference between good and evil, positive and negative, right and wrong, just and unjust, and so on. If one does not know the difference, it is time to do a little homework. Why? Unfortunately, with outright respect, most Believers do not know the difference between them, while pretending or assuming they do. As a result, they are NOT *Blessed To Be A Blessing* because they are spewing out evil without knowing it, leaving rotten fruits all over the place, being mean as a junkyard dog, and engaging in things that God hates.

To become *Blessed To Be A Blessing*, we must ask ourselves the hard questions to ensure our heart and mind postures are aligning with what PLEASES God. If *Asking Questions* is not a part of who we are, then it is time to step up our game in this area. Why must we step up? If we do not step up, we will more than likely have to step down. Here is what James 1:5 clearly says, *"If any of you lacks wisdom, let him ask of God, who gives to all liberally and without reproach, and it will be given to him."* So, if foolery is coming forth as a *Black Sheep*, it means we are not properly querying God, ourselves, and others. Let us talk about this a little more...

Asking Questions

In *The Black Sheep Power: As It Pleases God®*, the human psyche knows what our flesh denies. For this reason, when self-correcting, this is why we need the Holy Spirit for Divine Guidance, along with the covering of the Blood of Jesus as Spiritual Atonement on a moment-by-moment basis.

The Black Sheep Power

When *Asking Questions*, no one is exempt from good and evil, right and wrong, or just and unjust factors, even if we pretend we are. Once again, we are grafted into Spiritual Duality; therefore, we are all a constant work-in-progress, dealing with equals and opposites continually. Thus, with *The Black Sheep Power*, we must know what we are working on and the reasons why.

How do I know so much about seeking answers and asking questions? Experiences and uphill battles will teach us a few things, especially when we have a listening ear to Divine Wisdom. Here is what I learned from Proverbs 2:3-5 about Divine Wisdom and Clarity: *"Yes, if you cry out for discernment, and lift up your voice for understanding, if you seek her as silver, and search for her as for hidden treasures; then you will understand the fear of the Lord, and find the knowledge of God."*

What is the purpose of knowing, seeking, and searching, especially in the what, when, where, how, why, and with whom formational queries? First, it helps to provoke thought-provoking conversations with God, *Spirit to Spirit*, with ourselves, self to self, and with others, one to another. Secondly, it keeps us from lying and turning on ourselves when deception is in our camp or within us. And finally, it prevents us from hiding from our Spiritual Responsibilities as the Voice of God whispers Divine Instructions, Information, Plans, or whatever.

What if we were told not to question God as Believers? If we do not ask Him, then who should we ask? The devil? Come on...we have to do better than this! According to our DNA, questioning is a fundamental aspect of our human curiosity and intellectual growth process. If we do not ask questions, Divine Wisdom and Understanding are SILENCED within the human psyche, stifling our Creative Genius.

The Black Sheep Power

Distractions or deceptive measures are on the horizon when we are told NOT to query or seek God in a matter, or when we are pressured to make a quick decision. According to the Heavenly of Heavens, we should inquire with God, asking fact-finding questions in a REPENTANT, HUMBLE, and FORGIVING state of being, pleading the Blood of Jesus, and invoking the Holy Spirit. Plus, if Jesus questioned His disciples to keep them on their toes, what makes us think we are any different? We must ask questions to get answers, especially when it comes to dealing with *The Black Sheep Power*, period!

Hearing God

Can we really hear God? Of course, just as Adam and Eve heard God walking in the Garden, we can hear Him if we pay attention. Here is the hidden secret we need to know: *"And they heard the sound of the LORD God walking in the garden in the cool of the day, and Adam and his wife hid themselves from the presence of the LORD God among the trees of the garden."* Genesis 3:8. How is this a big secret? We have forgotten how God communicates with us, yet the instructions are hidden in plain sight. If we connect ourselves back to NATURE, we will find the Voice of God speaking without saying one word, we will spend less money seeking fulfillment, and it will heal the psyche in ways money cannot buy. But what do we do? We fear nature.

Some of us figured out the connection back to nature; some are too good to get their hands dirty. But if we take notice, children will naturally gravitate to outdoor activities, getting dirty, or playing with animals, unless we teach them otherwise. If we lock them in the house all day, they will become somewhat disassociative or dysfunctional, while we think we are protecting them from the world. Then, we wonder why our children get buck wild when they leave home. All in all, connecting to nature saves us money, Mentally, Physically, Emotionally, Spiritually, and Financially, especially when dealing with the human psyche.

Why do we need to connect ourselves back to nature? Adam and Eve made a free will choice to disconnect from their Source, while everything else God made remained connected. Therefore, we must choose to connect back to the Source through the Sacrificial Lamb, Jesus Christ, and allow the Holy Spirit to govern us accordingly. If not, we will continue with the cover-up, deception, hiding, pretending, and blaming game contributing to Spiritual Blindness, Deafness, Muteness, Dullness, and a Stiff Neck without learning the Spiritual Principles associated with tilling...Spiritually Tilling, to be exact!

Are we really designed to till our own ground? Of course, Spiritual Tilling is mandatory to embrace Eternal Life in Earthen Vessel and to use our Gifts, Callings, Talents, Creativity, and Purpose the way God intended, according to our Predestined Blueprint. As I align, once again, here is the Spiritual Seal we must know: *"Then the LORD God said, 'Behold, the man has become like one of Us, to know good and evil. And now, lest he put out his hand and take also of the tree of life, and eat, and live forever'—therefore the LORD God sent him out of the garden of Eden to till the ground from which he was taken."* Genesis 3:22-23.

Upon opening the above Spiritual Seal, *As It Pleases God*, we must continually work on ourselves to become better, stronger, and wiser. The moment we stop learning and think we have arrived, the Divine Well of Wisdom or the Tree of Life residing within each of us becomes guarded again.

Here is what happens when we stop tilling: *"So He drove out the man; and He placed cherubim at the east of the garden of Eden, and a flaming sword which turned every way, to guard the way to the tree of life."* Genesis 3:24. Simply put, we will turn on ourselves, bringing forth rotten fruits Mentally, Physically, Emotionally, Spiritually, or Financially.

When dealing with being about our Father's Business, *As It Pleases Him*, we cannot omit the Spiritual Principles associated with it. If we do, we will find ourselves with many personal issues that money cannot solve. Thus, as *Black Sheeps*, let us learn about *Finding Our Voices* and how to query ourselves while creating a win-win out of everything and with everyone.

Finding Our Voices

In *Finding Our Voices* as *Black Sheep*, we must ask ourselves, 'Are we learning without listening?' 'Are we listening without learning?' Or, 'Are we responding without listening, learning, growing, or sowing back into the Kingdom, *As It Pleases God*?'

As my ear has been to the ground, I have noticed people taking more time to comment about the life of another without reading or proactively writing their own script. While at the same time thinking God is failing them and not asking these questions, 'Are they failing God?' 'Have they found their voice?' Or 'Are they being about their Father's Business?"

God has expectations for us, and if we DO NOT take the time to engage in *Finding Our Voices* from the inside out, we can miss the mark, lose our identities, make bad decisions, have a hard time processing our emotions, or have a constant bout with interpersonal conflicts and relational boundaries.

Finding Our Voices as *Black Sheep* has everything to do with the VOICE from within (The Conscience), engaging with our inner thoughts, desires, and struggles. All of which are designed to help us with our Blueprinted Purpose or reason for being, which will also assist us with our values, passions, creativity, and dreams. To be clear, this Voice has Spiritual

The Black Sheep Power

Duality associated as well, bringing forth life or death if not governed properly, *As It Pleases God* or outright neglected.

What if we do not have a Voice from within? If we are breathing the Breath of Life, we have a Voice from within. Actually, it is the inner Voice that connects us to our Spirit Man, the Spirit of God, and the Spiritual Discerning Faculties associated with what we term as our intuition, conscience, inner guide, or Spiritual Compass. Then again, some would say it is more like a feeling in our gut, a nagging thought, a red flag, or a quiet whisper urging us to act or not to do something.

Even if we allow our Voice to chat away, know nothing about it, or demand its silence, it remains as a VIABLE CONDUIT for all mankind. How so? According to our Divine Design, this is the same Voice used to:

- ☐ Speak inaudibly to God, *Spirit to Spirit.*
- ☐ Speak to ourselves in (self-talking) engagements.
- ☐ Speak to others, one to another (inaudibly).
- ☐ Speak to life itself.

Is this humanly possible? Yes...I would say it is humanly plausible, happening more than we care to think. For instance, this is one of the reasons why John 10:27 says, "*My sheep hear My voice, and I know them, and they follow Me.*" Also, Isaiah 30:21 says, "*Your ears shall hear a word behind you, saying, 'This is the way, walk in it,' whenever you turn to the right hand or whenever you turn to the left.*"

For *The Black Sheep Power: As It Pleases God*®, we will remain on the positive side of the spectrum for the Greater Good of mankind. For the record, this is not a forced effort; however, to extract the Divine Power hidden within the pages of this

The Black Sheep Power

book, the Spiritual Contingencies are as follows, but not limited to such:

- ☐ We must remain on the positive side of all things.
- ☐ We must engage in goodwill gestures.
- ☐ We must use the Fruits of the Spirit.
- ☐ We must willfully self-correct.
- ☐ We must operate in the Spirit of Righteousness.
- ☐ We must behave Christlike.
- ☐ We must forgive and extend mercy.
- ☐ We must operate with lovingkindness.
- ☐ We must pray, repent, and fast occasionally.
- ☐ We must remain grateful in all things.
- ☐ We must be willing to share.
- ☐ We must operate with respectfulness.
- ☐ We must operate in the Spirit of Truth.
- ☐ We must operate in the Spirit of Excellence.

What if we do not operate with these Spiritual Contingencies, *As It Pleases God?* We will begin operating selfishly, doing things our way instead of God's way. Based on Spiritual Dualism, here is how this list will work in reverse, but not limited to such:

- ☐ We will begin operating on the negative side of things.
- ☐ We will engage in ill-willed gestures.
- ☐ We will become surrounded by rotten fruit.
- ☐ We will be unable to self-correct.
- ☐ We will operate in the Spirit of Unrighteousness.
- ☐ We will behave waywardly or hatefully.
- ☐ We will be unable to forgive and extend mercy.
- ☐ We will operate in unkindness.
- ☐ We will avoid praying, repenting, and fasting.

The Black Sheep Power

- ☐ We will become ungrateful and full of complaints.
- ☐ We will become unwilling to share.
- ☐ We will become disrespectful and rude.
- ☐ We will operate in the Spirit of Deceit.
- ☐ We will operate in the Spirit of Debauchery.

After continuously operating in excessive indulgences and sensual pleasures WITHOUT *Finding Our Voices*, we will begin engaging with people, places, and things that are morally questionable or socially unacceptable. All of which will fall into one or more of these categories: the lust of the eyes, the lust of the flesh, and the pride of life.

One day, you might look into the mirror, and to your surprise, there it is—a strand of gray hair. While asking:

- ☐ Where is the Gift?
- ☐ Where is my Talent?
- ☐ What am I called to do now?
- ☐ Have I lost the Gift?
- ☐ Has my Gift given up on me?
- ☐ How long will it wait?
- ☐ Am I too old?
- ☐ Is it too late?

How can we miss the mark, especially if we must live our own lives and God does not make mistakes? Missing the mark is a matter of perception, not *As It Pleases God*. Some would say, 'I am exactly where I need to be.' And one would be correct; however, we must ask ourselves, 'What are we doing with or learning from our current situation?'

What is the purpose of querying ourselves in such a manner? We may be in a cycle of déjà vu with little or no progress, but the longing or thirst within the human psyche tells our story without our participation.

On the other hand, if we hoard our Spiritual Gifts, they will become dormant, or we may lose them altogether. Now, if the CALLING is strong, it is essential to Global change, or it is time-sensitive, God will shut our lives down until we heed the CALL. Will God really shut our lives down?   Absolutely! Unfortunately, this means nothing will work as it should until we get on the right track.

Once we get on the right track, everything will begin to fall into place. Until then, this individual will feel like Jonah in the Belly of the Fish in Jonah 1:17. As a word of caution, if you are walking with a serious Spiritual Calling on your life, it is better not to run from a Divine Calling in the Spirit of Disobedience. From experience, it is better to run toward it with a work-in-progress mentality. Why? You will never have peace, causing the psyche to remain in a state of unrest with a cloud hovering over you, penetrating your environment in due time.

For example, we have a lot of people wanting to write books but have not taken the initiative to do so. To add insult to injury, they consistently post on social media, then turn around, proclaiming or complaining that they do not have enough time. Or, they refuse to take the time to document their *Spirit to Spirit* conversations with God as a Testament or Testimony for the Kingdom. In my opinion, a book can be written if we proactively compile all of the comments we post on someone else's feed or channel for recognition. At the same time, they do not realize that the book they are seeking to write is already within them, in seed form.

Listen, every Divine Blueprint has a prewritten script (book), and if we do not take the time to document our experiences, lessons, Blessings, and testings, we can indeed bury the book we are inspired to write. What if we do not have the resources to write our Testimony or Testament? As long as we have breath in our bodies, the provisions are available, but we must Spiritually Till our own grounds to stir up the GIFT or develop a *Plan of Action*. Listen, God is not asking us to be perfect; He is asking us to become Christlike and usable for Kingdom Purposes. Why is a Plan of *Action* important in the Eye of God?

- ☐ He BLESSES us to be a Blessing.
- ☐ He FEEDS us to feed others.
- ☐ He LOVES us so that we can share the love.
- ☐ He GIVES us peace to be at peace with others.
- ☐ He GRANTS us mercy so that we can become merciful.
- ☐ He OFFERS us the wisdom needed to share with others.
- ☐ He ALLOWS us to have trials in our lives so we can become the Teacher or Mentor.
- ☐ He PROVIDES us with provisions for us to provide for others.
- ☐ He PROTECTS us so we can become protectors.
- ☐ He OPENS doors for us so that we can open doors for others.
- ☐ He is KIND to us to ensure we understand how to be kind to others.
- ☐ He has GIVEN us life to understand the value of life.

I am not here to pull the wool over anyone's eyes; instead, I am here to remove it with *Divine Preparation*.

Divine Preparation

As Believers, we count on or depend on faith as we should; however, our faith incorporates proactiveness, which is commonly overlooked. Then, once something happens, we run to the church for help, when the real CHURCH is within us. I am not saying the church should not assist; we must exhaust our resources in preparing for our seasons of drought. In my opinion, this is similar to Joseph preparing Egypt for its drought by effectively storing and preparing, *As It Pleased God*.

We often use the story of Joseph as a story of triumph, but we must also use it as a Divine Blueprint of PROACTIVENESS and LEVERAGE. How do I get proactiveness and leverage from Joseph? While Joseph was in his father's house, he was learning, understanding, and preparing. When Joseph was sold into slavery, ending up in Potiphar's house, here again, he was learning, understanding, and preparing. When Potiphar's wife lied on Joseph, landing him in prison, he was still learning, understanding, and preparing. He did not know what God was going to do or how, but he remained on the proactive learning curve, building the leverage needed to facilitate his Blueprinted Purpose.

Suppose we do not learn, understand, prepare, and grow. In this case, we can become God's Chosen Elect in a famine depending upon someone else's provisions, subjecting ourselves to all types of cruelty and abuse for not having what we should have prepared for.

For the record, I am not here to point the finger; through many experiences, I can bring forth such Divine Information for such a time as this. Rest assured that my famine seasons have prepared me with the Divine Wisdom to facilitate the process of getting us Mentally, Physically, Emotionally, Spiritually, and Financially ready for whatever, with whomever. And then, training the next in line, passing the Torch of Wisdom, allowing the next generation to become better, stronger, and wiser without tripping over themselves.

The Black Sheep Power

How do we know what to do, *As It Pleases God*? Each man's Spiritual Negev (Underground or Hidden Reserve) is different based upon their Predestined Blueprint; therefore, we must incorporate God into the equation, covering ourselves with the Blood of Jesus and allowing the Holy Spirit to guide us.

Nonetheless, to get the Spiritual Negev flowing, *As It Pleases God*, we must use the Fruits of the Spirit and Christlike Character, allowing Him to unkink our qualmish kinks. What does this mean for Believers, according to Kingdom Standards? We all have something to work on; however, the psyche will hide things from us to stay in control. Frankly, this is why we cannot see our own issues as they are; yet, we are quick to point the finger at someone else, not realizing we are subjected to the same thing under a different label, blinded by our wants, needs, desires, conditioning, and biases. More importantly, this is why I write inclusively, excluding no one, including myself, because we are all subjected to Spiritual Error or Omission!

So, in the next chapter, we are going to talk about *Doing Real Business*, capturing the Divine Essence of how to put our Divine Blueprint to work in real-time. What is the purpose of doing so? In a world marked by disparity and inequality for *The Black Sheep*, it can often appear that Believers, who actively embrace faith, find themselves at a disadvantage compared to their worldly counterparts. And, now is the time to reverse this divisive plank, hindering our Kingdom's Prosperity.

Chapter Eight
Doing Real Business

As we delve into *Doing Real Business*, it becomes clear that in the Eye of God, Believers should not only experience Spiritual Wealth but should also thrive in every aspect of living life to the fullest.

What is the problem with doing Kingdom Business? Is it that we cry holy, holy, holy without helping others? Is it that we cry holy, holy, holy with the crabs in a bucket mentality? Is it that we cry holy, holy, holy, oppressing those appearing beneath us to pad our pockets? Is it that we cry holy, holy, holy without providing a road map for success for the next in line? Is it that we cry holy, holy, holy, forcing Believers to use worldly means to facilitate Kingdom Building? Is it, Is it, Is it?

In this chapter, we are going to get down to the nitty-gritty regarding all of the Undiscovered Talents, Untapped Potential, Hidden Gifts, Outlandish Creativity, and Supernatural Provisions hidden in the pews. How do I know? I am one of them...Respectfully speaking, I am indeed *The Black Sheeped* POWERHOUSE overlooked, abused, or misused by the church, which was my TRAINING GROUND.

Why was I overlooked? Who knows? I can only speculate. Maybe I was too flawed to be HOLY, maybe I was too cute to be HOLY, maybe I was too sexy to be HOLY, maybe I was too smart to be HOLY, maybe I was too creative to be HOLY, maybe I received too much attention to be HOLY, maybe I was

Doing Real Business

too kind to be HOLY, or maybe I was too ANOINTED to be HOLY. Regardless of the reason, my Divine Holiness kept me in the Spiritual Classroom to bring forth the Divine Information to change the trajectory of CHURCH RELATIONS until the end of time. I never want another one of God's precious sheep to endure the blatant rejection of those who could not bring more to the table than what I had to offer.

Undoubtedly, I am not against the church; actually, I am for the church. However, I am the Divine Messenger sent to provide the Heavenly Wakeup Call or Spiritual Shakedown for the Sake of the Kingdom. Had the experience not been so intense, I would not have been able to SEE accurately with my Spiritual Eyes, HEAR properly with my Spiritual Ears, and SPEAK eloquently with my Spiritual Tongue, conveying Divine Authority from the Heavenly of Heavens. With my hands-on experience, this is why we are getting ready to *Do Real Business* God's Way!

Let me say this before moving on: But by the Grace of God, with my 'Battle Scars and All,' I am here to set the record straight in *Doing Real Business*, helping those who are in need of what I could never get from those who could have helped me, but opted not to help for whatever reason.

How did I get the Battle Scars? Most of my Battle Scars came from those proclaiming to be Believers. Conversely, most of my help came from unbelievers, who wanted nothing to do with the church whatsoever. For this reason, I learned how to stop judging people while paying close attention to their fruits.

We most often will never know who or what God is going to use to give us a helping hand out of the mud or the trenches. Then again, we may not know where the fountain of information may originate. As we align with the Will of God, as *Black Sheep*, it is wise to use Spiritual Discernment instead

Doing Real Business

of judgment while paying attention to the USE of our Spiritual Fruits and the ones they are displaying. Here is what Matthew 7:1-2 says, *"Judge not, that you be not judged. For with what judgment you judge, you will be judged; and with the measure you use, it will be measured back to you."*

Is not paying attention to their fruits, not judging? Remember, there is no law against the use of the Fruits of the Spirit, according to Galatians 5:22-23. Whereas, the analysis of our Spiritual Fruits and those of another is used in our Spiritual Discernment Process. For this reason, Matthew 12:33 says, *"Either make the tree good and its fruit good, or else make the tree bad and its fruit bad; for a tree is known by its fruit."*

In this chapter, as *The Black Sheep*, when *Doing Real Business*, we are going to focus on good fruits, while dealing with a few items to enhance our Divine PowerGrid, such as:

- ☐ The Significance of Mind Mapping.
- ☐ Ways to uncover our Passions.
- ☐ Discovering True Purpose.
- ☐ Creating a Blueprint.
- ☐ Formulating a Business Plan.

By utilizing *The Black Sheep Power* Mind Mapping techniques when *Doing Real Business*, it will assist you in uncovering your passions, clarifying your purpose, creating a blueprint, and formulating a business plan. When *Building Bridges*, with the most potent aspects of *The Black Sheep Power: As It Pleases God*®, when following instructions, *As It Pleases Him*, you can equip yourself with the DIY tools needed to not only dream big but also take the steps needed to make those dreams a reality.

Doing Real Business

The Significance of Mind Mapping

In an increasingly multifaceted world, where information overload is at our beck and call, finding effective ways to organize and process our thoughts, enhance our creativity, and improve our memory is paramount. In *The Black Sheep Power: As It Pleases God®*, we do not take Mind Mapping lightly because it really can help us wrap our minds around our thoughts, ideas, concepts, precepts, or whatever.

Can we become powerful without Mind Mapping? Of course, we can. At its core, whether personally or professionally, it makes life a lot easier for those who are extremely creative, requiring a lot of assessing and re-evaluating. Plus, it helps in uncovering insights, thoughts, or ideas that would have otherwise remained hidden.

The Significance of Mind Mapping is wrapped up in how we take the mind on a journey to some sort of accomplishment or a *Win-Win*. In addition, it is also associated with building, dismantling, revamping, or regrafting our thoughts, ideas, concepts, precepts, and so on.

Using a Mind Map enhances our ability to visualize strategically, instead of allowing the mind to wander aimlessly or ungoverned. If the mind is not governed correctly, it creates illusions, be it true or untrue, giving way to our perceptions, biases, traumas, conditioning, or limitations. By allowing this to happen, we unawaringly transfer our God-Given Rights for our psyche to take over. With a Mind Map, we can rationally document while understanding the *What*, *When*, *Where*, *How*, *Why*, and *Whom* formational questions.

When *Doing Real Business* as a *Black Sheep*, being that we are always under a microscope, a Mental Mind Map is crucial, helping us deal with more facts than fiction. Of course, a little fiction may be necessary to break the ice, create a little humor, or develop our momentum. Still, the underlying foundation must be built upon factual information. Why? If a Mind Map is predicated on the Seeds of UNTRUTH, then the Harvest will eventually follow suit.

As the *Black Sheep*, we often do not think that questioning ourselves is essential, but let me be the first to say, 'It is.' I know that questioning ourselves may feel a little uncomfortable initially. Still, *The Significance of Mind Mapping* is a crucial step in building resilience, promoting growth, and discovering our true selves. So as we lean into the discomfort, let us go deeper.

A Mind Map is ideal in helping us to envision the vision, assisting in honing in on our imaginative efforts from the inside out. What is the difference between vision and envision? The vision is an outward manifestation, and envisioning is an inside one. In all simplicity, vision refers to the ability to perceive the physical world through the eyes. Frankly, it is the act of seeing things as they are in the present moment. On the other hand, envisioning is the ability to perceive things beyond the physical world, seeing things in the mind's eye that do not yet exist in the physical realm as of yet.

So, for the sake of *Doing Real Business*, a Mind Map helps us to bridge the gaps between the two, or it can also assist us in unblocking them as well. Amid all, we must understand the underlying desire for whatever or whomever. What does this mean for us? We must know the 'Why' behind our efforts. It limits our sincere efforts if we fail to understand this one fact.

How can we limit ourselves when we are putting in the work? If we fail to connect to the PASSION from within, it cannot connect to us. Nor can it feed us the necessary information to fuel our inner drives or tap into the infinite potential of it. For this reason, most people give up; they may jump from one thing to the next or live their dreams through someone else. The bottom line is that if we fail to connect relationally, we will find ourselves doing the right things for all the wrong reasons, creating disconnects from the inside out.

On the other hand, if we properly connect ourselves using the *Doing Real Business* approach to Mind Mapping, there are no limits to what we can achieve. Really? Yes, really! Listen, a Mind Map is a Spiritual Tool of simplicity, allowing us to structure or restructure based on our present-day information. Simply put, the instructions may change based on the level of our understanding, environment, conditioning, training, teachability, comprehension, resistance, and so on. All in all, we must PAY ATTENTION, period.

According to the Heavenly of Heavens, we cannot allow any form of frustration to detour us from our Spiritual Journey. Our Mind Map serves as a tangible source of information, getting us back on track when we suffer a detour. Also, it assists in recalling what we may have forgotten when placed under pressure. Of course, we will all have our moments, so when it does happen, do not feel bad. We simply must dust ourselves off, jump back on the path, and keep it moving toward Greatness in the Spirit of Excellence.

When using a Mind Map, if we redirect our focus to PURPOSE or our Divine Blueprint, we will have less time trying to please, coax, or cater to those who are not a part of the plan, who are wreaking havoc, or who are intentionally sowing discord. As a result, we have more time to provide a service, solve problems, or regraft negatives into positives, creating a *Win-Win* for all we come in contact with.

When developing a Mind Map, we must find one that caters to our unique Blueprint. Listed below are a few ways to create one that will work in our favor, but not limited to such:

Doing Real Business

- [ ] We must place the goal, idea, thought, purpose, or concept in the center of the page to develop FOCUS on the SEED.

  ← **GOAL** →

- [ ] We can use images, colors, symbols, or whatever we desire to keep us CONNECTED or CENTERED on the primary goal.

- [ ] We must create BRANCHES connecting us to the SEED, asking the *What, When, Where, How, Why*, and with *Whom* Formational Questions.

- [ ] We can have as many boxes as we like, providing different answers to each question. For some, a page will do, but for others, they may need a wall, depending upon the desired vision, goal, purpose, or whatever.

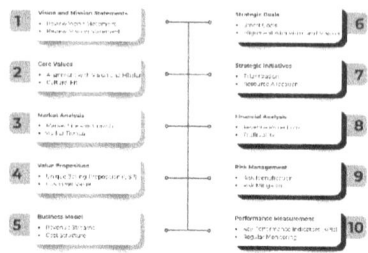

- [ ] We must document the Take-Away or Ultimate Achievement desired.

- [ ] Once done, for six days a week, we must provide the Reflective Thoughts regarding the primary reason for the Mind Map.

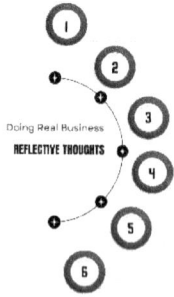

Doing Real Business

- [ ] We must use positive affirmations over the Mind Map, squashing all negative interjections. Mind Mapping for the *Win-Win* is a Positive Zone only!

- [ ] We must be willing to revamp often. No Mind Map is set in stone; it is a constantly evolving process of COMMITMENT. Why? Without growth, we are already symbolically defeated until we unblock ourselves or awaken from our slumber.

If our Mind Map from the first day looks the same way a month later with the same information, this should be a RED FLAG of some form of stagnation or blockage.

A Mind Map can be used in any way we desire. So, outside of our goals or purpose, we may use a Mind Map for a few other things, but not limited to such:

- [ ] Brainstorming.
- [ ] Projects or Presentations.
- [ ] Studying or Research.
- [ ] Relationships or Marriages.
- [ ] Self-development.
- [ ] Decision-making.
- [ ] Power moves.
- [ ] Family or Event planning.
- [ ] Problem-Solving.
- [ ] Inner Growth.
- [ ] Note-taking for writing an article, book, script, and so on.
- [ ] Unveiling our hidden Gifts, Callings, Talents, Purpose, or Creativity.

Doing Real Business

Regardless of how we use a Mind Map, it will prevent whatever we are doing from becoming messy or disorganized while we become crystal clear about 'What' we are doing and our reasons 'Why.' Most often, it is the power behind our 'Why' that makes the Win-Win GREAT, creating an overflow of Blessings for the Greater Good.

So, if we need to pinpoint the areas in need of revamping, additional questioning, or pruning, do it. Do not waste precious time wandering when you have the same opportunity to subdue, conquer, and WIN with the Spiritual Tools you already have in your hands.

By leading and Mind Mapping in outright humility, servanthood, self-control, diligence, love, and wisdom, we will not only become effective, but we can create Win-Wins. Yes, Win-Wins benefit the lives of others, creating Double and Triple-Portion Blessings. What does this mean? Putting in the work will not only benefit us, but it will BLESS others to become a Blessing as well, causing our act of diligence to keep giving to create an OVERFLOW with a Legacy of Impact.

Here is the deal: It is always best to understand our Divine Blueprint, *As It Pleases God*. Why should we add Him into our equational efforts as Believers? Our Divine Blueprint includes our prepackaged Gifts, Callings, Talents, and Creativity as the Spiritual Tools needed to facilitate them, which He has the key to. Without Him, we have limited access instead of Divine Access.

If we do not have a clue about who we are and why we are, then it is our responsibility to become clued in on what is already within. It will take a little soul-searching on our behalf, but it is indeed well worth the effort. Personally, with *The Black Sheep Power: As It Pleases God*®, I am not writing this book for us to get half of a portion; the goal is to receive FULL PORTIONS, period! Furthermore, when dealing with our

Doing Real Business

Divine Birthrights as *Black Sheep*, we want all that God has already PREDESTINED for us to have from the Beginning.

Now, with or without a Mind Map, we can use the questions below to get the ball rolling on pinpointing our Spiritual Gifts:

- ☐ Make a list of WHAT we love doing.
- ☐ Make a list of WHY we love doing it.
- ☐ Make a list of WHEN we love doing it.
- ☐ Make a list of HOW we love doing it.
- ☐ Make a list of WHERE we love doing it.
- ☐ Make a list of THOSE we love doing it with.
- ☐ Make a list of our TAKEAWAYS.
- ☐ Make a list of our GIVE BACKS.
- ☐ Make a list of our POSITIVE FRUITS.
- ☐ Make a list of our NEGATIVE FRUITS.
- ☐ Make a list of the CONVERTING negatives to positives.
- ☐ Make a list of the WIN-WIN without setting limits on the mind.

Our lists will vary from person to person with different meanings and instructions; therefore, it is always best to put in the hands-on work ourselves first. Why should we complete these lists ourselves? It ensures that someone else's inner desires do not lead us. Plus, if they have not gone through the previous chapters, educating themselves from the Heavenly of Heavens on *The Black Sheep Power: As It Pleases God*®, contamination can occur. So, exercise extreme caution when incorporating those who have not gone through Spiritual Processing or lack the understanding of the importance of having and maintaining a Positive Mental Mindset.

Doing Real Business

When Mind Mapping with our Divine Blueprint, we must follow the Spiritual Rules, exhibit Christlike Character, and be willing to move into our Purpose, utilizing our Spiritual Gifts, Fruits, Creativity, or Talents. Once again, we must also correctly discern between right and wrong, positive and negative, just and unjust, as well as good and evil. Without being able to discern people, places, and things properly, we can become an easy target of prey for predators. So, we cannot be ignorant of the devices used to sift us Mentally, Physically, Emotionally, and Spiritually. What makes this so important? If we are all over the place in or out of our Mind Mapping Sessions, we can subconsciously compromise a few things, but not limited to such:

- ☐ We can compromise our Spiritual Connection.
- ☐ We can compromise our Spiritual Receivers.
- ☐ We can compromise our Spiritual Queries.
- ☐ We can compromise our Spiritual Answers.
- ☐ We can compromise our Spiritual Astuteness.
- ☐ We can compromise our Spiritual Integrity.
- ☐ We can compromise our Spiritual Understanding.
- ☐ We can compromise our Spiritual Respectfulness.
- ☐ We can compromise our Spiritual Boundaries.
- ☐ We can compromise our Spiritual Depth.
- ☐ We can compromise our Spiritual Protocols.
- ☐ We can compromise our Spiritual Compatibilities.
- ☐ We can compromise our Spiritual Fruits.
- ☐ We can compromise our Spiritual Journey.

Often enough, as *Black Sheep*, we take many things for granted, but when it comes down to our Mind Mapping Sessions, we should not play around. Why? It is the Spiritual Tonic we need to satiate the inner thirst of the unnecessary, potentially

Doing Real Business

debilitating issues of life. If we do not perfect this process to the point of having a direct connection to God in or out of our *Spirit to Spirit* Relations, we cannot fault anyone. We all have the same opportunity to receive all God offers; we simply need to get out of our own way.

When doing our due diligence in Mind Mapping, it is imperative to step into its flow to gain access to the Secrets of Wisdom, Hidden Treasures, or Divine Insight. Plus, to better understand Spiritual Truths from God's point of view, we must also avail ourselves, *As It Pleases Him*.

When Mind Mapping according to our Divine Blueprint, the Heavenly of Heavens wants us to double-check a few areas consistently:

- ☐ Double-check our thoughts.
- ☐ Double-check our emotions.
- ☐ Double-check our motives.
- ☐ Double-check our habits.
- ☐ Double-check our behaviors.
- ☐ Double-check our attitude.
- ☐ Double-check our decisions.
- ☐ Double-check our accountability.
- ☐ Double-check our idols.
- ☐ Double-check our lusts.
- ☐ Double-check our pride.
- ☐ Double-check our state of repentance.

If we need to do a Mind Map for each one, do not be afraid to do so. It is our responsibility to take charge of our relationships with ourselves, ensuring we can request help in the areas of need or lack.

Doing Real Business

What if we are experts on ourselves? Then congratulations! Nevertheless, those who desire to be their BEST self know what they have to do to achieve the *Win-Win* from within.

According to our Divine Blueprint, we must become a Spiritual Magnet when doing business, allowing others to gravitate toward us freely. Amid doing so, we cannot force our Divine Purpose on others, making them feel bad for not supporting us, or have our countenance fall when we do not receive what we expected. More importantly, once we master the ability to listen and obey instructions, we will find our lives doing an about-face, giving our magnets a little more pulling force.

A Mind Map is designed to keep us from living with regret by getting rid of the inferiority complex. Never allow the thoughts of you not being good enough, the perception of you not being an expert, the fear of making mistakes, or the idea of you not being famous enough hold you back from succeeding. Of course, there very well may be someone better than you, but who cares?

I made mistakes, and still do, but I do not allow it to stop me. Nor do I allow it to cause me to second-guess what I am good at or my Purpose. I simply understand, learn, make the corrections, share the wisdom, and move on as an EXPERT in my Giftings, Talents, and Calling with NO REGRETS! If you are dealing with this inferiority complex, open and honestly ask yourself and answer these questions:

- ☐ Who am I?
- ☐ Why am I here?
- ☐ What is my purpose in life?
- ☐ What do I really want out of life?
- ☐ What are my strengths?
- ☐ What are my weaknesses?
- ☐ What am I afraid of? Why?

Doing Real Business

- ☐ What are my values?
- ☐ What are my priorities?
- ☐ What motivates me?
- ☐ What discourages me?
- ☐ What makes me happy?
- ☐ What makes me sad?
- ☐ Am I honest with myself?
- ☐ Who do I need to forgive? Why?
- ☐ What type of effect do I have on others?
- ☐ What opportunities do I have available to me?
- ☐ What steps should I take to get what I want?
- ☐ How can I improve the quality of my life?
- ☐ How can I improve the quality of life for others?
- ☐ Are there any real roadblocks on my path? Why?
- ☐ What do I need to change about myself in order to grow?
- ☐ What are my responsibilities?
- ☐ Am I willing to live a fulfilled life of integrity?
- ☐ Am I willing to brand myself uniquely?
- ☐ What will be the difference in my branding?
- ☐ What is the desired outcome for my brand?

We are the brand that leaves a positive or negative stamp on a person's heart, determining our believability, genuineness, deceptiveness, insecurity, or fear. Remember, every story has three sides—your side, the other person's side, and the truth. When making decisions or *Embracing Your Passion*, you must evaluate all three; if not, you will make permanent decisions on one-sided information, or you may negatively judge what is designed to BLESS you.

Doing Real Business

Embracing Your Passion

What is your PASSION? Are you connecting to it? Is it speaking and guiding you? Do you even know what it is or is not? Whether you are in the know or out of it, *The Black Sheep Brainstorming* can help you become crystal clear about what is needed to PASS ON to the next in line. More importantly, by removing the 'I' from passion, understanding that it is not about you, eliminates selfishness while ushering in humility, teachability, flexibility, and shareability. Passion is all about the PASS ON, solidifying the difference between being great in our own eyes or operating in documented and legitimized GREATNESS. Simply put, the difference exists between being verified with a SEAL OF AUTHENTICITY or blowing smoke with vaporizing effects.

Whether operating with smoke or a seal, as *The Black Sheep*, we are here to ask the RIGHT questions to bring FORTH or PROVOKE the Creativity of Greatness and be about our Father's Business! More importantly, in *Doing Real Business*, we are here to unveil that PASSION from within, helping you get out of your comfort zone and into your Divine Purpose or Predestined Area of Expertise.

When *Embracing Your Passion*, you must find a way to stimulate your mind. Stimulating creative thinking leads to unexpected insights, especially in this ability and agility process. Another strategy is to approach the problem from different perspectives. The approach can involve looking at the issue from the perspective of multiple or mirrored views, diverse participants, opposing forces, and so on. Just keep it positive and non-problematic, or without causing harm.

For example, for a cop to catch a criminal, he must think like a criminal to outsmart or catch them for the greater good or prevent further harm to the innocent. If not, a cop will 'get got,' looking like boo boo the fool for not doing their homework. When it comes down to thinking proactively, they are held to a higher standard, and so are you.

Incorporating playful, fun, or unconventional elements into *The Black Sheep Brainstorming* process is ideal, promoting stimulative interaction. Doing so may involve using games, puzzles, or other activities to stimulate creative thinking. By approaching the problem in a playful and lighthearted manner, you can help break down mental barriers and foster a more creative and innovative mindset.

Even if someone tries to convince you that your communicative efforts do not matter...well, let me be the first to say, 'It does matter!' The art of communication is a vital skill that everyone needs to master. At its core, communication requires a combination of verbal and nonverbal skills, emotional intelligence, and an understanding of cultural differences. Artful communication allows you to choose the right words to convey your message, become mindful of your tone, body language, and communication style, and adjust your approach accordingly.

Why must we go through all of this when *Embracing Our Passion*? Once again, we do not have to do anything. We always have the free will to opt out of *Doing Real Business* to do our own thing. Nonetheless, to be more adaptable and resilient in the face of challenges, you must be able to think on your feet instead of flat on your face or back.

As *The Black Sheep*, by learning to identify and address problems, *As It Pleases God*, you become better equipped to handle unexpected situations confidently. Plus, you can navigate your way through complex and uncertain environments a whole lot better. More importantly, you can easily use a Mind Map from your documented information. Also, you can create a vision for the future that aligns with your values, purpose, and higher self with *The Black Sheep Brainstorming* techniques at your fingertips.

The Black Sheep Brainstorming

Throughout years of being about my Father's Business, *As It Pleased Him*, I have found that *The Black Sheep Brainstorming* will help you get your wheels turning in the correct direction, regardless of where you are, what you are doing, why you are doing it, how you got there, and with whom.

Now the question is, 'What is brainstorming?' Brainstorming on a personal level is a creative technique used to generate ideas, concepts, and solutions to problems. Frankly, it is a powerful tool used for generating new ideas, thoughts, and insights to develop creative solutions to complex issues. It involves one person or a group sharing thoughts, concepts, and ideas on a particular topic without judgment or criticism.

The goal is to produce as many documented ideas as possible, regardless of how feasible or practical they seem. Here are a few examples of questions to ask when engaging in *The Black Sheep Brainstorming* Session on a personal level:

- ☐ How do you define success?
- ☐ What are your top three career aspirations?
- ☐ What are your top three personal ambitions?
- ☐ What are your greatest strengths?
- ☐ What areas do you need to work on to improve yourself?
- ☐ What skills do you need to develop to achieve your goals?
- ☐ What motivates you to keep going?
- ☐ What are your core values that guide your decisions and actions?

Doing Real Business

- ☐ How do you stay motivated?
- ☐ How do you overcome challenges?
- ☐ How do you handle setbacks and failures?
- ☐ What steps do you take to accomplish your goals?
- ☐ What kind of support do you need to achieve success?
- ☐ What habits do you need to develop to become successful?
- ☐ What habits do you need to break to achieve success?
- ☐ What routines do you need to establish to achieve success?
- ☐ What routines do you need to eliminate to achieve success?
- ☐ What resources do you need to achieve success?
- ☐ Who can be your mentors or role models to help you achieve success?
- ☐ What risks are you willing to take to achieve success?

The Black Sheep Brainstorming is a formal question-and-answer idea session that can be done in person or online, and it is often used in business, education, and other fields where innovative thinking is required. The process typically involves a facilitator who guides the discussion and encourages participants to build on each other's ideas.

Nonetheless, if you must do it alone, make sure you develop a *Spirit to Spirit* Relationship with your Heavenly Father, invoke the Holy Spirit, and cover yourself with the Blood of Jesus before documenting. Why is this necessary for Believers? It gives you Spiritual Leverage, connecting you to the SOURCE.

In *Doing Real Business*, here is what to use to preface *The Black Sheep Brainstorming* session: "*My heart is overflowing with a good theme; I recite my composition concerning the King; My tongue is the pen of a ready writer.*" Psalm 45:1. Why must we use this scripture?

Doing Real Business

You do not have to do anything...you have free will to use it or not. I cannot force this upon you, nor should you force it upon someone else, especially when *Doing Real Business*.

Why must we separate business from personal? Businesses constantly face new challenges and obstacles that require innovative solutions. Plus, the querying sessions are different. Most often, they entail a collaborative process that leverages the power of a group to generate fresh ideas with unique, innovative, and breakthrough solutions. Meanwhile, on a personal level...only one person is needed.

Nevertheless, in *Doing Real Business*, we are going to focus more on the business aspects because we are being about our Father's Business. Simply put, we are teaming up with the Holy Trinity and the Heavenly of Heavens to brainstorm on a level, putting our internal or external enemies to boot.

How will *Doing Real Business* Brainstorming Session help us as *The Black Sheep*? With this book, we approach from a Spiritual Perspective, getting our mental juices flowing by adding PASSION into the equation. Doing so allows us to tap into the diverse perspectives, thoughts, and experiences of team players, and it creates a platform for Spiritual Growth and Development.

Unlocking new levels of recognized or unrecognized Passion provides a nest egg of creativity, sustainability, and productivity, enabling teams to achieve their goals and transform their company's success. By harnessing the power of collective intelligence, businesses can overcome challenges, achieve their goals, and thrive on a level that sets them apart from the rest.

In the Eye of God, *The Black Sheep Brainstorming* is our way of jumpstarting the creative process used to generate ideas and solutions to a problem, product, event, task, or direction. It is a valuable tool for anyone, especially writers, designers, singers, business leaders, entrepreneurs, or anyone needing fresh, new, or reformed ideas. Here are some steps to follow when brainstorming:

- ☐ Set a clear goal or objective. Before brainstorming, ensure you know what you are trying to achieve. Please write down the problem or task you are trying to solve so you can keep it in mind as you generate ideas.

- ☐ Establish a secure setting. Brainstorming is often done in a group setting, but you can also do it alone. If you are working with a group, ensure everyone is clear on the session's goal and is on one accord.

- ☐ Establish an open floor, leaving their feelings at the door. Brainstorming works best when there are no rules or criticism of ideas. Encourage everyone to speak up and share their ideas, no matter how wild or unconventional they may seem.

- ☐ Encourage free thinking. This will help you and your team feel more comfortable sharing thoughts and ideas, no matter how unusual or impractical they may seem. When your mind is free, it will produce more radical thoughts that can be used now or later; therefore, do not despise the day of small thoughts, people of small thoughts, or the diamonds in the rough.

- ☐ Use a variety of techniques. You can use many techniques during brainstorming to TRIGGER the mind, such as mind mapping, road mapping, word association, or random word generation. Experiment with different approaches to find the best that works for you and your team.

Doing Real Business

- ☐ Generate and document ideas. Start by writing down as many ideas as possible without judging or evaluating them. Use a whiteboard or flip chart to capture all the suggested ideas, or designate someone to document on paper.

- ☐ Encourage the Build-An-Idea Mentality. One of the benefits of brainstorming in a group is that you can build on each other's ideas. Encourage everyone to listen to each other and then build on or expand the presented ideas, repeating this process. With each repeat, the information, thoughts, beliefs, or ideas should become stronger and stronger. If not, it means the conveyance system is blocked. Freedom and comfort must be re-established with a TRIGGER word, thought, belief, or a relevant story. What does this mean? Reset the expectations and reconnect by telling a story with triggered, encouraging, and comforting words of motivation.

- ☐ Listen actively. Listen carefully to what others are saying and ask questions to clarify their ideas. Active listening will help ensure everyone is on the same page and prevent misunderstandings.

- ☐ Stay focused. It is easy for brainstorming sessions to go off on tangents, wasting precious time. For this reason, it is wise to stay focused on the objective while overcoming viable distractions. If the discussion goes off-topic, gently steer it back to the main objective.

- ☐ Use visual aids. Visual aids such as whiteboards or flip charts can help to organize ideas and keep the discussion on track. Being that we are visual beings,

Doing Real Business

they can also help to stimulate creativity and encourage participation in those who are anti-social by nature.

- ☐ Take breaks. Do not be afraid to take breaks during brainstorming sessions. Sometimes, stepping away from the problem for a few minutes can help you come back with fresh ideas and a renewed perspective.

- ☐ Refine and evaluate. Once you have generated a list of ideas, start evaluating them. Look for the ones that are most promising and refine them further. You can also combine ideas to create something new.

- ☐ Take action. Once all the ideas have been generated, they can be evaluated and refined to determine the most viable or practical. Once done, decide on a plan of action and assign tasks to team members, if necessary.

When being about our Father's Business, *As It Pleases Him*, rest assured, it will take time and practice. According to the Heavenly of Heavens, do not be afraid to experiment and try new techniques to encourage free-flowing, spontaneous thinking, and to explore all possibilities and develop viable solutions, even those that may seem far-fetched or impossible.

Storming the Brain is crucial because it allows people to think inside, outside, around, through, over, and under the box and develop innovative ideas as building blocks to create a whole. When broken down into stages, it helps break down mental barriers without criticism or judgment in multiplicity forms.

Doing Real Business

For example, this analogy is similar to fixing a car; something must be broken down or removed to fix the issue, and then put back together to complete the job. The mind is the same way; some form of dissection must occur to enhance, repair, or fix someone or something, from the least to the greatest or vice versa. Therefore, when someone says, 'They have it all together,' or 'They do not have anything to work on,' I know it is not true, because deception is one of the greatest downfalls of humanity. For this reason, it is to our advantage to develop a work-in-progress mentality, enabling productive and fruitful growth.

The work-in-progress mentality also helps build team cohesion and improves communication among ourselves and others. When people work together to brainstorm, they learn to listen to each other's ideas, respect different perspectives, and collaborate to find the best solutions. Doing so helps to create a positive environment and fosters a sense of unity and shared purpose, developing our innovative people skills.

When properly governing your leverage and being about your Father's Business with *The Black Sheep Brainstorming*, if you dare to take this up a notch to incorporate positive mind-storming, thought-storming, word-storming, action-storming, and character-storming, it will make you uniquely UNSTOPPABLE. Whether doing so alone or with someone else, it is a powerful tool guaranteed to revolutionize your life. Here are the benefits of brainstorming in conjunction with your mind, thoughts, words, actions, and character, but not limited to such:

- ☐ Increased Creativity.
- ☐ Improved Communication.
- ☐ Enhanced Problem-Solving.
- ☐ Increased Motivation.
- ☐ Greater Productivity.

Doing Real Business

- ☐ Improved Decision-Making.
- ☐ Increased Confidence.
- ☐ Greater Sense of Ownership.
- ☐ Increased Innovation.
- ☐ Improved Problem-Identification.
- ☐ Increased Teamwork.
- ☐ Enhanced Learning.
- ☐ Increased Engagement.
- ☐ Improved Time Management.

Sparking your creative juices from within and with others is one effective technique to encourage free association, allowing ideas to flow freely without judgment or evaluation. However, it is imperative to lock in on the win-win instead of the cynical lose-lose. What makes this so important when increasing our capacity? The win-win mindset expands your capacity, whereas the lose-lose mindset restricts and binds. Even if you are dealing with the appearance of losing, the WIN is hidden amid it, amid them, or amid you.

Finding Real Purpose

In dealing with the Four Corners of the Divine Mindset, we must approach it strategically in the Spirit of Excellence, cleaning out the negative cobwebs. In excelling with the Eye of God hovering over *The Spiritual Negev*, we must begin to think positively and proactively with a SUPPORTIVE demeanor.

What does support have to do with our mindsets? Support has everything to do with the Four Corners of one's Divine Mindset, especially when dealing with their Predestined Blueprint. Listen, our lives have Divine Instructions; through the mind, we can Spiritually Download the specifics for the

Doing Real Business

Spiritual Legs supporting it. What does this mean? Most items created by man contain four legs, points, or corners to hold them up. For example, a car has four wheels; a chair has four legs; a desk has four corners; a stove usually has four burners; our computer or television has four corners; a cross has four points, and so on. As humans, we can add more when extending a little creativity. Still, under normal circumstances, four usually get the job done unless excessive weight is carried, such as tractor-trailers moving big things.

Now, getting back to the Four Corners of the Divine Mindset, if it is overloaded with negativity or self-defying thoughts, we cannot download, *As It Pleases God*. The bottom line is that we need outside help, Spiritual Help, to be exact! If not, we will feel as if we have a ton of bricks weighing us down, especially when there is not one brick in sight.

When dealing with the mind, it does not calculate tangibly; it calculates INTANGIBLY first. Why? We are Spiritual Beings having a human experience. If we are unaware of this one fact, we can operate in Spiritual Error, building with worldly tools when God requires Spiritual Ones.

Here is what we need to know: *"The workmanship of the wheels was like the workmanship of a chariot wheel; their axle pins, their rims, their spokes, and their hubs were all of cast bronze. And there were four supports at the four corners of each cart; its supports were part of the cart itself."* 1st Kings 7:33-34. When we put the 'Cart before the horse,' we will find ourselves operating without instructions, feeling our way through life with Spiritual Blindness without realizing we are blind in the Eye of God. Now, to get our mental wheels turning in the right direction, *As It Pleases Him*, we must develop ourselves from the inside out, beginning with the thoughts we think, building quality and credibility.

For this Spiritual Journey, we need to MASTER putting our positive thoughts in ACTION form. We can speak about

Doing Real Business

positivity all day long, but if we do not put actions behind our thoughts, we will fall short without realizing it.

How do we operate with a Four Corner Mindset when dealing with others? Everyone is different; therefore, we must add the Holy Trinity into the equational effort when dealing with people. Why? When someone has low self-esteem or is emotionally bankrupt, they can misread the Fruits of the Spirit based on their perceptional expectations.

For example, I am strategic, analytical, and forthcoming, so if someone is wishy-washy, problematic, or has a problem with someone questioning their behaviors, thoughts, or beliefs, they would be offended by my method of operation. Meanwhile, for someone possessing a business mindset like myself, I am perceived differently and aligned with integral values, standards, and excellence.

From the *Four Corners*, when transitioning from our people skills, how do we develop a Business Plan, Plan of Action, or Mind Map, PINPOINTING our Spiritual Gifts, Callings, or Divine Purpose? We must understand that a Spiritual Journey is involved in unveiling them. According to the Heavenly of Heavens, to obtain the full portion of our Predestined Blueprint, we must dig deep, Mentally, Physically, Emotionally, Spiritually, and Financially, aligning each area *As It Pleases God*.

Why are our Spiritual Gifts, Callings, Talents, Creativity, Passions, or Purpose hidden deep within our life's journey? It is often said, 'Nothing ventured, nothing gained.' In the Eye of God, this cliché is applicable and relevant. Being *The Black Sheep* or not, without a commitment to the outcome, we tend to give up, become ungrateful, or become disrespectful at the slightest notion of defeat or resistance. For this reason, they are often hidden under our 'something else' or weaknesses that need development before attaining them. Here are a few

Doing Real Business

questions to answer when attempting to *Find Real Purpose*, but not limited to such:

- ☐ What are your strengths, interests, and weaknesses?
- ☐ Why do you enjoy your strengths?
- ☐ How do your interests benefit you and others?
- ☐ What are people saying about your weaknesses?
- ☐ How do you feel about your weaknesses?
- ☐ Are your weaknesses making you feel insecure, doubtful, or angry? Why?
- ☐ Why are your weaknesses a weakness?
- ☐ Where do you exhibit your weaknesses?
- ☐ When is the best time to work on your weaknesses?
- ☐ With whom do you exhibit weaknesses?
- ☐ How can you make your weakness a strength?
- ☐ What type of training is needed to become better at your weaknesses?
- ☐ What can your weaknesses teach you?
- ☐ What can you do to create a win-win out of your weaknesses?
- ☐ How can your weaknesses bring joy and satisfaction to you or someone else?
- ☐ What can you do to feel more confident with your weaknesses?
- ☐ How can you intertwine your weaknesses with your Spiritual Gifts, Calling, Talents, Purpose, Passion, or Creativity?
- ☐ How can you make an old weakness a newfound strength?
- ☐ Are you willing to practice on your weaknesses daily?
- ☐ Are you ready to turn your weaknesses into Greatness?
- ☐ What are the applicable scriptures regarding your weaknesses?
- ☐ What does the Bible say about this weakness?

Doing Real Business

- ☐ What is God revealing to you in your *Spirit to Spirit* private time with Him?
- ☐ What are some positive words you can speak over your weaknesses?
- ☐ Are you willing to read through the answers to these questions daily and update them often?

What is the purpose of answering these questions thoroughly? Most of our issues lie in the questions we DO NOT ask and the answers we DO NOT receive. With *The Black Sheep Power*, if we desire to overcome, *As It Pleases God*, we must MASTER how He thinks. Really? Yes, really!

The Bible is riddled with questions and answers we often overlook. Why are they overlooked or not pointed out to Believers? The Divine Unveiling depends on our readiness in the Eye of God. Plus, we are not formally trained to query and answer, giving the Vicissitudes and Cycles of Life permission to share the information needed for the Spiritual Classroom without us abusing it or indulging in idolatry.

I am Dr. Y. Bur, The WHY Doctor, for a reason. I have embarked on a transformative Spiritual Journey to uncover what lies beneath the surface of our daily lives. With *Finding Real Purpose*, I have tapped into my *Spiritual Negev*, rich with Divine Insights and Clarity, making anyone's baby leap from within.

How can I make someone's baby leap, especially if they are a full-grown adult? This Spiritual Leaping Process is done by asking the right questions and documenting the answers, similar to what we are reading right now. There is beauty and resilience in harsh conditions, and it is our responsibility to find it, share it, and capitalize for the Greater Good, especially when *Doing Real Business*.

Doing Real Business

Regardless of whether we have been *Black Sheeped* or not, what seems barren, desolate, or underexplored holds the potential for growth and enlightenment, once we add God into the equation, *As It Pleases Him*. It is this that I now share with those daring to DIG DEEP in *Finding Real Purpose*. Once we answer the questions above honestly, we will easily find the information for our Plan of Action, Business Plans, or Mind Maps, to relay or document accordingly. How is this possible, especially when we are clueless about everything? With *The Black Sheep Power: As It Pleases God®*, everything we need is already hidden within, like *Diamonds In The Rough*.

When *Doing Real Business* or *Finding Real Purpose*, the goal is to get the DIALOGUE started...God has a dialogue, we have a dialogue, life has a dialogue, purpose has a dialogue, and so on. All we need to do is get them to SPEAK to us, as we DOCUMENT what they are saying.

Diamonds In The Rough

Our layers of debris are our only weaknesses, covering the diamonds within, blocking the value we hold. How do I know? Every weakness I had was intertwined with my Spiritual Gifts, Calling, Talents, Creativity, and Purpose for a time such as this. However, I had to know this for myself. More importantly, I had to Spiritually Till my own ground, challenging my weaknesses to PUT UP or SHUT UP! How did I do this? I had to learn the difference between positive and negative words, thoughts, beliefs, reactions, desires, and behaviors.

Here is the deal: I trained my mind to accept the positive as food for the brain while challenging or rejecting the negative. Thus, if the negative could not justify its reason, prove its case, or give me a LESSON or TESTIMONY for others to glean, it had to SHUT UP, period! Can we really train the mind to do

Doing Real Business

this? Absolutely! Once again, as *The Black Sheep*, I am living proof. Nevertheless, when challenging negativity to PUT UP or SHUT UP, we simply must know the DIFFERENCE in a positive, actionable form. As a *Diamond In The Rough*, with this understanding based on Spiritual Duality, it will determine how we will internally shut it down within the human psyche to prevent its penetration.

Most people become externally reactive when combating negativity. Whereas, unbeknown to most, the POWER lies in the ability to become INTERNALLY PROACTIVE without becoming jealous, envious, prideful, greedy, covetous, competitive, or comparing ourselves. By far, it helps to release the genuine DIAMOND of AUTHENTICITY.

How do we become Internally Proactive, releasing our Divine Shine? In our documenting efforts when dealing with *Doing Real Business*, here is an Internally Proactive Checklist, *As It Pleases God*, but not limited to such:

- ☐ We must IDENTIFY the problem.
- ☐ We must INVOLVE the Holy Trinity in the equation.
- ☐ We must REMAIN positive, productive, and fruitful.
- ☐ We must ACCOUNT for our role.
- ☐ We must PLAN for whatever, with whomever.
- ☐ We must REFUSE to allow doubt, fear, anger, or regret to yoke us.
- ☐ We must SET goals, reviewing and updating often.
- ☐ We must DETERMINE the next step.
- ☐ We must PRIORITIZE what is important and what is not.
- ☐ We must BECOME consistent and persistent.
- ☐ We must become WILLING to ask for help, receive help, or take risks.

Doing Real Business

- ☐ We must FOCUS on the solution.
- ☐ We must LEARN from whatever, with whomever.
- ☐ We must PRACTICE on whatever, with whomever.
- ☐ We must VISUALIZE the win-win or positive outcome.
- ☐ We must SHARE our findings to build another.
- ☐ We must SURROUND ourselves with positive people, places, and things.
- ☐ We must REWARD ourselves amid all, gearing up for what is next.

In transitioning from a Spiritual Mindset to *Doing Real Business*, I will put on my business hat for the remainder of this chapter. I will also close it with specific instructions to maximize our Heaven on Earth expenditures, *As It Pleases God*, especially since we have established the foundational WHY of *Mind Maps, Passions, Brainstorming, Purpose*, and being *Diamonds in the Rough*. Knowing how to put our Spiritual Tilling efforts to work for us is imperative, opening the Promised Greatness from the Ancient of Days, and releasing it into our NOW. With this in mind, let us move on to put our Spiritual Gifts, Talents, and Creativity in a workable ACTION form through an occupational or entrepreneurial format.

Overcoming Business Doubt

When *Doing Real Business*, regardless of whether we feel like *The Blacksheep*, the no sheep, the shepherd, or the goat, our *Predestined Blueprint* is designed as a TOOL! When living real life, waiting until we have all of our ducks in a row or everything to be perfect may not be the best option.

Doing Real Business

Why should we not have perfect conditions, especially when we do not know what we are doing? When Spiritually Tilling our own grounds or when becoming a work-in-progress, *As It Pleases God*, we must learn, grow, and sow back into the Kingdom as we go, while developing our faith along the way. In my opinion, this makes 2 Corinthians 5:7 all the more relevant: *"For we walk by faith, not by sight."*

Here is the deal: If we do not learn, we cannot grow. If we do not grow, we cannot sow or expand our mindsets beyond where we are, causing wavering faith. James 1:6 even says, *"But let him ask in faith, with no doubting, for he who doubts is like a wave of the sea driven and tossed by the wind."* Simply put, it is the mental and emotional tossing that gets the best of us, especially when dealing with some form of stunted growth or fear paralysis.

Nevertheless, I have a great story aligning with wavering faith. We have an employee working for a company for over 20 years, and the company went up for sale 1 year before being publicly posted. This employee wanted to buy the company but complained that they did not have the money to do so; therefore, they tried to recruit buyers from their circle of friends. I advised this individual to purchase the company because they knew the company inside out, and I would help them with the process. Here is what I recommended for their 1-year plan:

- ☐ Make their interest in purchasing the business known.
- ☐ Work on their credit while developing a strategy.
- ☐ Save as much money as possible from the employee status to finance the transition to the employer status.
- ☐ Get a *Business Plan* to envision their vision.
- ☐ Work on a *Plan of Action* to obtain funding for a business already making money.

Doing Real Business

They declined because of fear, a limited mindset, and the conditioning of being an employee, not an employer. As a result, this employee had to train the individuals who eventually purchased the business. A few months later, once trained and having gotten the information needed to function, they fired this employee. Why would they do such a thing? The employee was hung up on the old system of doing business, trying to boss them around. Therefore, the new owners got tired and decided to bring in a new crew to make their vision work.

Work experience means very little if it is misappropriated, underdeveloped, misused, or used to bully. Our experience on a job, in a business, or in our personal lives must be appropriately leveraged. If not, it can become kryptonite, halting our ability to *Do Real Business*. Why would we become blocked? By not combining our work, home, business, or personal experiences with our Spiritual Gifts or Divine Blueprint, we may think we have it going on. When in reality, we cannot hit a lick at a crooked stick. Who am I to judge, right? Absolutely. No judgment is intended; nevertheless, while becoming an expert on someone else's vision, we must also work on our Predestined Blueprint, developing the God-Given Expert from within ourselves.

Let me put this in perspective: Everyone wants to be successful, whether as a business owner or a millionaire, without understanding what it takes or accounting for the price, stressors, pressures, injustices, and responsibilities of being one. Nevertheless, throughout my journey, there is a preconceived notion that millionaires know everything. Truthfully speaking, this is not true at all; as a matter of fact, no one knows everything!

If we take this a little further, 80% of millionaires do not have degrees! But here is the kicker: 90% of their employees do! So, what does this tell you? Being a millionaire is a

Doing Real Business

MINDSET comprised of systems, strategies, concepts, obedience, perseverance, the quest for know-how, delegation, and what is written or documented in black and white.

The millionaires without degrees are not stupid by a long shot. When they have an idea, project, or concept, they are Genius enough to get someone with a degree or specialization who knows what they are doing to implement, guide, or tell them what to do with what they ENVISION.

Now, the keyword is **ENVISION** (In Your Vision). How do we make this make sense? Okay, let me break this down for you: An already millionaire pays someone to take the ideas of what they have in their mind, put it on paper, develop a system or strategy, and get their approval when it is done. If it looks right, sounds right, and makes money, it is a go, and everyone gets paid. Simple enough, right? On the other hand, if it does **NOT** look right, if it does **NOT** make money, then it is back to the drawing board, and nobody gets paid until it is correct.

If you want to tell people what to do or boss them around, this is not a millionaire or business mentality! From a business perspective, most often, this is why we miss the mark with our people skills, or we become hated by those we work for or work with.

Listen, we do not need to be pocketable millionaires to obtain a millionaire mindset while proactively putting in the work. Once we establish this mindset, *As It Pleases God*, the Divine Provisions Mentally, Physically, Emotionally, Spiritually, and Financially will come in due season with no shame attached.

From the Ancient of Days until now, here is the FIRST SECRET most overlooked: The goal is to acquire a team of individuals to TELL us and DOCUMENT what to do about what we Envision. Why do we need a team? For the simple fact that we DO NOT have all the answers, and we may need a third party involved to trigger our Inner Genius or uncover our buried Wisdom. While simultaneously documenting it in black and white, capturing this actionable Biblical Principle: *"Write the vision and make it plain on tablets, that he may run who reads it."* Habakkuk 2:2.

The SECOND SECRET is that while making provisions on a job, setting aside time to develop what is already within is imperative. What if we do not have time? If we have time to talk on the phone, watch television, use social media, and so on, we have time! We simply need to rethink how we spend it and why, helping us to fill in the blanks of whatever, with whomever. Here is the Spiritual Seal and actionable Biblical Principle needed: *"For the vision is yet for an appointed time; but at the end it will speak, and it will not lie. Though it tarries, wait for it; because it will surely come, it will not tarry."* Habakkuk 2:3.

Business Savvy

The goal of this Divine Principle regarding *Doing Real Business* as *The Black Sheep* is designed to teach you how to take the ideas, thoughts, or vision out of your mind, get them on paper, build a roadmap, and give you an idea of what it is going to take to achieve it. How can this help, especially when having zero business savvy? First, from a Spiritual Perspective, *Business Savvy* is developed. And secondly, when rooted in Spiritual Values, dealing with *Predestined Blueprints*, and a wholehearted commitment, listed below is how *Business Savvy* can work for you, but not limited to such:

- ☐ *Business Savvy* is established by operating *As It Pleases God*.
- ☐ *Business Savvy* is established by allowing the Holy Spirit to GUIDE.

Doing Real Business

- ☐ *Business Savvy* is established by COVERING all things with the Blood of Jesus.
- ☐ *Business Savvy* is established by ALIGNING with the Word of God.
- ☐ *Business Savvy* is established by being AUTHENTIC.
- ☐ *Business Savvy* is established by finding your NICHE.
- ☐ *Business Savvy* is established by understanding your PURPOSE.
- ☐ *Business Savvy* is established by using Godly Principles of BLESSING your business.
- ☐ *Business Savvy* is established by exhibiting INTEGRITY.
- ☐ *Business Savvy* is established by being GRATEFUL.
- ☐ *Business Savvy* is established by SERVING others.
- ☐ *Business Savvy* is established by being PATIENT.
- ☐ *Business Savvy* is established by sharing KINDNESS.
- ☐ *Business Savvy* is established by being HUMBLE.
- ☐ *Business Savvy* is established by being BALANCED.
- ☐ *Business Savvy* is established by DECIDING the type of business to set up.
- ☐ *Business Savvy* is established by continuing to LEARN.
- ☐ *Business Savvy* is established by establishing a Spiritual Marketing System.
- ☐ *Business Savvy* is established by setting GOALS.
- ☐ *Business Savvy* is established by building TRUST.
- ☐ *Business Savvy* is established by SOLVING problems.
- ☐ *Business Savvy* is established by KNOWING what to do with what you have in your hands.
- ☐ *Business Savvy* is established in LEADING by Example.

Doing Real Business

- ☐ *Business Savvy* is established by being RESILIENT.
- ☐ *Business Savvy* is established by OPERATING in the Spirit of Excellence.
- ☐ *Business Savvy* is established by developing the WISDOM on how to Work, Present, and Sell your dream, idea, or concept.

In establishing a business, at some point, we must take the time to think, rethink, and become succinct. If not, we cannot develop the vision, establish longevity, build our business credit to finance it, or create the leverage needed to become one of the Business Elites. If we have someone else do all the work without our involvement, we will not know what is going on, leaving us open to deceptive measures or having the wool pulled over our eyes.

In *The Black Sheep Power: As It Pleases God*®, the ultimate goal is to place ourselves on the Leading Edge, where our competitors try to emulate but cannot duplicate. How is it possible for our competitors not to duplicate? We must tap into our reason for being, releasing our Spiritual Gifts according to our Divine Blueprint, Spiritual Fruits, and Christlike Character while being about our Father's Business.

On the other hand, we can become duplicated if we miss a part of this Spiritual Equation. Why can we become duplicated as Believers? We do not have a Spiritual Seal, which leaves us and our business open to counterfeit fingerprints.

Once we place a Spiritual Seal, *As It Pleases God*, it grants our business endeavors a unique fingerprint called the Real Deal. Unbeknownst to most, when one is the Real Deal, people will come in droves, trying to discredit or assassinate our character, fruits, or mission without realizing what they are

Doing Real Business

doing. How can they not know? The enemy will use anything or anyone, especially the ones we love, to cause the mind or psyche to jump the track or to make us feel like *The Black Sheep*. So, we must stay on ready, knowing and understanding our Divine Passion or Blueprint. However, we must make sure that our character traits are up to par, *As It Pleases God*, leaving NO STONE UNTURNED to sustain and maintain where we are going.

Once again, we cannot put the cart before the horse, especially when starting a new business. If we do not know or understand our Divine Passion or Blueprinted Purpose, we can become easily manipulated or traumatized, shaken to the core. For this reason, I will share the *Business Info, Tips, and Know-How* that I have picked up along the way.

Business Info, Tips, and Know-How

When engaging in *Doing Real Business*, the questions on your paperwork will ask you for some of the same information from your Business Plan or Plan of Action. The goal is to prepare you for those questions in advance to ensure you are not overwhelmed with the process. So, if you have not completed your mind map, answered the questions in the previous sections about your Passion, Brainstorming, and Real Purpose, it behooves you to go back and do so. You are going to need that information later on down the line as you progress in *The Black Sheep Power: As It Pleases God*®.

In *Doing Real Business* as *The Black Sheep*, God is adamant about having our Spiritual Fruits, Character, and Predestined Blueprint documented and checked consistently. Why is God so meticulous about our Spiritual Fruits and Character? People may not buy us, our brand, or our product for a few reasons, but not limited to such:

Doing Real Business

- ☐ We may not be buying ourselves.
- ☐ It may not be adequately packaged.
- ☐ We may lack the ability to connect with them.
- ☐ We are not presenting what they need.
- ☐ We may not be showing the benefits associated.
- ☐ They may not like our approach.
- ☐ Our vibe may be off.
- ☐ We may lack sincerity.
- ☐ Our character sucks!

Most people dislike selling as much as they avoid salespeople, without realizing that we sell and promote ourselves whenever we open our mouths, with every move we make, etc. Regardless of how we try to rationalize and justify, we all sell ourselves in some way, shape, or form, making everyone a salesperson whether we like it or not.

So, if you are not getting what you want, simply check or adjust what you are doing and why you are doing it. Your attitude, actions, and reactions reveal the quality of your product and how you make people feel. Today, take the time to choose your words carefully; you never want to sell yourself short when you are quality at its best. Plus, there is no reason why you should not be able to succeed at what you do best. If you follow the process that I am laying out for you…you will thank me later because business professionals capitalize on newcomers for their lack of knowledge. So, I am here to walk you through, especially with the domain names.

If you are starting a new venture, do not, and I repeat, do not submit paperwork on that business before you purchase the domain name. Make sure you buy the domain name first. Why? Suppose you file the paperwork for a business on a city, county, or state level without purchasing your desired domain name first. In this case, it will most likely no longer be

Doing Real Business

available to you at a reasonable price. A company will purchase the domain name at $21.99 or less, and sell it back to you for $500.00 or more.

For example, I filed for a county license for my company called xye3, and then a week later, tried to purchase the domain www.xye3.com; it said the domain name had already been taken, but it is for sale for $500.00. Yet, last week the domain was available for $21.99. Nevertheless, you must decide on your process or way of doing things relating to your business.

In *The Black Sheep Power: As It Pleases God®*, I can only lead you and reduce the headache or heartache associated with the cost of *Doing Real Business*. In tapping into your underground cisterns from a business perspective or to establish a measure of credibility, here is what you need, but not limited to such:

- ☐ You must UNDERSTAND or have an idea of your Gifts, Callings, Talents, Creativity, Passion, or Purpose.

- ☐ You must DECIDE on the type of business endeavor.

- ☐ You must DETERMINE the products you intend to sell.

- ☐ You must ESTABLISH a business name. When deciding on the name of your business, write out 20 different names and then narrow it down to one based on the domain search process or company name availability. Make sure you do a Division of Corporations free online search to ensure your new business name is not already being used in the state where you will be doing business. Try to keep your web address as a dot.com, if possible.

Doing Real Business

☐ You must PURCHASE your Domain Name. I prefer using Wix or GoDaddy to purchase my domains. Beware: GoDaddy's method of operation will try to upsell you on products you DO NOT need through solicitation.

☐ You must SET UP your email address. You will need all of this information when filling out your business paperwork. Gmail accounts work great because they have many features that help promote your business and connect to your Social Media accounts.

☐ You must develop a professional logo.

☐ You must get a website with Wix or GoDaddy. It is best to choose a plan that accepts credit card payments. Beware: GoDaddy's method of operation will try to upsell you on products you DO NOT need through solicitation.

☐ You must have your Business Plan and Plan of Action documented. SBA and SCORE have a lot to offer you regarding help with your small business. It is the U.S. Small Business Administration; they assist with startup costs and help with your Business Plan.

☐ You must DETERMINE where you are going to set up your business. Please check the zoning laws before committing to a specific location. You must do your homework on a location before investing in one that cannot pass zoning restrictions predicated on the type of business. Depending on the type of business, you can always use the Post Office as a great alternative; their P.O. Boxes are not expensive, but bank and state

Doing Real Business

agencies will require brick-and-mortar addresses. In addition, you can always use a virtual office if you cannot find an office. Check your local listings for the Virtual Office Spaces in your area, which give you options to cut costs or offer space sharing! If you are just beginning, you can set up a temporary business mailing address and phone number to get the ball rolling before establishing a permanent one.

- ☐ You must make sure your personal credit is separate from your business credit.

- ☐ You must decide on a business structure by setting up a Corporation (for-profit or non-profit), LLC (Limited Liability Company), or Sole Proprietorship.

- ☐ You must get an EIN number from IRS.gov.

- ☐ You must open a business checking account with the suggested banks, Wells Fargo, Chase, or Regions. Make sure there are no insufficient funds linked to this account.

- ☐ You must establish a business phone line.

- ☐ You must register your business with Dun & Bradstreet to get a DUN's number.

- ☐ You must master the ability to track your expenses using your credit card statements.

- ☐ You must complete your business budget forms.

Doing Real Business

- ☐ You must SET UP Facebook, YouTube, Instagram, Snapchat, Reddit, Pinterest, LinkedIn, Google+, and X (formerly Twitter) accounts. In my opinion, this is the best time to set up your social media accounts.

- ☐ You must ESTABLISH a good marketing plan.

- ☐ You must get professional-looking promotional material such as business cards, company letterhead, invoices, and brochures.

What is the purpose of adhering to this list? Before establishing any form of Business Credit, we must establish a credible business. Although some people are in business making money, it does not mean they are credible or legal. Why not, especially if they are making money? They do not have the proper paperwork in place, especially a business plan, website, EIN number, Dun's number, business checking account, business phone, or the proper filings with the state where they live.

Defining the requirements for a new business startup from state to state can be perplexing and time-consuming. Many agencies have different regulations and various aspects of business operations; however, each state will also have its own guides. These are the basic requirements that apply to all businesses, such as:

- ☐ Sole Proprietorship
- ☐ Partnership
- ☐ General Partnership
- ☐ Limited Partnership
- ☐ Limited Liability Company (LLC)
- ☐ Corporation

Doing Real Business

Sole Proprietorship is an unincorporated business consisting of one owner who pays taxes on the profits from the business. This type of business is very simple, with few government regulations; however, it has the greatest risk and liability. Although it may be less paperwork and easier to set up, it is also the easiest to take down. Most new businesses that do not understand the liabilities involved opt for this initially, but later change their minds to form an LLC.

Partnership is when two or more people are involved in the ownership of an unincorporated business. This setup is similar to the Sole Proprietorship, but with two or more people contributing to all aspects of the business, sharing in the profits, losses, and the same liabilities of the company. Unfortunately, it exposes the owners to personal liabilities as well.

General Partnership is when two or more individuals own a business, intending to earn profits. Profits are presumed equally distributed among the partners unless otherwise stated in a written contract. This partnership exposes the owners to personal liabilities as well.

Limited Partnership is when two or more individuals own a business, and are two different partners. One is a general partner, and the other is a limited partner for specific responsibilities based on the agreement outlined in the file elections. Example: The General Partners are involved in the day-to-day management of the business, and the Limited Partners are usually the investors with limited personal liability.

Limited Liability Company (LLC) is where the owners are called members and have limited liability. What this means is they are not totally liable for all debts and liabilities of the LLC. They are not bound by the same strict rules set forth when having a corporation. Most states do not restrict members; they can be an individual, corporation, another LLC, or a foreign company. It can be as simple as a single or husband/wife-owned LLC. It is a popular choice for smaller businesses because it is a little easier, and it protects your personal assets from your business assets. When doing business, it is always good to separate the two. The only companies NOT allowed to form an LLC are Banks, Non-Profit Organizations, Certain Financial Institutions, and Insurance Companies.

Corporation is the most complex organization to form due to the amount of paperwork required and the fact that the corporation has shareholders. There are four types of corporations: C corporations, S corporations, Non-Profit Corporations, and Professional Corporations, which are structured and taxed differently. They all have their advantages and disadvantages. Shareholders play a vital role in the company and contribute to the capital, taking on the roles and responsibilities of a person. However, an individual can contribute to, perform on behalf of, or speak for the corporation. Yet, the bottom line is that the shareholders are indeed the entity with the power, duty, and rights of the corporation.

Sadly, this is how the local Mom and Pop, without any prior business knowledge, get sucker punched into signing a contract to go public with a chain of stores. Although they may have more leverage, a more comprehensive platform, and big money, now they have no say-so in their business or are outright benched! So, exercise extreme caution when deciding what type of company you would like to set up.

Each state has laws regarding the sections, and tax purposes vary from state to state for the corporation. Each structure has advantages and disadvantages; please seek legal counsel to ensure you select the best choice for your business.

Doing Real Business

Once again, SBA and SCORE are great alternatives for you as well. They have great counselors/mentors who will assist you with little or no cost. As you can see, it can get pretty lengthy; however, you have to decide what is best for you and your business. Nevertheless, we must invest in a Business Plan, allowing others to visually see our vision documented. Listen, it does not need to be perfect; it just needs to be documented with a work-in-progress mentality.

Writing A Business Plan

When writing a Business Plan, the goal is to document, document, document. According to the Heavenly of Heavens, it helps to build our FAITH, CONFIDENCE, and COURAGE in all areas. Writing a plan may not be an overnight process, but we can invest in documenting one word at a time to build a sentence. A few sentences will make a paragraph. A few paragraphs will complete a section. With each section completed, we will eventually have a Business Plan, one step at a time.

To view a Business Plan as a whole can become overwhelming at times, but if we break it down into words, paragraphs, and sections, in the end, we will have what we need. When embarking upon each section, we need to know the *What, When, Where, How, Why,* and with *Whom*. Some may apply, and some may not, but it does get our mental wheels turning in the right direction, breaking the stagnation to bring forth a FLOW of *Doing Real Business*.

According to the Heavenly of Heavens, our Divine Vision has a voice, and if we place a Spiritual Demand on it, *As It Pleases God*, it must speak! When it does, we must capture it on paper; if not, it will become silent again. Once again, here is the Spiritual Seal to leverage when doing so: *"For the vision is yet for an appointed time; But at the end it will speak, and it will not lie.*

Doing Real Business

Though it tarries, wait for it; Because it will surely come, It will not tarry." Habakkuk 2:3. Amid all, our Predestined Blueprint belongs to us for others. It is our responsibility to extract and convert it and then present it to the Kingdom in Earthen Vessel based upon the Law of Reciprocity or Seedtime and Harvest.

Your Business Plan will have different topics, along with supporting material. The topics are:

- ☐ Executive Summary
- ☐ Profile of Business
- ☐ The Company
- ☐ Mission Statement
- ☐ Company's Vision
- ☐ Objectives
- ☐ Management
- ☐ Organizational Structure
- ☐ Organizational Management
- ☐ Business Credentials
- ☐ Company licenses
- ☐ Company Accreditations
- ☐ Market Analysis
- ☐ Market Location
- ☐ Market Description
- ☐ Market Qualifier
- ☐ Competition
- ☐ Marketing Strategy
- ☐ Pricing and Profitability
- ☐ Product or Service Distribution
- ☐ Sales Strategy
- ☐ Operations
- ☐ Financial Statements
- ☐ Startup Requirements
- ☐ Budget

Doing Real Business

- ☐ Cash Flow Statement
- ☐ Conclusion

What is the purpose of leveraging our business in such a manner? Most businesses fail due to improper financial management, not having access to capital, a lack of business credit, the fear of pursuing business leverage, or cluelessness about the company's objectives. Most businesses do not have a Business Plan to guide or remind them of their vision; as a result, they find themselves all over the place, doing this or that for the dollar.

When *Doing Real Business* as *The Black Sheep*, we have a reason for doing what we do, *As It Pleases God*. Doing anything with anyone for the dollar is not wise, especially when tapping into what is Divine, according to our Predestined Blueprint. Really? Yes, really. The Streams of God are not for those easily strayed by the dollar sign. Nor is it for those who jump into anything without a sense of Spiritual Discernment. For this reason, we must manage our finances accordingly.

When exhausting our personal credit for business purposes, we overload ourselves with too much debt. Therefore, funding for the business needs to be on a business line of credit or credit card, and our personal needs must go on our personal credit, creating a balance between the two. In addition, it helps us to leave a paper trail of our expenditures for tax purposes with itemized statements accepted by the IRS, even if we have lost the receipt or it has faded. So, it behooves us to keep our personal and business credit separate.

To develop and maintain financial power and freedom, we must build our business portfolio, even if we are not fully ready to embark upon it. What does this mean? We should not wait to begin the process; we must take baby steps, building our strength and endurance while gainfully

Doing Real Business

employed. In so many words, while working on a job, we should also carve out time to build a business or work on a roadmap.

To get started, follow the steps from the above checklist. Once a business is registered with state and federal agencies, it can begin building its credit line. Here are the goals:

- ☐ 1 Bank loan or line of credit. Secured or Unsecured.
- ☐ 3 Business credit cards with American Express, Chase, Capital One, Sam's Club, or Wells Fargo for unsecured.

Vendor trade lines for a net 30, 60, or 90-day terms with Amazon Business, Quill, Uline, Crown Office Supplies, Office Depot, Staples, Home Depot, Lowes, or Nav. All of which helps us gain *The Divine Advantage*, regardless of where we are, what we have going on, or what we have to overcome.

Chapter Nine
The Divine Advantage

The Divine Advantage of grace and mercy is available to all, but if we do not take a chance on our Spiritual Gifts, Predestined Blueprint, or be about our Father's Business, they will remain dormant. Is this fair? Absolutely. With the *Divine Advantage* comes Divine Diligence in Spiritually Tilling our own ground (Putting in the Work), *As It Pleases God.* Here is what Proverbs 12:11 specifically says about this non-negotiable: *"He who tills his land will be satisfied with bread, but he who follows frivolity is devoid of understanding."*

In contrast, using grace and mercy as an excuse to sit on our hands, twiddling our thumbs, and doing nothing for the Kingdom is not wise. Plus, grace and mercy do not support or endorse this behavior. Nor does it endorse chasing fleeting desires, pleasures, or distractions, while outright ignoring or downplaying our reason for being. How can I say such a thing, right? Well, according to Luke 9:62, it says, *"But Jesus said to him, No one, having put his hand to the plow, and looking back, is fit for the kingdom of God."* Most often, we pretend we are doing something for the Kingdom of God, but we are really doing it for ourselves, for a show, to stroke our egos, or for the money.

As Believers, we are called to be active participants in the Kingdom, being about our Father's Business. In addition, we are also called to love and serve others, share the gospel, and use our talents and resources for the Glory of God, not to glorify ourselves. However, some Believers may use the concepts of grace and mercy as an excuse to exist or wallow in folly, breathing in the Breath of Life as if they do not need to do anything in return. Based upon this misconception, in *The Divine Advantage*, we pride ourselves on this Spiritual Principle: *"Freely you have received, freely give."* Matthew 10:8.

Grace and mercy are not a license to be lazy or complacent, and not to take chances. Here is the deal: Grace is the unmerited favor of God, given to us despite our sins and shortcomings, for REFINEMENT. Mercy is the compassion of God, shown to us even when we deserve punishment. These concepts are not meant to be an excuse for inaction but rather a MOTIVATION for us to live out our faith and serve Him with all that we have, being about His Business first and doing what we were sent here to do in Earthen Vessels.

Why must we place God first, especially when He has given us free will? If God served us what we deserved, we would hang our heads down in shame. Better yet, if He released the skeletons hidden in our closets, we know that we would get a severe side-eye. Instead, we can walk in boldness and confidence that He has our backs with our heads held high...thus we should never come with the 'woe unto me' mentality in this lifetime or the next.

Furthermore, the Bible teaches us that faith without works is dead in James 2:17. We cannot simply claim to believe in God and then do nothing to show it, or see a fallen brother or sister and not help them back up, kick them when they are down, plot their demise, or spitefully air out their dirty laundry, especially when we have our own underlying quirks.

In the Eye of God, our faith must be accompanied by ACTION, positive action to be exact. However, with *The Divine Advantage*, when taking action, *As It Pleases Him*, we must understand two things:

The Divine Advantage

- ☐ The Risk.
- ☐ How to Overcome Deceptive Measures.

Here is what Jesus said about *The Divine Advantage* in John 14:15, '*If you love Me, keep My commandments.*"

The Risk

With that out of the way, let us get back on track with *The Divine Advantage*. We must consciously choose to Spiritually Till our own grounds, taking a RISK on ourselves, according to our Predestined Blueprint. Why is a risk required of us as Believers? Whether we are a *Black Sheep* or not, every seed planted in or out of season must take a risk at living, and we are no different in Earthen Vessels.

When someone says to me, 'I do not believe in chances.' I am like, 'Speak for yourself!' I believe in them because I am living proof of several occurrences. If one has never experienced making a conscious choice to come back from the other side to complete their Divine Mission, it becomes easy to judge what we do not understand. More importantly, if I had not taken a chance at writing with my flaws and all of my idiosyncrasies, pushing beyond my self-imposed limitations, we would not have this TIMELY information about *The Black Sheep Power: As It Pleases God*®.

What is the big deal about grace, mercy, and taking chances? We need them all. When taking a risk or chance, we will need grace and mercy working on our behalf. For those opting to use grace and mercy without taking a chance, it is like buying an 'As Is' product without a warranty; come on...this manipulation of Believers must stop. As long as grace and mercy remain, so will the element of risk.

The Divine Advantage

Our Forefathers took risks for us, and we should never forfeit the element of chance. Regardless of how we play on words, there is a time and season for everything under the sun; whether we are given another chance at living, as I have been given, or we take a chance on something or someone as a formal risk, it is indeed a chance!

Before ending this section on a note of chance, please allow me to Spiritually Align this squeamish debate: *"Whatever your hand finds to do, do it with your might; for there is no work or device or knowledge or wisdom in the grave where you are going. I returned and saw under the sun that—The race is not to the swift, Nor the battle to the strong, Nor bread to the wise, Nor riches to men of understanding, Nor favor to men of skill; But time and chance happen to them all."* Ecclesiastes 9:10-11.

So, what do we have working in our favor aside from grace and mercy? It is TIME and CHANCE! In order for them to work in our favor, *As It Pleases God*, we must engage in *Overcoming Deceptive Measures* to ensure we do not self-sabotage ourselves or our Bloodline.

Overcoming Deceptive Measures

In an age pigeon-holed by rapid and instant exchange of information, the presence of misleading tactics and deceptive measures can significantly impact our decision-making and understanding process. All of these tactics mislead the psyche if we do not find ways to *Overcome Deceptive Measures* and the strongholds associated.

In *The Black Sheep Power: As It Pleases God*®, to gain *The Divine Advantage*, here are a few types of common *Deceptive Measures* we must know about, but not limited to such:

The Divine Advantage

- **Emotional Manipulation**: In *Overcoming Deceptive Measures*, this tactic is used to influence or control someone's feelings and actions by exploiting their emotions. Sadly, this can involve playing on someone's fears, insecurities, guilt, traumas, or desires to achieve a specific goal. Then again, some manipulators may create situations or narratives designed to evoke strong emotional responses, often aiming to persuade the individual to act in a way that benefits the manipulator rather than themselves or God Almighty. The emotional coercion may also include playing the victim, guilt-tripping, or gaslighting someone to control them.

- **Selective Manipulation**: In *Overcoming Deceptive Measures*, this tactic refers to the practice of presenting information in a way that emphasizes certain aspects while downplaying or omitting others, leading to a skewed or biased understanding of a situation. This method is commonly used in various contexts, including advertising, politics, and media reporting, to achieve specific goals or persuade an audience. The selective coercion may include cherry-picking information, biasedly framing information, or outright omitting facts to narrow perspectives instead of expanding our perspectives with the truth.

- **Misinformative Manipulation**: In *Overcoming Deceptive Measures*, this tactic refers to the deliberate use of false or misleading information to influence perceptions, beliefs, or behaviors without necessarily being overtly deceptive. It combines the elements of misinformation and manipulation, aiming to steer individuals' thinking in a particular direction or achieve specific outcomes.

The Divine Advantage

The misinformative coercion may include twisting the facts, selective exclusion, contextual distortion, and emotional appeal. This distortion is found in our homes, advertising, politics, and media, and often aims to exploit cognitive biases and emotional triggers to achieve its goals.

☐ **Visual Manipulation**: In *Overcoming Deceptive Measures*, this tactic refers to the deliberate alteration or arrangement of visual elements within an image, video, or presentation to influence perception or convey a specific message. It often involves techniques such as editing, distortion, or selective framing to evoke emotional responses, emphasize certain aspects, downplay others, or play on our senses. This form of visual coercion is frequently used in advertising, politics, and media to exploit cognitive biases and emotional triggers, ultimately shaping their audience's attitudes, responses, desires, habits, triggers, urges, weaknesses, and beliefs.

☐ **Cognitive Manipulation**: In *Overcoming Deceptive Measures*, this tactic refers to techniques or strategies used to influence an individual's thoughts, perceptions, and behaviors through psychological means. Clearly, this can involve altering how information is presented, framing issues in a particular light, or exploiting cognitive biases to shape opinions and beliefs. This hidden kryptonite is often used in our family dynamics without realizing it. But it is also used in contexts like advertising, politics, workplace relations, and media outlets. This form of cognitive coercion seeks to evoke emotional responses, play on the conscience, and guide decision-making without the individual being fully aware of the influence. The goal of this power play is to persuade or control how individuals process information and respond to specific messages.

☐ **Faith-Based Manipulation:** In *Overcoming Deceptive Measures*, this tactic refers to the use of religious beliefs, symbols, or cultural practices to influence individuals' thoughts and behaviors for specific purposes. In addition, this can occur when leaders or organizations exploit the trust and conviction that their followers have in their faith in them, or in God Almighty. In all simplicity, when someone engages in acts to persuade others to act in ways that may benefit the leader or organization, rather than the individual's best interests, God's Divine Standards, or operate with outright integrity...there is manipulation at play here. In reality, such manipulation can manifest through various means, including selective interpretation of scripture, hiding the truth, emotional appeal, board appeal (people pleasing), moral discrepancy, pimping or prostituting God, and advocating personal reliance instead of God Reliance. Faith-based coercion is focused on blurring the lines between genuine Spiritual Guidance and coercive influences. Of course, this should not happen, but it is happening in real time.

☐ **Psychological Manipulation:** In *Overcoming Deceptive Measures*, this tactic refers to a process where one individual influences another person's thoughts, feelings, or behaviors in a deceptive or exploitative way. It often involves tactics aimed at creating confusion, fear, or guilt within a person, ultimately leading them to act in a manner that serves the manipulator's agenda. By getting into someone's head like this, it can manifest through various strategies, such as gaslighting, emotional blackmail, setting traps, or using misleading information to control or dominate the relationship. This type of psychological coercion may seek to undermine the autonomy of the person being manipulated, making it difficult for them to discern the truth and maintain their own decision-making power.

- ☐ **Dream-Killing Manipulation**: In *Overcoming Deceptive Measures*, this refers to a tactic used by individuals to undermine someone else's aspirations, goals, desires, dreams, passions, or ambitions through negative comments, doubts, or discouragement. This type of manipulation typically stems from envy, jealousy, pride, greed, coveting, competitiveness, insecurity, or a desire to maintain control over someone. The individuals employing this tactic may intentionally or unintentionally diminish the confidence of others, thereby stifling their dreams and potential. For the most part, dream-killing coercion can be introduced as doubt to make us second-guess ourselves, or it can cause us to accept negative feedback as being normal. Then again, it can also make us comfortable with those who withhold support or minimize the achievements of those who are wholeheartedly and legitimately putting in the work.

- ☐ **Love Manipulation**: In *Overcoming Deceptive Measures*, this tactic refers to a form of emotional manipulation where one person uses affection, love, or emotional ties to influence or control another person's thoughts, feelings, or actions. This can include tactics such as guilt-tripping, emotional blackmail, or conditional love, where affection is given or withheld based on compliance with the manipulator's desires or expectations. Love coercion often stems from an imbalance of power in the relationship, where the manipulator seeks to maintain control or instill dependency in the other person. Such behavior can undermine an individual's self-esteem and autonomy, leading to toxic dynamics or outright bullying in the relationship.

☐ **Black Sheep Manipulation:** In *Overcoming Deceptive Measures*, this refers to a tactic where an individual is portrayed as the outsider or the misunderstood *Black Sheep* within a group, often used to elicit sympathy or to deflect criticism. This manipulative victim strategy is commonly employed by individuals who feel marginalized. Then again, it is also used by those who want to gain attention and support by emphasizing their uniqueness or perceived victimhood. *The Black Sheep* coercion can involve exaggerating personal struggles or presenting oneself as the only one who understands certain issues, thereby influencing others' perceptions and eliciting loyalty or empathy from them. Whereas, in this book, we do not manipulate in this manner, we simply turn our *Black Sheep* Experiences into POWER.

☐ **Materialistic Manipulation:** In *Overcoming Deceptive Measures*, this tactic refers to a situation where individuals or societies are influenced or controlled by the pursuit of material possessions and wealth. It suggests that people's values, behaviors, and decisions are driven by a desire for financial gain and tangible goods, often leading to a neglect of Spiritual Relations. Materialistic coercion can manifest in various ways, such as consumerism, where people feel pressured to buy more than they need. In addition, it can also appear as an exaggerated form of neediness to be happy. For the record, by not being content with who we are as a Spiritual Being, having a human experience is a big slap in the face to our Creator.

- ☐ **Pimped Manipulation**: In *Overcoming Deceptive Measures*, this tactic refers to a situation where an individual is exploited or controlled by others, often by using deceptive tactics, persuasive techniques, or emotional coercion. Pimped coercion can occur anywhere, especially in our homes, relationships, churches, workplaces, or societal structures, where the individual may feel pressured to perform or act in ways that benefit the manipulator rather than themselves. Being used for someone else's gain, whether it is financial, social, or emotional, while our own needs and desires are sidelined, is not what God intended for us.

All of these forms of manipulation weigh on the psyche of mankind. If not recognized or counteracted, *As It Pleases God*, we will have issues, while finding ourselves at a disadvantage within our very own psyche.

What is the psyche designed to do? It is designed to rule over us with all types of impulses, deception, denial, and blaming until we awaken from our slumber, *As It Pleases God*. The more we ignore this one factor, the bigger the gap becomes between the ONE God of all, within us all. In addition, it also impacts our thought patterns and how we communicate with ourselves from the inside out. The most

The Divine Advantage

prominent example is when the mind says one thing, the heart says another, and our conscience also weighs in, causing an internal battle or extreme exhaustion. Here is what James 4:1 says about this: *"Where do wars and fights come from among you? Do they not come from your desires for pleasure that war in your members?"*

If we have not noticed by now, our tangible communication tools, such as our eyes, ears, mouth, and nose, are closer to the mind than the soul (the core of our being) for a reason. It allows us to rationalize or govern what is going on in the MIND, or evaluate our brainial functions before involving the intangible heart (soul).

On average, amid using less than 10% of our brainial functions, if a soulish trigger occurs, it still allows us to interject positivity and rationale, or the negativity and defeat of our choosing based upon our mindset, as well as our people and problem-solving skills. All of these are based on what we see, hear, speak, taste, and smell before connecting the power of touch or engagement. Why do we need to know this? It gives us the ability to shut it or them down, safeguarding ourselves to be about our Father's Business, *As It Pleases Him.*

How is this possible when the soul(psyche) is one with the mind? Here is where Spiritual Erring takes place. Just as the body is one in itself, it has many members. If we go to the doctor, they do not treat the entire body; they treat the members of the body, such as the head, eye, arm, finger, heart, chest, leg, knee, foot, toe, and so on. Therefore, when dealing with the psyche, it is imperative to deal with the MIND separately. Why? It is where the Realm of Spirituality takes place, serving as a Spiritual Filter before depositing whatever or whomever within the soul or reacting to emotions. More importantly, it is where SCIENCE has not tapped into yet.

Why does Science have limited access to the components of the mind? Spiritual Death from the Garden of Eden was not with the body, as most would think. It was through the

The Divine Advantage

Divine Connection back to the Kingdom of God in an Earthen Vessel through our mental communicative capacity. Blasphemy, right? Wrong!

In Genesis 3, when the serpent beguiled Eve, he planted a seedful thought in her mind, and she had the choice to accept, reject, or ponder on it. Nothing happened to her Mind, Body, Soul, or Spirit until she put ACTION behind the seedful thought planted with a question of contempt from the most cunning beast of the field. As a result of her acceptance of the seedful thoughts, the cunned individual became cunning, feeling right or justified in her own eyes.

With the implantation taking effect with the same Seed of Deception, she gave the Forbidden Fruit to her husband to keep the cycle going. Once Adam took part in this act of disobedience, it changed the trajectory of how the Mind's Eye connects to the Mind of God and His All-seeing EYE as the cycle continues.

What does the cycle have to do with the Mind's Eye or Eye of God? In all simplicity, nothing has changed up until now with the Seed of Deception. It is still seeking its dominance and relevance, preventing us from being about our Father's Business, *As It Pleases Him*. However, the Blood of Jesus and the Holy Spirit are our RECONCILIATION and SALVATION factors, merging the two back together as ONE with Spiritual Conditions.

Moreover, it is available to all, making no one exempt as long as we meet the basis of the Covenantal Agreement from the Heavenly of Heavens. Thus, being that we do not fully understand this information, it causes the battle for the mind to occur within the human psyche and for the Believer to bogart, control, or prostitute God with deceptive intentions.

In the Eye of God, being that the cycle of deceptive measures has not stopped yet, therefore, it has Spiritual Laws, Protocols, and Principles protecting the Divine Access to

The Divine Advantage

certain Spiritual Realms, Wisdom, Secrets, Treasures, and Knowings, regardless of who we are or why we are. Really? Yes, really! Although God loves us all, for this profound reason, from the Ancient of Days until now, Spiritual Tilling must occur, *As It Pleases Him*. If not, we will have limited access, even if we go to the dark side to obtain the counterfeit version and suffer the consequences of this Spiritual Violation.

In moving forward in the Spirit of Excellence, even if someone says we do not have to do anything to become or remain a Believer, it is a LIE. We need God, the Blood of Jesus, and the Holy Spirit involved in our daily lives to unfold the reason for our being or unveil our Predestined Blueprint. More importantly, we need the Fruits of the Spirit and to behave Christlike to gain Spiritual Access, *As It Pleases Him*. Why must we *PLEASE Him* to gain Spiritual Access? Illegal Access comes with curses, yokes, and strongholds seeping into the Bloodline of the violators.

As a rule of thumb, we must work on ourselves to AVOID becoming deceitfully negative or cunning and to prevent people from getting in our heads. What is the purpose of doing so? The enemy will plot and set traps to ruin our credibility, especially in the minds of those who are gullible.

Suppose we are not strong Mentally, Physically, Emotionally, Spiritually, or Financially. In this case, we can become consumed, crushed, or thrown under the bus by the cunning voices whispering in our ears, catering to our weaknesses, insecurities, lack, or traumas.

How do we know if we are being deceived? First, deception is recognized through the questions being asked, often creating doubt, the fear of missing out, or the attempt to dismantle our Spiritual Assignments. Secondly, it is known by the language spoken, whether it is positive, negative, intrusive, fact-finding, or illuminating light or darkness.

Thirdly, it is identified by whether it leads us to the truth or lies about ourselves or others. Fourthly, whether it guides us to or away from the Fruits of the Spirit, Christlike Character, the Word of God, or straight into the PIT. And lastly, it prevents us from operating in the *Freedom of Authenticity*. The moment we want to be other than what God created us to be, as if He made a mistake, then there is a bigger problem on the horizon. Nevertheless, here is what Galatians 5:1 tells us to do: *"Stand fast therefore in the liberty by which Christ has made us free, and do not be entangled again with a yoke of bondage."*

Chapter Ten
Freedom of Authenticity

In the *Freedom of Authenticity* lies us, with the free will to choose between being who we are or to be an imitation of someone else. At its core, authenticity is about being true to oneself, but what if we do not know the truth? What if we are being lied to? What if we do not know how to stop lying to ourselves about who we are? Well, in *The Black Sheep Power: As It Pleases God*®, our qualities, values, and beliefs rest IN HIM. It does not lie in seductive traps or mind games, offering the temporary comfort of acceptance to feed the lust of the eyes, the lust of the flesh, or the pride of life. We are indeed the Tree of Life, and the moment we awaken from our slumber to embrace what we already are in Earthen Vessels, life will begin to serve us very well.

According to the Heavenly of Heavens, the way to the Tree of Life within us and back to our Heavenly Father is HEAVILY guarded. Why is there a need for guards? God's most precious commodities, such as gold, silver, diamonds, oil, and Chosen Ones, will always be hidden in plain sight, not appearing as such. Then again, the cultivation of the authenticity of something or someone, or the quality of being genuine, may cause us to put in the work to unveil them.

When it comes to Divine Authenticity, how we THINK with the MIND can protect or destroy the Body and Soul, affecting our *Spirit to Spirit* Relationship with our Heavenly

Freedom of Authenticity

Father. For the record, and before moving on, just because we think right does not mean we are correct, and just because we are in right standing with God, it does not mean we are thinking right, *As It Pleases Him*. How would we know the difference? Simply put, it is noticed by what slips off our tongues, our hidden or open actions, and our internal or external reactions, which are predicated on our THOUGHTS and MINDSETS.

According to the Heavenly of Heavens, the problem with getting one-sided information from man's perspective, not from God's Divine Perspective, is that it leaves room for the lack of authenticity and deceptive measures to gain a chokehold on our weakest links. The bottom line is that we must know where we are, Mentally, Physically, Emotionally, Spiritually, and Financially, to govern our next moves or Bloodline. Is any of this Biblical in the pursuit of *Freedom of Authenticity*? I am so glad you asked. It says, *"Be diligent to know the state of your flocks, And attend to your herds; For riches are not forever, Nor does a crown endure to all generations."* Proverbs 27:23-24.

Whether we have or do not have, we cannot lose ourselves amid whatever or with whomever. If we lose ourselves, deception is waiting to overtake us with negative thoughts, emotions, actions, behaviors, and beliefs. Really? Yes, really! This condition is why, when some people get a little taste of money, they become a force to be reckoned with in a bad way. How do we make this make sense? The negative character traits were already flowing through their veins, and money allowed them to become comfortable with cutting loose, removing the mask, or treating others like they had once been treated.

As *The Black Sheep* in the *Freedom of Authenticity*, I suggest proactively working on our fruits and character before tasting the Promises and Blessings. Why should we work on our

Freedom of Authenticity

fruits and character if we are Believers? Regardless of who we are, where we are, or what we believe, the material gain associated with power, money, and sex MAGNIFIES who we really are at the core, eventually costing us in the long run. For the record, it can cost us Mentally, Physically, Emotionally, Spiritually, or Financially with a flaming arrow, especially if we do not find a way to add the Holy Trinity into the equation. Nonetheless, it behooves us to tread with caution while developing *Authentic Balance* along the way. Here is what Romans 12:3 says to us: *"For I say, through the grace given to me, to everyone who is among you, not to think of himself more highly than he ought to think, but to think soberly, as God has dealt to each one a measure of faith."*

The Flow

Being authentically ourselves helps us with *The Flow* from the core of our being. According to the Ancient of Days, the moment we begin to pretend, *The Flow* becomes dammed. But of course, as Believers, we most often will not admit that we are blocked. Plus, if we are faking it, I mean, really faking it, we definitely will not share that we are Spiritually Blocked, Blind, Deaf, or Mute. As a result, we continue in our folly with rotten fruits all over the place with 'zero to no' self-control, especially with our tongues. Who am I to judge? No judgment intended, but know this:

- ☐ Our words speak louder than what is being said.
- ☐ Our actions speak louder than what is being done.
- ☐ Our thoughts speak louder than what is envisioned.
- ☐ Our beliefs speak louder than what is conveyed.
- ☐ Our reactions speak louder than our responses.
- ☐ Our servanthood speaks louder than what is done.
- ☐ Our seeds speak louder than our harvests.

Freedom of Authenticity

- ☐ Our hearts speak louder than what we share.
- ☐ Our eyes speak louder than what the psyche masks.
- ☐ Our lusts speak louder than what meets the naked eye.

All of the 'speak louder than' works positively and negatively. In the Spirit of Wisdom, we should keep all of them on the positive side of the spectrum. Whatever is not positive, then it is our responsibility to work on it or reverse engineer it into a win-win for the Greater Good. If not, it can become our underlying kryptonite, canceling out our positive attributes by default.

Why do the negative qualities cancel out our good ones? Once TRUST and INTEGRITY are lost in one area, it has a domino effect in the others. Even if we are good people or have good intents, the psyche of mankind is very fickle, holding on to the negative while overriding all the positive. For this reason, it is always BEST to use the Fruits of the Spirit and behave Christlike continuously to reverse-engineer the negative domino effects associated with just being human, and to avoid tainting *The Flow*.

According to the Heavenly of Heavens, if you desire to unleash *The Flow* of your Divine Blueprint, you must go Spiritually Till your own grounds. In *The Flow* as a *Black Sheep*, here is the Spiritual Seal you need to adhere to: *"Let him who stole steal no longer, but rather let him labor, working with his hands what is good, that he may have something to give him who has need. Let no corrupt word proceed out of your mouth, but what is good for necessary edification, that it may impart grace to the hearers. And do not grieve the Holy Spirit of God, by whom you were sealed for the day of redemption. Let all bitterness, wrath, anger, clamor, and evil speaking be put away from you, with all malice. And be kind to one another,*

Freedom of Authenticity

tenderhearted, forgiving one another, even as God in Christ forgave you." Ephesians 4:28-32.

The Spiritual Reservoir of others is designed to inspire, motivate, encourage, TRIGGER, or get our wheels turning in the right direction, similar to putting oil in our cars to keep the engine running properly. The moment the car decides it does not need oil or has a leak, it will begin to fail because it is not designed to produce oil. More importantly, a car needs to stay in its lane of being a car, doing what it is designed to do, and getting the maintenance or updates designed by its MANUFACTURER to function correctly. With this analogy, the same applies to us in real-time. How so? Our Spiritual Manual or Blueprint is within us; we do not need to take it from anyone—it is already there.

Now, based on my Predestined Blueprinted Purpose, it is my JOB and reasonable service to TRIGGER or UNBLOCK *The Flow*, allowing you to tap into what is already. Plus, by Divine Design, you are the only one who can do something about it or naturally FLOW in it, whatever your 'it' is.

How can we tap into our Spiritual Gifts if we are not triggered or remain blocked? In the same way, oil is extracted from the earth, fruits, or vegetables; it knows what it has without doubting. We will never find the earth, fruits, or vegetables saying, 'I think I have oil.' It is a KNOWING hidden from within, and it is our job to locate it and then capitalize on it. If not, it does not change the fact of the hidden commodity. It simply keeps recycling itself (Cycle of Déjà vu) until we EXTRACT the oil or awaken from our slumber.

The Well of Wisdom does not discriminate! Suppose we extract the Lesson, Blessing, Testing, or Revelation, converting it as we should. In this case, *As It Pleases God*, what is Predestined Within us (our reason for being) will begin to run over, getting everyone drenched with our Gifts, Callings, Talents, Purpose, or Creativity. What does this mean? They

Freedom of Authenticity

will multiply through others. Remember, Psalm 23:5 says, *"You prepare a table before me in the presence of my enemies; You anoint my head with oil; My cup runs over."*

How do we make the overflow happen as Bloodwashed Believers? We must make sure we positively GIVE out of *The Flow*. If we are having a hard time sharing with others, it will pump the brakes on our Spiritual Gifts. Therefore, if we desire favor in our lives, here is what Luke 6:38 says, *"Give, and it will be given to you: good measure, pressed down, shaken together, and running over will be put into your bosom. For with the same measure that you use, it will be measured back to you."*

To understand how the overflow process works in the Kingdom, I have a perfect example. The ocean sharingly branches out into other bodies of water, such as the seas, rivers, lakes, streams, lagoons, creeks, and so on. All of them are affected by the Law of Gravity, flowing together to create a rhythmic systemic cycle of motion. When movement ceases, the body of water becomes septic unless it is a frozen glacier moving under its own weight as a form of LEVERAGE.

What does water have to do with us, especially as Believers? According to *The Flow*, our bodies are 60% water, sometimes a little more or less, which is a vital element that sustains life in numerous ways. Moreover, it is the only element on Earth that exists naturally in three states: solid, liquid, and gas. The Universal Laws of flexibility and the circulation process, as they pertain to water, are also applicable to us. Regardless of whether it is the circulation of blood, the transmission of signals in our nervous system, the exchange of nutrients at a cellular level, or our Divine Blueprint, they are all related in the Eye of God.

In all simplicity, just as water can adapt to different environments through its interconnectedness, doing what it is designed to do, so can we. Just as every drop of water is

Freedom of Authenticity

connected to a larger system, so are we. If the waters know and respect their boundaries, why do we pretend as if we do not have any? The moment we think that we do not need anyone or anything, and we are more comfortable rolling solo, it means that we are already defeated in the Eye of God. Now, if I take another dig, if everything we do, say, or become stops with us, then why are we here? Wait, wait, wait, do not answer this question yet...just think about it for a moment as I dig a little deeper.

Please allow me to paint a picturesque view for the mind's eye. Symbolically, our Blueprinted Purpose is the ocean, containing resources to the seas, rivers, lakes, streams, lagoons, and creeks to facilitate the lifeline to our Spiritual Gifts, Callings, Talents, Fruits, and Creativity. All of which are designed to create ANOTHER lifeline for something or someone else. Now, with it, *As It Pleases God*, it allows us to FLOW or give us the ICEBERG LEVERAGE above or beneath whatever, with whomever for the Greater Good of mankind.

Here is the deal: If we are NOT flowing or gaining leverage, then what are we doing here? If you do not know, then it is time to get *In The Know*! You cannot sit around making up stuff as you go along. In *The Flow*, as a *Black Sheep*, you must become INTENTIONAL.

To break free from this cycle, I ran into a gentleman who had enough capital to finance his dreams on a level that would make the best dreamer shake their head in dismay. But for some odd reason, he could not sustain *The Flow* in becoming a sought-after writer, putting in the necessary work. As I probed a little further, asking fact-finding questions, I found that he was more focused on material gain than on making his dream a reality.

In all simplicity, being that he did not INVEST in his dream, he did not see the VALUE in it; therefore, he spent his time, energy, emotional commitments, and finances elsewhere.

Freedom of Authenticity

By lacking the commitment to invest in his aspirations to unlock a wealth of opportunities, he found himself trapped in a cycle of secret longings, a bed of illusions, and continual discontentment. Underneath the wealth, he was good at talking a good game, but lacked the execution to facilitate the process while developing the Spirit of Coveting. To my surprise, it was tinged with a little frustration and envy toward those who do not have the capital and still make their dreams a reality.

I advised that he should not focus on things to buy; instead, the wisest thing to do is invest that money into himself, fulfilling the desires of his heart. After our little talk, he had a choice to make: Forge ahead toward the fulfillment of his dreams by taking a leap of faith or remain stagnant, plagued by regret. Now, the question is, 'What was his choice?' Let me say this: Everyone has a story to tell, and now he is well on his way to telling his.

Although he is dragging his feet in the documentation process, this is not uncommon for those who are busy doing their thing or living real life. Nevertheless, from my perspective, despite the reluctance or slow pace, with positive encouragement, he is still one step ahead of doing absolutely nothing at all or being completely stagnant. For this reason, *Strength In Community* is a game-changer for those who are not accustomed to breaking their dreams down into bite-sized pieces.

According to the Heavenly of Heavens, for sustainable and lasting success with achievable goals and favorable outcomes, with patience and perseverance at the forefront, we must take one step at a time, leaving no stone unturned, *As It Pleases God*.

Chapter Eleven
Strength In Community

The Divine Prescription to build *Strength In Community* is hidden in your GIVE BACK, breaking the poverty mentality and strengthening your backbone. What makes this so important? God does not want to open up the Windows of Heaven for you and is not able to use you as a VESSEL to open up the Windows of Heaven for someone else.

What is the big deal about giving back as Believers? God uses people to accomplish His wondrous works. If He Blesses you, and you are **NOT** able to Bless someone else, that one Blessing stops at YOU, which means you robbed Him! I believe God needs people who will keep tithing on what He is Blessing to keep the Blessings in motion.

Most people think tithing is just money, and it is NOT! Let me repeat, 'It is N.O.T.' Most people do not want to hear the truth, but I am not most people. Tithing is one of the rules of the Covenant that most of us do not really understand, yet it is the MOST MANIPULATED and ABUSED. As a part of the Covenant, a Tithe means you are partnering with God to accomplish a specific Mission in which you both have a vested interest.

Being about our Father's Business is indeed the Highway to Heaven, building the Strength in Community. But, the question is, 'Why are so many Believers missing the bus on this?' Well, someone has to answer this question, so it may as well be me. We often talk about losing our SALVATION, but what about salvaging it? Reclaiming what rightly belongs to us is not losing it! Although it may feel as if we have lost it, once the Wrath of God is upon us. Still, what Jesus did on the CROSS for us is SEALED in the Heavenly of Heavens.

When most speak about losing our salvation, it is more like having it lie dormant, similar to the Holy Spirit lying dormant within us. Due to our lack of understanding, we are quick to condemn and throw someone into the Pit when we do not know what God is using to train, teach, test, or chastise, unless the Holy Spirit reveals it to us. For this reason, when building *Strength In Community,* we must evaluate and work on our FRUITS and CHARACTER when being about our Father's Business.

According to the Heavenly of Heavens, you must invest (Tithe) back into your Spiritual Gifts to keep them flowing or producing, similar to how water evaporates from the earth and gives back to it through the rain. In reality, I do not know of one bank that would finance a company with nothing vested or that is unwilling to invest in its potential! Then we sit around mad at God for not doing what we neglect to do for ourselves.

As a matter of fact, while we are sitting around thinking or feeling as if God has abandoned us, we do not attempt to Spiritually Till our own ground to gain the SEEDFUL KNOWLEDGE of why we are in this condition. Nor do we even know about the Spiritual Tilling process in itself and why it is necessary to develop *The Black Sheep Power: As It Pleases God*®. Before going any further, I want to say that God is our best and most faithful cheerleader, proactively providing the Spiritual Tools needed in our reason for being and for our Heaven on Earth Experiences, *As It Pleases Him.* Still, as a Spiritual DIY Project, we must selflessly put in the work while

Strength In Community

building *Strength In Community* without being outright selfish, prideful, and unmerciful.

Yes, we do have free will in the Spiritual Tilling Process or opting out of it altogether. But by golly, we cannot lay the blame on God when our seeds are not producing what we think we deserve. Nor should we resort to taking what does not belong to us, using people to get what we want, or leveraging the privilege card to oppress another to break down the community.

Although exhorting privilege to override properly building *Strength In Community* or outright negating the Spiritual Tilling Process, seemingly works in the worldly realm. However, it still does not make it right or worthy of the calling in Christ Jesus. How do I know? Matthew 18:4 clearly says, *"Therefore whoever humbles himself as this little child is the greatest in the kingdom of heaven."* So, if anyone thinks they are really GREAT without humility while breaking people down or destroying them while gleefully sowing bad and deceitful seeds, in the Eye of God, it is a LIE. Really? Yes, really! Even James 4:10 tells us how real GREATNESS is viewed in the Eye of God: *"Humble yourselves in the sight of the Lord, and He will lift you up."*

As *The Black Sheep*, when it comes to the Kingdom of God, He weighs the heart and mind postures associated with our seeds, fruits, and character traits. All of which solidifies Matthew 20:16: *"So the last will be first, and the first last. For many are called, but few chosen."*

When building *Strength In Community*, why does God require us to sow good, righteous, and ethical seeds, especially when we have no control over them in a dog-eat-dog world? First, a seed reproduces after its own kind. Secondly, we do not want to engage in foolery because it has shame attached to it. Here is what 1 Corinthians 1:27 says, *"But God has chosen the foolish things of the world to put to shame the wise, and God has chosen the weak things of the world to put to shame the things which are mighty."*

The Spiritual Moth

As our actions, thoughts, beliefs, desires, and words shape our lives, there is one thing that we do not often talk about is *The Spiritual Moth*. It metaphorically weaves together the fabric of our daily existence and defines our experiences from within, whether good, bad, or indifferent, with a tendency to destroy our valuable resources externally.

If we want to sow bad seeds and engage in all types of foolery, while wanting our dreams to fall out of the sky and not have to work for them, rest assured that delayed gratification, ungratefulness, and discontentment will become our portion. To be clear, as *The Spiritual Moth* silently nibbles away, I do not wish ill will upon anyone. As the Divine Messenger of the Most High God, I must bring forth the Heavenly and Timely Warning on the hidden forces that are quietly eroding our strengths, values, aspirations, and Divine Promises from the Heavenly of Heavens.

Now, getting back to what I was saying about willful foolery found in our negative thoughts, sensitive feelings, unresolved fears, and toxic relationships, from a Kingdom Perspective, we cannot fully enjoy whatever with whomever in community or private. Why not? It becomes like an internal *Spiritual Moth* eating away at our self-worth with all types of insecurities, paranoia, and doubtfulness. If left unrecognized or undealt with, *As It Pleases God*, this will cause us to lose sight of our reason for being or unawaringly fall into a state of slumber.

Can the *Mothing Effect* really happen to us as Believers? It is happening in real time; thus, we need to stop with the lies! I wish someone would have shared this information with me

Strength In Community

when I was younger, but now that I am older, wiser, and Kingdomly Usable with all types of Battle Scars, as I learn, I TEACH to feed God's precious sheep.

When not prioritizing our lives, *As It Pleases God*, only to please ourselves, our underlying negative self-talk, limiting beliefs, lack of authenticity, and the comparison to others often ignites the *Spiritual Mothing Effect*. Even if we lie about this *Spiritual Moth* eating away at the psyche, it is happening, especially behind closed doors. As we continue to lie and dwell on past failures or circumvent our oppositions, this Spiritual Parasite is gnawing at our confidence, integrity, peace, and character. At the same time, it creates a fertile breeding ground of decay while we appear right in our own eyes. In Spiritually Aligning this Divine Truth, I gleaned this information from Isaiah 51:8: *"For the moth will eat them up like a garment, and the worm will eat them like wool; but My righteousness will be forever, and My salvation from generation to generation."*

We must put in the work, Spiritually Tilling and confronting our Spiritual Moths because *"To whom much is given, much is required."* Luke 12:48. Even if we go to the dark side to accomplish our dreams, wants, needs, and desires, it will still cost us. If one is willing to pay the price...then the warning still stands.

Remember, you must share your Spiritual Gifts from WITHIN and the proceeds of overcoming a lesser law with a GREATER ONE to keep the Spiritual Moth at bay. Why? It is God's capitalizing way of getting your Mental, Physical, Emotional, Spiritual, and Financial Systems flowing through you. Here are some rules that will help you safeguard your BLESSINGS while being *'In PURPOSE on Purpose'* or Intentionally Purposeful:

☐ Do not take from something, and not give back.

Strength In Community

- ☐ Do not take from a person, and not give back.
- ☐ When you receive a Blessing, BLESS someone else.
- ☐ If you need a Blessing, create a BLESSING for someone else.
- ☐ When entering a person's house as a visitor, BLESS them with a gift.
- ☐ When someone visits you, BLESS them with a gift before they leave.

Although these rules seem so simple, they are continuously overlooked. These few rules have so much power I cannot begin to tell you about...you must experience it yourself. God is very strategic, and He has designed everything to reproduce after its own kind. Nevertheless, there are a few things we often forget:

- ☐ We must TAKE CARE of it.
- ☐ We must NURTURE it.
- ☐ We must PREPARE it.
- ☐ We must RESPECT it.
- ☐ We must SHARE it.

Whatever our 'IT' is or is not, we cannot ignore it because it will not get resolved. Then again, it can create a life of its own without our permission due to our ignorance or lack of understanding. For this reason, we must own our truth regardless of whether it is good, bad, or indifferent while understanding *The Power of Intent*.

Chapter Twelve
The Power of Intent

The Power of Intent is rooted in WHY we do what we do. Then again, it is also grafted in WHY we are not doing what we should do as well. In a world filled with distractions and unimaginable obligations, it is easy to lose sight of the deeper meanings of real life from a Divine Perspective. Although we are Spiritual Beings having a human experience, we are still mere flesh and blood, having real emotions, feelings, thoughts, beliefs, and desires, with a struggle with Spiritual Duality. According to Ephesians 6:12, it says, *"For we do not wrestle against flesh and blood, but against principalities, against powers, against the rulers of the darkness of this age, against spiritual hosts of wickedness in the heavenly places."*

According to the Heavenly of Heavens, the struggle of mankind is real, even if we pretend as if we are perfect, needing nothing from anyone. So, regardless of how we feel or think, Galatians 5:17 says this: *"For the flesh lusts against the Spirit, and the Spirit against the flesh; and these are contrary to one another, so that you do not do the things that you wish."* The hidden struggles between fleshly desires and our moral compass are real; therefore, it is our responsibility to understand the differences. If not, we will begin lying to ourselves and pretending while covering all of it up with our habits, lusts, and ungoverned behaviors.

The Power of Intent

According to the Heavenly of Heavens, the Veil of Pretense is now being lifted from the pews to the pulpit and anything in between. Simply put, as we say in the south, *'It is time to straighten up, and fly right!'* If we need to self-correct, then do it. If we need to awaken from our slumber, then wake up. If we need to develop our character, then use the Fruits of the Spirit. If we need covering, then use the Blood of Jesus. If we need guidance, then use the Holy Spirit. If we need healing, then pray, repent, and forgive. If we need encouragement, then use the Word of God.

In understanding *The Power of Intent*, in both success and failure, we can change the trajectory of our lives in ways beyond human reasoning if we opt to operate *As It Pleases God* instead of pleasing ourselves. For instance, we have two options:

- ☐ **Option 1**: We get what we want on the front end and lose on the back end with the underlying fear of failure, obsession with perfectionism, extreme bouts with pridefulness, or secret doubts about one's capabilities.

- ☐ **Option 2**: We can surrender to God on the front end and get what we desire on the back end with confidence, peace, authenticity, understanding, and humility.

In the Eye of God, we have free will to choose what best suits our intents. However, we cannot become fickle with the repercussions associated with our choices, whether positively or negatively.

When dealing with Divine Self-Control and Divine Alignment, *As It Pleases God*, we must always operate for the Greater Good of mankind. If not, or if we make a willful choice to operate in the lesser good, our Divine Status can be removed like a demotion, but in the Realm of the Spirit. This type of unseen demotion may not be seen with the naked eye, but it is felt from within the conscience, even if we remain silent about it. In addition, it can also be detected by those who have been Spiritually Unveiled to see what most cannot.

How do we know if they know our Spiritual Status? If the Holy Spirit does not advise us of them being Divinely Aware, then we may never know. Why not? They will not say a word to us about it…but will offer Divine Wisdom instead, while sharing the Fruits of the Spirit and Leading by Example. Simply put, the REAL DEAL, and I mean the REAL DEAL, will NOT bodaciously insult God's precious sheep, regardless of whether they are in or out of the Spiritual Fold. What makes them so cautious? It is due to them harnessing *The Black Sheep Power: As It Pleases God*® to build, empower, and inspire others to become better, stronger, and wiser.

Spiritual Loop

With the *Power of Intent*, the MEAN SPIRITED Religion is not what gets the Spiritual Elites seated at the Divine Table—It is their PEOPLE SKILLS. They develop their people skills to lay down the truth in a manner that convicts and corrects simultaneously without leaving people hanging in a *Spiritual Loop*.

What is a *Spiritual Loop*? We all know what Spiritual Loops are, even when we pretend we do not, as that slight eye roll says what the mouth will never voice out of respect. Nevertheless, a *Spiritual Loop* is when the same information is repeated over and over for a Spiritual High. And then, followed by a letdown with nothing to go on or reflect on for tangible results; thus, leaving us empty, confused, or frustrated.

The Power of Intent

For instance, we have someone who is saying God is good, and all the time, God is good. And, we are in AGREEMENT with this statement, but the one who is getting us hyped up, their fruits are rotten, mangled, and unpalatable, and their character is highly questionable. In this questionable state, here is what they missed:

- ☐ They never stated HOW God is good.
- ☐ They never shared WHY God is good to them.
- ☐ They never talked about the times WHEN God was good to them.
- ☐ They never spoke of the moments WHERE God showed them kindness.
- ☐ They never revealed WHAT the source of the goodness that flowed into their lives was.
- ☐ They never disclosed WITH WHOM the flow of goodness impacted.
- ☐ They did not share the WAYS to keep the flow of God's goodness flowing into our lives and the lives of others, *As It Pleases Him.*
- ☐ They did not UNVEIL the Divine Expectations or Contingencies associated, if applicable.

According to Kingdom Standards and Protocol, we must give instructions or roadmaps on how to self-correct, not only telling others what to do, but also how to do it. While at the same time containing a free-willed *Baited Hook*, leading all things back to the Kingdom of God. Is this being somewhat manipulative? In my wording, it may appear so, depending on our perception of the word bait.

Nevertheless, in our approach with *The Power of Intent,* 2 Timothy 3:16-17 says, "*All Scripture is given by inspiration of God, and is profitable for doctrine, for reproof, for correction, for instruction*

The Power of Intent

in righteousness, that the man of God may be complete, thoroughly equipped for every good work." In all simplicity, to avoid veering into a *Spiritual Loop*, here are a few things to do, but not limited to such:

- ☐ We must make whatever it is inspirational.
- ☐ We must make it worthy, fruitful, or positive.
- ☐ We must speak the truth in love and with concern.
- ☐ We must correct without scolding or shaming.
- ☐ We must provide understandable instructions.
- ☐ We must operate in the Spirit of Righteousness.
- ☐ We must properly prepare or equip others as well as ourselves for the Greater Good.

In the hustle and bustle of life as *Black Sheep*, we can figure out the above list on our own, or we can use the Fruits of the Spirit and Kingdom Standards, *As It Pleases God*. Once approached in this manner, manipulation is not necessary because God will defend Himself. He only needs our WILLINGNESS and OBEDIENCE to feed His sheep, *As It Pleases Him*, and He will do the rest without us force-feeding anyone. Remember, Matthew 4:19 says, *"Follow Me, and I will make you fishers of men."* He has not changed His mind...now the question is, 'Have you changed yours?'

Baited Hook

Whether we teach others how to fish, fish for ourselves, or when doing business, *As It Pleases God*, baiting the hook is mandatory. Why must we provide bait? It is in our nature to become drawn to some form of lure, attraction, or temptation instigated by our wants, needs, desires, or the lack thereof. All of these are governed by the Gravitational Pull, which is based

The Power of Intent

upon our Divine Blueprint, how far we are straying away from it, or what is inside the core of our being.

More importantly, everyone's BAITED HOOK will not be the same. Why not? One man's treasure is another man's trigger, and the other man's trigger is the treasure for the next person. Listen, we are all created differently with varying fingerprints, footprints, and mind prints, even if we pretend to be alike. If we do not master this Divine Principle, our enemy gains leverage to capitalize on our weaknesses as we pretend to be strong. Why would this happen to us as Believers? Humility is our true strength. When we exhibit overzealous strength or become a know-it-all, the enemy can set traps to trip us, proving we are NOT who we say we are to create doubt, disbelief, or insecurity.

On the other hand, if our hidden strengths have a *Baited Hook* of humility, *As It Pleases God*, the enemy's tricks become a Lesson, Blessing, Testing, or Nutrition for the Kingdom of God. Really? Yes, really! For this reason, in a *Spirit to Spirit* Relationship with our Heavenly Father or when in a Spiritual Classroom, we must document, document, and document, capturing the information for His sheep. Not our sheep, not their sheep, but HIS sheep!

Why must we know about the *Baited Hook* and God's sheep? Simply put, we have Believers praying wicked, deceptive prayers or trying to become Spiritual Bosses over other people's stuff not belonging to them for the come up while insulting His sheep behind their back. After all, they think this behavior is rightfully justified, whereas it is NOT in the Eye of God. Why is it not justifiable? It is based upon deceptiveness.

We do not need anyone to tell us when we are behaving unwisely or debaucherously. The psyche knows, overriding our sense of good judgment, leaning toward what appears right in our eyes without TRUTHFULLY involving the Holy

The Power of Intent

Trinity. How do we know the difference? If there is any form of selfishness, untruths, or biases in this equation, more than likely, the Father, Son, and Holy Spirit may not be involved, and repentance needs to occur.

Why must we repent if we feel deceived or ousted? According to the Heavenly of Heavens, deceptiveness is derived from jealousy, envy, pride, coveting, or greed. For the record, being deceitful is an act, whereas feeling deceived or thinking we are getting the short end of the stick is a matter of perception. Unfortunately, this is one reason we operate in Spiritual Error without knowing it. For example, repentance must occur when we say one thing as being pro-holy, and our behaviors, demeanors, words, thoughts, or beliefs prove otherwise. Without self-correcting, we will turn on ourselves, getting the short end of the stick while appearing right in our own eyes.

Let us go deeper, or better yet, deeper than deep. A non-correcting and non-repentant mindset will cause us to turn on ourselves from the inside out. Why would we turn on ourselves, especially when we are pro-self? Although the psyche is very fickle, it keeps account of the good and bad, right and wrong, just and unjust, as well as our differences and avoidances. Unbeknown to most, to negatively turn on others without compassion or mercy, we must turn on ourselves first from within, spreading outwardly, even if we proclaim to love ourselves.

What is the purpose of the psyche keeping track of what we do or do not do? It contributes to us walking uprightly, *As It Pleases God*, or meandering with a topsy-turvy effect as it pleases self. Listen, the psyche has an internal file cabinet waiting for the right moment to gain leverage, especially when we do not know how to release our hidden issues to God Almighty. It also happens when we are clueless about how to Spiritually Counteract our negatives into positives using the

The Power of Intent

Word of God and the Fruits of the Spirit. Without taking the time and energy to pray, repent, self-correct, or invoke our Spiritual Gifts, Divine Blueprint, Spiritual Provisions, or Supernatural Alignment regarding our own stuff, *As It Pleases God*, it will cause us to feel like a victim or pretend as if we are one.

Then again, if we do not walk in the LIGHT, it may cause us to operate in Spiritual Error or opt for a grab bag full of tricks, causing the *Baited Hook* to become a PRUNING HOOK instead. Please allow me to align: "*Many people shall come and say, 'Come, and let us go up to the mountain of the LORD, To the house of the God of Jacob; He will teach us His ways, And we shall walk in His paths.' For out of Zion shall go forth the law, And the word of the LORD from Jerusalem. He shall judge between the nations, And rebuke many people; They shall beat their swords into plowshares, And their spears into pruning hooks; Nation shall not lift up sword against nation, Neither shall they learn war anymore. O house of Jacob, come and let us walk In the light of the LORD.*" Isaiah 2:3-5.

Pruning Hook

When walking in the LIGHT or becoming Spiritually Illuminated, if we do not take the initiative to exhibit the Fruits of the Spirit or use Christlike Character, only sharing the victim mentality, we will have issues with ourselves and God. Why? Siccing God on others or pimping God to appeal to our illusional visions, bogus paybacks, or the downfall of another, we will fall short Mentally, Physically, Emotionally, Spiritually, or Financially. Unfortunately, with the *Baited Hook* becoming a pruning one, it will bring forth after its own kind, baiting the bait for another to satiate the longing hidden within the psyche.

The Power of Intent

What is the big deal about *Pruning Hooks*? A pruning hook can become dangerous, especially before the season of harvest. Here is what we must know before moving on: *"For before the harvest, when the bud is perfect And the sour grape is ripening in the flower, He will both cut off the sprigs with pruning hooks And take away and cut down the branches. They will be left together for the mountain birds of prey And for the beasts of the earth; The birds of prey will summer on them, And all the beasts of the earth will winter on them."* Isaiah 18:5-6. For this reason, it is imperative to ensure the psyche is not secretly sour or repulsive amid the growth process. When the cutback occurs, we do not want to ooze all over the place, trying to hold on to dead people, places, and things, getting caught in our self-made snares.

As a Word to the Wise, when we bait our hooks to ensnare the RIGHTEOUS, we can become an Enemy of God, so beware. Why must we exhibit caution? When the Holy Spirit leads, He will advise us when to be extremely cautious with the thoughts of casting ill will, misguiding, or setting a trap of doom and gloom over someone He is using for Kingdom Purposes, or it is unjustified. In addition, He will also send a warning when attempting to lead them into Spiritual Error intentionally. When this type of warning goes out in the Realm of the Spirit, the cautionary Spiritual Decree goes out to the person we are attempting to mislead as well. Sometimes they get it, and sometimes they may not, due to some form of Spiritual Blindness, Deafness, or Muteness. However, the question is, 'Would we want to risk our plots backfiring?'

For the record, when engaging in a *Spirit to Spirit* Relationship with our Heavenly Father, the Holy Spirit will not warn us without warning them, and vice versa. Why would God inform anyone of a deceptive *Baited Hook*? First, it allows us to suit up with the Whole Armor of God to

The Power of Intent

withstand the enemy's wiles. Once again, He knows, *"We do not wrestle against flesh and blood, but against principalities, against powers, against the rulers of the darkness of this age, against spiritual hosts of wickedness in the heavenly places."* Ephesians 6:12. Secondly, He advises them to stand down, allowing them to retreat, rethink, repent, recalibrate their mindset, forgive, or add Him into the equation. Thirdly, if any involved parties miss their Spiritual Cue or Warning, with or without the *Baited Hook*, they are still accountable!

Although, as a Child of God, we should NOT behave as if we do not have home training, try to ensnare others, or prey upon their weaknesses. However, if we decide to behave in such a manner, here is what can happen: *"Because you have forgotten the God of your salvation, And have not been mindful of the Rock of your stronghold, Therefore you will plant pleasant plants And set out foreign seedlings; In the day you will make your plant to grow, And in the morning you will make your seed to flourish; But the harvest will be a heap of ruins In the day of grief and desperate sorrow."* Isaiah 17:10-11. I do not wish grief and sorrow upon anyone. Therefore, I am giving you the information to decide whether the seedling is sown in or out of season.

In building leverage, *As It Pleases God*, we will all have our moments in the learning process or when in a Spiritual Classroom. As *Black Sheep*, this is where the Holy Spirit will correct or recalibrate us, leading us into forgiveness and a state of repentance. Why do we need the help of the Holy Spirit when on a learning curve? It helps us to avoid pridefulness, worldliness, turning on ourselves, or self-destructing. All the curvature behaviors we unawaringly overlook may cause us to become stiff-necked, dull, lukewarm, a flaming sword, consumed with idolatry, or esteeming ourselves on power, money, or sex.

The Power of Intent

Unbeknown to most, the enemy's *Baited Hook* categorizes everything under the lust of the eyes, the lust of the flesh, and the pride of life, hidden in *The Power of Intent*. Unfortunately, these are the contributing factors to becoming the Enemy of God. Is any of this Biblical? Once again, I would have it no other way; we need to know this because it does not make sense how some of us carry ourselves in the Name of God. *"Where do wars and fights come from among you? Do they not come from your desires for pleasure that war in your members? You lust and do not have. You murder and covet and cannot obtain. You fight and war. Yet you do not have because you do not ask. You ask and do not receive, because you ask amiss, that you may spend it on your pleasures. Adulterers and adulteresses! Do you not know that friendship with the world is enmity with God? Whoever therefore wants to be a friend of the world makes himself an enemy of God."* James 4:1-4.

We must set aside our differences for the Kingdom of God, coming together as ONE, being about our Father's Business. As I move about, I have to shake my head in dismay. Asking God and myself...Where is the kindness? Where is the love for one another? Where is the respect? Where is self-control? Where is it, where is it, where is it? Have we totally lost ourselves in the whitewash? Please, someone, tell me...the *Spiritual Hook* is seriously bent!

While writing this book, *The Black Sheep Power: As It Pleases God*®, my eyes have seen much from both sides of the spectrum. Believers throw each other under the bus without exhibiting the Fruits of the Spirit or Christlike Character, while being quick to check someone or pinpoint flaws without checking themselves first. On the other hand, I see worldly individuals controlling their temper, working together, staying calm, resolving conflicts amicably, and joining forces against Believers to take them down.

The Power of Intent

To say the least, I am totally flabbergasted when comparing the two (Worldly versus Kingdom). Watching the Kingdom Seekers openly spread curses, talk down to others, airing out people's dirty laundry, and mistreat God's sheep is unsettling at times. Primarily, when I see us, as Believers, excluding people based upon certain biases, conditioning, or terminology as if this is normal, I have to shake my head in dismay. Here is what we must know before moving on, but not limited to such:

- ☐ If we DO NOT submit to God, our Heavenly Father, the *Baited Hook* will become tainted.

- ☐ If we resist God and DO NOT resist the devil, we will become misdirected, deceived, and easily manipulated.

- ☐ If we DO NOT consciously attempt to operate with clean hands and a pure heart, we will become double-minded, chaotic, and contradictory.

Is this Biblical? Absolutely! According to Scripture, *"Therefore submit to God. Resist the devil and he will flee from you. Draw near to God and He will draw near to you. Cleanse your hands, you sinners; and purify your hearts, you double-minded."* James 4:7-8.

In conclusion, with *The Black Sheep Power: As It Pleases God*®, you are now prepared with enough Divine Information and Spiritual Ammunition to do what you were called to do while valuing the simple things in life.

More importantly, based on your ability to reverse engineer Spiritual Duality, if you have been mistreated as a *Black Sheep*, do not mistreat others. If you have been abused as a *Black Sheep*, do not become an abuser yourself. If you have been

The Power of Intent

hated on as a *Black Sheep*, do not become a hater. If you have ever felt unloved as a *Black Sheep*, do not be unlovable or unloving. If you have been brought to shame as a *Black Sheep*, do not intentionally bring shame to another. If you have been betrayed as a *Black Sheep*, do not become deceitful. If you have been insulted as a *Black Sheep*, do not insult others. If you have been treated mercilessly as a *Black Sheep*, do not be merciless or unforgiving. If you have been thrown under the bus as a *Black Sheep*, pull others from under the bus. If you have been left for dead as a *Black Sheep*, bring LIFE and HOPE to others. With the essence of your empowerment, *As It Pleases God*, these are all doable. As you very well know, life is a series of decisions; you only need to make a CHOICE to reverse the narrative and take positive action.

According to the Heavenly of Heavens, the SOLUTION lies within you, for indeed this is where your Divine Power as a *Black Sheep* lies. Your creative expressions, innovative thinking, bodacious courage, and Predestined Blueprint are waiting for you with a Transformative Impact to change lives for the Greater Good.

From this point onward, put on the Whole Armor of God, follow instructions, and work on your Spiritual Fruits and Gifts continuously. In the multiplicity of them all, do not allow anyone or anything to stop you from becoming the BEST VERSION of who you were created to be in Earthen Vessel.

Sheep to sheep, Shepherd to Shepherd, and *Spirit to Spirit*, I believe in you...You got this! I PROMISE you that your SPARK of Divine Power is waiting to be UNLEASHED. Grow Great and Many Blessings to ALL.

Dr. Y. Bur

www.ingramcontent.com/pod-product-compliance
Lightning Source LLC
Chambersburg PA
CBHW071658160426
43195CB00012B/1509